European Readings of
American Popular Culture

Recent Titles in
Contributions to the Study of Popular Culture

Hollywood as Mirror: Changing Views of "Outsiders" and "Enemies" in American Movies
Robert Brent Toplin, editor

Radical Visions: American Film Renaissance, 1967–1976
Glenn Man

Stanley Kubrick: A Narrative and Stylistic Analysis
Mario Falsetto

Ethnicity and Sport in North American History and Culture
George Eisen and David Wiggins, editors

The Neutral Ground: The Andre Affair and the Background of Cooper's *The Spy*
Bruce A. Rosenberg

Post-Franco, Postmodern: The Films of Pedro Almodovar
Kathleen M. Vernon and Barbara Morris, editors

Populism and the Capra Legacy
Wes D. Gehring

Auteur/Provocateur: The Films of Denys Arcand
Andre Loiselle and Brian McIlroy, editors

Dark Alchemy: The Films of Jan Svankmajer
Peter Hames, editor

Queen of the 'B's: Ida Lupino Behind the Camera
Annette Kuhn, editor

Film, Horror, and the Body Fantastic
Linda Badley

Lawrence of Arabia and American Culture: The Making of a Transatlantic Legend
Joel C. Hodson

EUROPEAN READINGS OF AMERICAN POPULAR CULTURE

EDITED BY
John Dean and Jean-Paul Gabilliet

Contributions to the Study of Popular Culture, Number 50
M. Thomas Inge, Series Adviser

Greenwood Press
Westport, Connecticut • London

Library of Congress Cataloging-in-Publication Data

European readings of American popular culture / [edited by] John Dean
and Jean-Paul Gabilliet.
     p.   cm. — (Contributions to the study of popular culture,
ISSN 0198-9871 ; no. 50)
    Includes bibliographical references (p.   ) and index.
    ISBN 0-313-29429-1 (alk. paper)
    1. Popular culture—United States.   2. Europe—Civilization—
American influences.   3. Popular culture—Europe.   I. Dean, John.
II. Gabilliet, Jean-Paul.   III. Series.
E169.04.E84   1996
306.4'0973—dc20   95-31339

British Library Cataloguing in Publication Data is available.

Library of Congress Catalog Card Number: 95-31339
ISBN: 0-313-29429-1
ISSN: 0198-9871

First published in 1996

Greenwood Press, 88 Post Road West, Westport, CT 06881
An imprint of Greenwood Publishing Group, Inc.

Printed in the United States of America

The paper used in this book complies with the
Permanent Paper Standard issued by the National
Information Standards Organization (Z39.48-1984).

10 9 8 7 6 5 4 3 2 1

For American Studies scholars everywhere.

"What harm in getting knowledge even from a sot, a pot, a fool, a mitten, or an old slipper?"

François Rabelais,
Gargantua and Pantagruel 3

"The hierarchy of research areas is regarded as one of the most important areas in the sociology of knowledge, and one of the ways in which social censorships are exerted is precisely this hierarchy of objects regarded as worthy or unworthy of being studied. This is one of the very ancient themes of the philosophical tradition; and yet the old lesson of the *Parmenides*, that there are Ideas of everything, including dirt and body hair, has not been taken very far by the philosophers, who are generally the first victims of this social definition of the hierarchy of objects. . . . [T]here are scientific profits to be drawn from scientifically studying 'unworthy' objects."

Pierre Bourdieu, *Sociology in Question* 132

Contents

Part VII   Americanization

Acknowledgments

It takes a lot of people who give assistance down a long and winding road to put a book together. The actual inception of this collection stems from a conference entitled "Popular Culture in the United States," which the editors organized on behalf of the French Association for American Studies in Chantilly, near Paris, in 1993. The meeting proved so intellectually fruitful that we decided to produce a book furthering the reflection engaged in Chantilly.

For their institutional assistance we wish to thank the Université des Sciences Humaines de Strasbourg–Strasbourg II, the Strasbourg Institute of Political Studies, and the American Library in Paris.

For their goodwill and professional advice, we thank Claude-Jean Bertrand, James Gilbert, Rob Kroes, François Pitavy, and our editor Alicia S. Merritt of Greenwood Publishing Group.

John Dean wishes to express his professional gratitude to the fine people in the School of Journalism and Mass Communication, University of Colorado at Boulder, for much practical assistance given in the summer of 1994; to Patrick Adjedj for translation assistance; to Michel Cieutat and Francis Bordat for ever-helpful feedback on all things popular and cinematic; and privately for the patience and kind nourishment of Geneviève and Benjamin in Paris, the whole Dean clan in the U.S.A.

Jean-Paul Gabilliet wishes to express his private gratitude to his family and professional thanks to the past and present English faculty of Bordeaux's Université Michel de Montaigne, particularly Professors Ginette Castro, Jean Cazemajou, Bernard Gilbert, and Jean-Michel Lacroix. I am also especially grateful to my colleagues and friends at the Institute of Political Studies for their support and encouragement over the years. And for his transatlantic friendship and obligingness, David Thomson.

Finally, special thanks to M. Thomas Inge for his strong and positive support in getting this comparative crosscultural project launched in the first place. And to Jean-Claude Mézières for Chapter 4.

Preface: Ever the Twain Shall Meet

John Dean and Jean-Paul Gabilliet

There is a story that very early on D-day morning, June 6th 1944, one of the first American landing crafts to hit the beach at Normandy aroused the Germans with loudspeakers that played out Glenn Miller's "Moonlight Serenade"—and then the firing began. That invasion was not about the seductive melodies of swing music but about the sheer firepower of bullets, big guns, brute strength, and massive casualties.[1] Since that time, another kind of American assault on Europe has taken place—an assault of American popular culture—that has been rather more peaceful but no less effective in maintaining powerful pro- or anti-American attitudes among Europeans. Rich political and social connotations have accompanied American popular culture as it has made its way across Europe in modern times. For example, in the early 1990s a Levi's jeans ad appeared throughout Europe. This ad showed the powerful, lanky, long-legged back profile of a cowboy in a typical U.S. western desert setting. Beneath his sartorially splendid blue-jeaned legs, his boots crushed barbed wire. And he moved forward accompanied by the text: "La liberté finira un jour par aller à tout le monde. Levi's.®"[2] This conveyed at least three messages at once: a brand—"Levi's®"—that stakes out territory in the open range of a post–Berlin Wall Eastern Europe; a consumer invitation to be one of the free and buy the product; an informal expression of U.S. propaganda.

But two can play this game as well as one. At about the same time, in the late 1980s, the French Association for Cancer Research mailed out a request for donations accompanied by a huge, free poster. This poster showed an American cowboy, strong and handsome, bedecked with a white Stetson hat, wearing a blue jean jacket, and with the classic John Ford Monument Valley, Utah, background behind him. This wasn't just any cowboy, but a very clear imitation of America's own Marlboro Man. That cowboy was brazenly standing in the middle of a highway, leaning down slightly, lighting his cigarette. Just above his proud white Stetson was an enormous road sign with an arrow pointing down at him and the road on which he stood. The sign read "Cancer City," and the text beneath him read "In 1988, tobacco killed more than 66,000 people in France." The implicit message: Are you as dumb as the Marlboro Man?

American popular culture is not the same thing outside the United States as it is within. Domestically, "popular culture" primarily means the daily forms of recreation and entertainment, leisure and play activities, customs and life-styles that are practiced by or easily accessible to most Americans (Dean, 1992: 11–16). Outside the United States the selection of materials, marketing, audience reception, and use change radically; popular culture becomes an export culture wherein people lack experiential reference to the original, the daily, social frame of reference. America's popular culture becomes an end in itself, a language in itself, which others can use.

Like foreign affairs, diffusion of American culture abroad is a devilish thing for the exporters. It is foreign and will not conform to the American whim. Sometimes things sell; sometimes they don't. Has it brought the two worlds—Europe and the United States—closer together and ultimately diminished their differences? After all, shared interests are often the very stuff of conflict. Both sides want something—a market, cultural status. Yet they both sympathize about something—material needs and ideal desires; sympathy: a community of feeling, compassion; your pain in my chest. There is a genuine relation, and argument, established on the basis of American popular culture, between the United States and Europe. To paraphrase Woodrow Wilson: mutual interests do not always tie nations together; they sometimes separate them. But sympathy and understanding can help unite them.

European Readings of American Popular Culture offers a fair selection of current, indigenous European critical readings and thoughtful essays that assess America's cultural penetration of Europe. In no way do the editors believe the collection covers every major topic relating to this broad issue. But we hope we have creatively and positively contributed to Euro-American cultural relations. America for the European has always been a blend of fiction and truth—a fiction created from Europeans' own needs to imagine a better world; a truth that shocks them. But America is only one of many different alternative worlds to which European society and mass media have turned.

The diffusion of American popular culture in Western Europe is both a European story about America and an American story about Europe. It is a history replete with contradictions, seductions, and invitations. This is not an abstraction; it is a live issue. Western European news is regularly peppered with woeful stories about how American film or TV industries drown out the national mass media systems. European educators, politicians, and parents protest the violence of

American movies or rap music; the degrading influence of American materialism; or the sheer, hideous bad taste of American customs. University courses in both Europe and North America—Economics, Political Science, Sociology, Popular Culture, Cultural Studies, History and Mass Communication—all address the problem.

The problem is a process: cultural diffusion. This is what happens when the foreign penetrates the native and the native reacts; when that other person, object, or value from abroad gets to where it has not been and does not belong—and yet finds a place. The underlying principle of this study is that Western European governments and citizens have gotten what they wanted from the United States. American popular culture has been *given* a place in Europe—as much as that place has been taken. This has been a two-way street. The Western European way of life is remarkably sly, tough, and resilient. The Western European–American storyline is actually one obsessive tale told over and again: meeting, mutual seduction, and compromise as American forms of recreation and entertainment, leisure and play activities, customs and life-styles have met and mingled with those of Western Europe. Diffusion has meant the defusion of a potent threat. Did America really "colonize" the area of the world that taught the world how to establish empires? Western Europe has allowed itself to be enriched by the import of American popular culture, which has been selected with care and a keen eye for European comfort and practical advantage.

What explains the selling force of America in Western Europe? After all, the loudest complaint heard is that the American way of life is a cultural, social, and economic plague that Europeans cannot stop; it possesses a corrosive force of inertia. But which is more important: European invitations or American seductions? At the end of World War II, was America simply in the right place at the right time? It easily dominated both the world's monetary system and industrial production, as Paul Kennedy has shown in *The Rise and Fall of the Great Powers* (1987). Did American culture sneak into Europe in the slipstream of victory? Did the model of American business and culture fertilize a wasteland of European self-destruction or exploit the fallen ally? Why did America continue to dominate European culture for decade after decade, so that now, by century's end, this remains a subject of common, vital interest?

Numerous reasons have been given for the popularity of American popular culture in Western Europe since World War II. It was a welcome relief following the fascist regimes of the turbulent 1930s and the war years. Young Europeans in particular have used it to distinguish themselves from their parents. In Eastern Europe and the Soviet Union during the Cold War, American popular culture goods were vital symbols of social protest. The GIs of the 1940s were often accompanied by an abundance of material goods. The PX followed along wherever the GIs went, and those troops readily dispensed food and clothes as they traveled. One of many witnesses to this is the dialogue at the beginning of Simone de Beauvoir's 1954 novel *The Mandarins*:

"You were hungry during the war?" . . .

"Hungry? . . . I literally went mad over the first American who plunked his ration in my arms."

"Is that what made you like Americans so much?"

"That, and at first they used to amuse me." She shrugged her shoulders.

"Now, they're too well organized; it's not fun anymore. Paris has become sinister again." (74–75)

Many Europeans welcomed the American arrival, which—to this day—people of that generation remember in terms of American products they had never seen or heard of before. The American presence was filled out with the Marshall Plan, but also with movies, refrigerators, chewing gum, and Coca-Cola—which became the first grounds for the Euro-American modern culture debate. American popular culture spread throughout Western Europe in unprecedented waves as extensive new communication systems grew: radio, popular youth music, new styles of dress. Added to this was the mass onslaught of the American tourist. Indeed, American popular culture fueled the growth of a European material renaissance. But it was only one factor among many. The release of the colonial empires freed most European nations to concentrate on their own economic infrastructures—to their own benefit.

American popular culture is an exported culture that was not simply transfered whole. Indeed, cultural exports are transformed by native audience reception. As the Austrian author Reinhold Wagnleitner noted in his remarkably thorough *Coca-Colonization and the Cold War*, when Americans heard Bob Dylan's 1963 hit "Masters of War" they thought of the escalating Vietnam War, but in Europe "those who understood the lyrics were not reminded of Vietnam but of the Second World War" (Wagnleitner, 1994: xiii). One of the editors of this collection had a similar experience of the transformation that occurs in the export of culture. It was in London in 1975, during a showing of the movie *Dog Day Afternoon*, in which the favorite expletive was the all-American F-word. Al Pacino as "Sonny" and John Cazale as "Sal" spat out "F-this" or "F-ing that" every few minutes in the movie. Now, in England at the time this word was an uncommon public swear. The movie audience in London went wild with embarrassed laughter whenever it was used. Their reaction totally transformed the movie, turning it into an adolescent farce. But from a non-English, American viewpoint, the environment that shaped the experience of that American popular culture product (the movie) was all wrong. This phenomenon has been repeated across Europe: the strange French reception of Jerry Lewis; the idealization in Belgium of old, American junk-heap cars; the transformation of disco into the Euro-Trash rock music of everything from 1970s Abba to 1990s Ace of Base.

It is important to see how European culture has contributed to the American popular culture goods that have spread throughout Europe and the world. As Marianne Debouzy points out in her chapter, "American mass culture often drew its inspiration from Europe, but its products and stories have to be adopted in the United States before being marketed throughout the world." What is increasingly important as one looks closer, then, is the United States not as cultural source but as cultural generator and distributor, as place of go-between and not as place of genesis. Is "Americanization," as Rob Kroes argues in the introduction to this book, ultimately another form of Europeanization? Or, as Claude-Jean Bertrand maintains, has America since the 1960s adopted an increasingly European way of life that diminishes the uniqueness of its own popular culture? There is much room for debate. Some still persist in thinking that Europe has been straitjacketed into American popular culture; it dominates as a substitute culture, threatens as an unreal culture. There is the tradition of American popular cultural pessimism, which in the postwar years goes back at least to Clement Greenberg and Dwight MacDonald[3] in the United States, and to Raymond Williams and Graham Greene in Europe. This is linked to a long European tradition of seeing Americans as culturally disrupting European equanimity and traditions: from the time of Samuel Johnson's statement that Americans are "a race of convicts [who] ought to be thankful for anything we allow them short of hanging" (Boswell, 1927: 560) and Thomas Paine's friendship with Danton—down to the latest GATT (General Agreement on Tariffs and Trade) trade row. Citizens of the brave Old World read into American popular culture with both enhancement and enervation.

What of the academic outlook nowadays? Frankly, American popular culture is a marginal if not completely outlandish area in European academic traditions. Only since the 1970s have the British coined a brand of it called "Cultural Studies" (preceded by the magnanimous "Area Studies," the ingenue rubric "Pop Arts," and the ideological interpretations of the Open University). Prior to that on the Continent, American popular culture occurred in Europeanist, anti-Soviet magazines such as the Paris-based *Preuves* and Berlin-based *Der Monat*. These were heavy with the Cold War rhetoric of a U.S. cultural offensive and dabbled in U.S. "low culture" as the occasional spice in an otherwise high-minded brew of Faulkner and Camus, Philip Rahv and Luigi Barzini (Coleman, 1989). Certainly European artists, from Francis Picabia and Pablo Picasso to Stuart Davis and Richard Hamilton, made use of American popular culture; but in the institutional realm of higher education it was taboo.

Even for those who do not dismiss American popular culture as negligible, irrelevant, or despicable in the academies, it is still difficult to gain access to primary sources because most institutions, libraries, or research centers do not stock original materials. Imagine studying the Elizabethan theater if one only found reference books and tantalizing chapters in volumes about British civilization or the occasional play that passed through town. European scholars of American popular culture have therefore had to overcome both institutional and methodological hurdles, which their colleagues researching more "conventional" topics do not experience as acutely.

Critical structure and theory result both from the examined data and the native, cultural perspective of whoever does the examining. American Studies emerged in the various European countries after World War II thanks to the constitution by European scholars of a pluridisciplinary (although mostly literary) area mapped out by reference to the social, political, economic, and cultural specificities of the United States. The discipline evolved through the gradual realization of what Western Europe did and did not have in common with the United States. It is from this perspective that most European thinkers have developed their account of American popular culture.

The French sociologist Pierre Bourdieu has argued that "popular culture" does not exist as such because it is only a trivialized version of Culture—that is, elite culture, the only reference against which all cultural practices and productions are defined (Bourdieu, 1990: Chapter 7; Bourdieu, 1993: 1–7). This view echoes the canon defended by evangelical advocates such as T. S. Eliot, who, in "Tradition and the Individual Talent," held that tradition "involves . . . a perception not only of the pastness of the past, but of its presence [, a realization] . . . that the whole of the literature of Europe from Homer [onward] . . . has a simultaneous existence and composes a simultaneous order" (Eliot, 1920: 49).

This elite contention might have been tenable in Europe's case, but was it legitimately transposable to the United States? America was up to something different; it arguably constructed its culture and national psyche by asserting its difference to, not similarity with, the distant British model. From at least the antebellum period, much of the American cultural reaction—from Noah Webster's *American Dictionary* and Davy Crockett's *Sketches and Eccentricities* to the writings of Walt Whitman and Harriet Beecher Stowe—was consciously and distinctly non-European. The old hierarchies were denied. The problems weren't the same. The people were different. The land had another meaning. Simultaneously, huge numbers of immigrants came to American soil after leaving behind radically different cultural backgrounds. U.S. culture has consequently emerged less through hierarchical distinction than through economic determination. Uprooted mentally and geographically, newcomers and longtime Americans responded equally to newspaper-type populism, the only discourse that enabled the media to sell its products in such a heterogeneous market. As a worldview—more than a genuine ideology—populism advocated unqualified egalitarianism and held that those who availed themselves of more than their rightfully earned share threatened the American ideal and social order. Like all its precursors, the American utopian project equated social harmony with the quest for happiness. American popular culture is populism's legacy to the post–World War II "Western world," the eudaemonic dream that has successfully become the lingua franca of Modernity, an epoch's aspiration shared by all those who do not reject the Occidental model.

In this context, what Europeans read into American popular culture is provocative for three reasons. Europeans hail from countries that discovered egalitarianism and its cultural avatars fairly recently. The specifically American idea of the middle class arguably differs from the context of European bourgeois societies, which derived from the court society analyzed by the German historian and sociologist Norbert Elias. Finally, when Europeans scrutinize anything American, they stare at themselves through a distorted mirror but also provide insights that only outsiders can develop.

If anything, this collection is intended to be an exercise in the reading of a civilization's psyche. First, because—as Nietzsche said—"it takes two to find the truth"; in psychoanalysis, the truth or any semblance of it stems from an intimate dialogical relationship between two people (not one, three, or four; but two). Second, because—just as psychoanalysis relies on neglected or overlooked details—the study of popular culture rests on the scrutiny of the matter that minds, spirits, and souls foster, only to deny its existence subsequently. One English word perfectly epitomizes this specificity; popular cultural production is culture's *refuse*—the scraps and wastes that dominant discourses on culture self-consciously refuse to acknowledge as significant. This is what the Italian art historian Carlo Ginzburg (1980) has called the "paradigm of the clue," an interpretive method relying on any ostensibly "marginal" data considered as telltale. We believe this is the bottom line of popular culture scholarship: to allow for the surfacing and subsequent scrutiny of what a civilization prefers to leave unnoticed— occasionally by means of discursive rejection strategies—in its cultural output. Popular cultural production is to a civilization what fingerprints and repressions are to a human being: intimate, greasy smears that make it possible to track down and reconstruct a complete individual in a fuller and more meaningful fashion.

We hope our editorial work, like the entire collection, has exemplified this dialogical collaboration. Jean-Paul Gabilliet is a French citizen who has clocked in much time in North America, John Dean an American who has lived in Western Europe for half his life; we enjoyed and took advantage of each other's input in this pluricultural project. Some may find it symbolic that the two editors are affiliated with the University of Strasbourg, Europe's "capital." To us it has been a fortunate coincidence above all.

Finally, the purpose of *European Readings* is to allow academics to speak out about a range of topics still infrequently addressed from this side of the Atlantic. As we gathered our material, it turned out that the critical voices we heard from the most were those of Western and Middle Europe. We are thus aware of the significant areas of Eastern, Southern, and Northern Europe that still need to be heard from. We are also aware of the French accent in this collection, primarily because so much of the debate about American cultural influence in Europe has come from France, and practically because our immediate pool of resources was in the area around Strasbourg.

The book's organizational logic is user-friendly. The chapters fall into seven sections—Image, Music, Written Word, Food, Social Customs, Ethnic Cultures, and Americanization—that broadly cover recurring areas of European concern. Each chapter provides a selection of approaches that attempts to answer three questions: How does American popular culture *function*? What *forms* does it assume when it is imported to Europe? How do Europeans *respond* to it?

NOTES

1. From the oral history report of the fortieth anniversary of the D-day landing, *BBC-Radio 4 Long Wave*, April 1984—as received in Paris and as selected by Radio 4 from the oral history archives of the Imperial War Museum, Lambeth Road, London.

2. As included in the American propaganda pamphlet produced for the fiftieth-anniversary celebrations of D-day, edited by George Clack: *50 Years of the Atlantic Alliance: From D-Day to the Partnership for Peace* (Washington, DC: USIA, 1994) 36–37. The sentence contains a pun on the possible double meaning of *tout le monde*; it translates as "One day freedom will eventually fit everybody" or "One day freedom will eventually fit the whole world."

3. Compare these critics' essays in Rosenberg and White, 1957.

REFERENCES

Beauvoir, Simone de (1984). *The Mandarins* [1954]. London: Fontana.

Boswell, James (1927). *The Life of Samuel Johnson, LL.D.* [1775]. London: Oxford University Press.

Bourdieu, Pierre (1990). *Distinction: A Social Critique of the Judgement of Taste* [1979]. New York: Routledge.

——— (1993). *Sociology in Question* [1980]. London: Sage.

Coleman, Peter (1989). *The Liberal Conspiracy*. New York: Free Press–Macmillan.

Dean, John (1992). *American Popular Culture—La Culture Populaire Américaine*. Nancy: Presses Universitaires de Nancy.

Elias, Norbert (1985). *Court Society* [1969]. Oxford: Blackwell.

Eliot, T. S. (1920). "Tradition and the Individual Talent." *The Sacred Wood: Essays on Poetry and Criticism*. London: Methuen, 47–59.

Ginzburg, Carlo (1980). "Signes, traces, pistes. Racines d'un paradigme de l'indice" [Signs, tracks, trails: Roots of the paradigm of the clue]. *Le Débat* 6 (November): 3–44.

Gopnik, Adam, and Kirk Varnedoe (eds.) (1991). *High and Low: Modern Art and Popular Culture*. New York: Harry N. Abrams.

Kennedy, Paul (1987). *The Rise and Fall of the Great Powers*. New York: Vintage-Random.

Rosenberg, Bernard, and David Manning White (eds.) (1957). *Mass Culture: The Popular Arts in America*. New York: Free Press.

Wagnleitner, Reinhold (1994). *Coca-Colonization of the Cold War: The Cultural Mission of the United States in Austria after the Second World War*. Chapel Hill: University of North Carolina Press.

Williams, Raymond (1968). *Culture and Society 1780–1950* [1958]. Harmondsworth: Penguin.

SELECTED BIBLIOGRAPHY

Arciniegas, German (1986). *America in Europe: A History of the New World in Reverse* [1975]. New York: Harcourt Brace.

Bennett, Tony, Graham Martin, and Bernard Waites (1982). *Popular Culture: Past and Present*. London: Routledge/Open University Press.

Bertrand, Claude-Jean (1987). "American Cultural Imperialism: A Myth?" *American Studies International* 25.1 (April): 46–58.

Bigsby, C.W.E. (ed.) (1975). *Superculture: American Popular Culture and Europe.* Bowling Green, OH: Popular Press.

Dean, John, and Jean-Paul Gabilliet (eds.) (1994). "La culture de masse aux Etats-Unis." *Revue Française d'Etudes Américaines* 60 (May).

Evans, J. Martin (1976). *America: The View from Europe.* New York: Norton.

Hall, Edward T., and Mildred Reed (1990). *Understanding Cultural Differences.* Washington, DC: Intercultural Press.

Hoggart, Richard (1957). *The Uses of Literacy.* London: Chatto & Windus.

Kroes, Rob, R. W. Rydell, and D.F.J. Bosscher (1993). *Cultural Transmissions and Receptions: American Mass Culture in Europe.* Amsterdam: VU University Press.

Kuisel, Richard F. (1993). *Seducing the French: The Dilemma of Americanization.* Berkeley: University of California Press.

Lenz, Günter, and Kurt Shell (eds.) (1986). *The Crisis of Modernity: Recent Critical Theories of Culture and Society in the United States of America and West Germany.* Frankfurt: Campus.

Morin, Edgar (1988). *L'Esprit du temps* [1962]. Paris: Livre de Poche.

Portes, Jacques (1990). *Une Fascination réticente, les Etats-Unis dans l'opinion française, 1870–1914.* Nancy: Presses Universitaires de Nancy.

Robin, Ron (ed.) (1990). "On the Impact of U.S. Culture Abroad." *American Studies International* 28.2 (October).

Rollin, Roger (ed.) (1989). *The Americanization of the Global Village: Essays in Comparative Popular Culture.* Bowling Green, OH: Popular Press.

Rosenberg, Emily S. (1982). *Spreading the American Dream: American Economic and Cultural Expansion, 1890–1945.* New York: Hill & Wang.

Royot, Daniel, Jean-Loup Bourget, and Jean-Pierre Martin (1993). *Histoire de la culture américaine.* Paris: PUF.

Tomlinson, John (1991). *Cultural Imperialism: A Critical Introduction.* Baltimore: Johns Hopkins University Press.

Usunier, Jean-Claude (1993). *International Marketing: A Cultural Approach.* New York: Prentice-Hall.

van Elteren, Mel (1994). *Imagining America: Dutch Youth and Its Sense of Place.* Tilburg, Netherlands: Tilburg University Press.

Webster, Duncan (1988). *Looka Yonder! The Imaginary America of Populist Culture.* London: Routledge.

Wellek, René (1968). "The Name and Nature of Comparative Literature." *Comparatists at Work*, eds. Stephen G. Nichols, Jr., and Richard B. Vowles. Waltham, MA: Blaisdell-Ginn & Co.

Willett, Ralph (1989). *The Americanization of Germany: 1945–1949.* London: Routledge.

Introduction: America and Europe—A Clash of Imagined Communities

Rob Kroes

Where would Europe be without America? Probably where it is today, but only geographically so. Psychologically, America has always been Europe's "significant other," helping Europeans to define their sense of self by offering contrasts and counterpoints. Clearly, as a national culture, America stands within a larger framework of Western civilization. There are many continuities across the Atlantic in terms of cultural standards, aesthetic appreciation, and communities of taste. Yet at the same time America is not merely an offshoot of Europe in the sense that Iceland is. America is a cosmopolitan blend of many cultural repertoires, the result of a blithe bricolage that endlessly changes the context and content of culture as Europeans know it. Thus, not only has American culture developed into something that is predominantly contrapuntal to European views of culture, but also, retroactively, it has worked to instill a sense of Europeanness into Europeans. As André Siegfried pointed out in the 1920s, it took a trip to the United States to make him feel European. Equally, in the defense of their national identities and national cultures against the ongoing cultural penetration by America, many Europeans have raised the flag of an imperiled Europeanism, projecting their national fears onto a larger European screen.

When Europeans argue that they see America as a threat and a contrast to things dear to their hearts, what do they mean? It is never the case that they speak on behalf of all Europeans; indeed, for every European who has called for the rejection of American culture, another has welcomed it as a source of renewal and rejuvenation. Often it is a matter of generations clashing in Europe, of older generations rising in the defense of European culture as they see it, and younger generations defiantly adopting American cultural forms. Often it is also a matter of time before European views of American culture change from rejection to acceptance. More often than not it is Europeans who, after a certain interval, take a fresh look at American cultural forms (like jazz, B-movies, rock music, hardboiled detective novels) and start a process of cultural revaluation. Like the refuse from a throwaway culture, these cultural forms are picked up, recycled, made the subject of critical language; they are catalogued and stored and become part of a collective European cultural memory. There is a long history of the appreciation and appropriation by Europeans of American culture that one would assume to have undermined the established European rhetoric of cultural rejection. Yet it hasn't. The repertoire of cultural anti-Americanism is remarkably long-lived and stable in its argumentative structure. In the following discussion we propose to explore this repertoire. But as a further introductory note, let us review the main dimensions of an alleged American threat to Europe.

First, indigenous culture and the protection of national identities in Europe are concerns likely to be triggered by American cultural activities abroad. The American cultural presence beyond its own national borders is often seen as domineering and overbearing, forcing non-American competition off the market while undermining the taste and cultural standards of its foreign audiences. In this running *Kulturkampf* saga, the most recent installment occurred when the international GATT negotiations in the so-called Uruguay Round were nearing completion. When it began to look as if free trade principles might henceforth apply to cultural goods as well, European countries called for a cultural exemption clause, protecting their domestic markets from the American audiovisual industries. The reaction may well have been too late. As it is, up to 90 percent of the films shown in European countries are American. For the music and television industry the American presence is not quite as stark, yet trends show a continuing weakening of European shares of these mass entertainment markets. The reaction to this may be one of economic protectionism, yet the language used to justify such measures moves beyond the economic rationale. Protectionism in the cultural sphere is seen as an exception, justified by the larger goal of protecting the national cultural identity. Likewise, the European cultural identity is sometimes presented as being in its infant stage—and thus in need of protectionism in order to allow a European cultural industry to develop and to find its mass European audience.

Second, another pattern of European defensiveness against America focuses on issues of power and dependency. America's cultural expansionism is only one example of a more general American imperialism, and cultural hegemony only one tool in a wider strategy of political, economic, and military domination. Interestingly, and in spite of the fact that these repertoires of anti-Americanism are logically interrelated, people may actually use only one repertoire of rejection while supporting an American presence in Europe on other grounds. Thus, there have been those who welcome American mass culture, who do love jazz, blue jeans, and Elvis Presley, while at the same time demonstrating against America as an imperialist and capitalist state. Others, the European Atlanticists of the Cold

War era, have argued in defense of America's political and military presence in Europe while at the same time abhorring the cultural manifestations of that presence, which has been slowly but surely "Americanizing" Europe.

Third, America stands accused of what truly are the effects of larger, anonymous forces of modernization at work in the contemporary world. There is an almost metonymous relation between the two words—"America" and "Modernity"—that may make us forget that the connection is relatively new. Just over a century ago, as a recently discovered *inédit* (unpublished work) by Jules Verne may show,[1] Verne chose to project his fears of a world dehumanized by technology onto the French capital. In our century Verne would more likely have used America, as in fact so many observers and critics of the American scene have done. Yet at the same time as America is seen as the usher of "Modern Times," it is not always the setting for Chaplinesque nightmares. There are different faces of Modernity that outside observers have recognized in America and that they have appreciated rather than rejected. America, to them, was modern because it offered a humanistic counterpoint to Europe: in America people could truly be the masters of their own fate. There, as Crèvecoeur put it over two centuries ago, "they are become men." In the modernity of America promising fulfillment of Renaissance hopes of a new beginning, of man as his own free agent, outsiders also chose to recognize it as a non-Europe.

THE WEST AS WILL AND CONCEPTION

The reception that Europe has been offering American culture has been going on for centuries. It began even before Europeans put America on their maps. The idea of America had been conceived before the land itself was discovered. Europe had already produced many fantasy worlds, counterimages of itself, utopias. They could be places of hope such as a lost paradise or an imminent redemptive millennium, or places of darkness and doom, without civilization, given to barbarism.[2] But it was not until the Renaissance that the closed, self-contained world of Europe actually exploded into the unknown. It was as if people of their own free will opted for their own expulsion, for a self-inflicted exile, a free-fall off the known world. Not everyone could witness this without a feeling of horror. Consider the famous Florentine mural—literally a sign on the wall—by Masaccio, in which he depicts the expulsion of Adam and Eve from paradise. Rarely has the horror of facing the unknown been expressed so grippingly. Yet in spite of the fears and trepidation of some people, others eagerly engaged in the indomitable quest for the unknown. It produced the one voyage of exploration that, in epic concentration, would hold all the symbolism of this quest: Columbus's voyage toward the West.

The symbolism is so strong that it may appear at times as if Columbus himself is an invention, reminiscent of Noah who sent aloft a dove in search of land, a seafarer from Europe whose very name—Columbus—meant "dove." Like Noah's winged messenger, he returned bringing news of the discovery of land across the ocean. Of course, in spite of such mythical connections and connotations, Columbus stands squarely in historical time, at that critical juncture between the Middle Ages and modern times when people began to have a sense of being masters of their own fate. They made their own world by making the world their own.

The Genoese explorer Columbus relied on a blend of truth and fiction, of reality and fantasy. As he himself reported to his royal principals, he was convinced of having reached the terrestrial paradise. That traditional stories and old lore colored his perceptions and gave them sense and cohesion is truly the interesting point. For indeed, in the European conception of America, things have never been much different. A further dramatic element was the discovery of a populated New World. The European imagination at the time ranged from an early modern awareness of anthropological relativism, exemplified by Montaigne's "Everyone calls barbarity whatever does not fit into his custom," (*Essays* Book 1, chapter 31) to the mad projection of everything forbidden and taboo that lay in the European subconscious, such as Shakespeare's Caliban. The uncivilized, brute force of the savage, regardless of whether he eats men or rapes women, makes him "A devil, a born devil, on whose nature nurture can never stick!" (*Tempest* IV, 189). This image of the untamed savage as the embodiment of all the forces of evil, in compact with the devil and only to be subdued by force, would long endure as a view of America. Whites, in the early days of settlement, were haunted by fears of scalping and ravaging Indians. Later, the white upper stratum of European origin projected such images on a slave population that was African instead of Indian.

Interestingly, these repertoires of projection already freely mingle in Shakespeare's *Tempest*: older fears of African blacks blend into fantasies about the American Indian. Caliban, in the list of dramatis personae described as "a savage and deformed slave," combines a number of fantasies concerning the non-European "Other." Not only is he black, not only does his mother come from "Argier" (the Moorish Algier), but his mythological makeup also shows traits of Natives from the New World, of "Cannibals" from the Caribbean, of Patagonian giants that Magellan had seen, and of inhabitants of the Bermudas. On a symbolic level, a similar blend turns Caliban into an image of the monstrous: he represents every force opposed to Christianity and civilization and the dreams of freedom that people secretly associate with the infringement of cultural rules.

The Tempest is an early example of European fantasies about America after its discovery. In it we recognize a rejection of America and Americans as diametrically opposed to civilization and culture—a rejection that continued even after "the American" was no longer an Indian savage but a transplanted European. We also recognize in Shakespeare's imagination the vibrant, carnivalesque element of cultural revolt, the element of liberation that is precisely to be found in the shedding of Old Europe's civilization. Generations after Shakespeare have chosen to highlight this side of America and the possibilities it offered of becoming "a new man." In all such fantasies America once again becomes paradise, the fount of rejuvenation, the wondrous melting pot that turns servants and slaves into free beings. "Highday freedom!" The European attitude toward America is an ambivalent rejection that always borders on attraction. This ambivalence comes out clearly in Prospero's words when, turning to Caliban, he says: "This thing of darkness, I acknowledge mine" (*Tempest* V, 275–276).

AMERICA AS TABULA RASA

Shakespeare set his imagination to work when British settlement on the American continent had hardly begun. By nature uncivilized and uncivilizable, Caliban represents the danger of barbarous nihilism. When in a state of inebriation he rises in revolt, Shakespeare lends the event the wider contours of a "revolt of the masses." Sinister companions, which we might well conceive of as the rabble of the Old World, the riffraff of Europe, tell Caliban that he can break his master's power by getting at its source, his master's books. "Burn but his books" (*Tempest* III, 91). In his depiction of Caliban as "hooligan," Shakespeare clearly is inspired by old European fears of the nihilism of the lower classes, seen as a reservoir of chaos and destruction. He then projects these fears onto America as a place of uncouth savages. The image of civilization and culture as a threatened enclave in a ruthless surrounding would endure even after the first white settlers built a precarious existence for themselves on American soil. We recognize it most clearly in the case of the early Puritans in New England, who saw their life as a divine assignment to a handful of chosen people to build the New Jerusalem in America. The wilderness against which they had to secure their enclave was seen as the terrain of diabolic stratagems, of trials and tribulations, invented by the devil to obstruct their divine mission.

In such daring claims as those of Cotton Mather in *Magnalia Christi Americana* (1702) we can recognize the old European dreams about America as the Land of Promise, the terrestrial paradise, the place of redemption. Only through the settlement of white Europeans would America come into its own and be able to fulfill its potential. Only then and there, with the New Jerusalem, would the circle of providential history come to a close. In the view of Europeans and their descendants in America, America would become a tabula rasa, a blank page that they could fill as they saw fit. In the 1720s the Irish philosopher and Anglican bishop George Berkeley gave forceful expression to this tendency to weave America into the pattern of European expectations concerning the course of history. Inspired by ideas that extend back to the Roman poet Virgil concerning the westward shift of the center of the world, Berkeley wrote his famous lines:

> Westward the course of empire takes its way;
> The first four Acts already past,
> A fifth shall close the Drama with the day;
> Time's noblest offspring is the last. (Berkeley, 1957)

"Westward the course of empire" came to assume the force of a slogan in the conquest of the American West in the period from 1840 to 1870, although people tended to forget that Berkeley had something different in mind. He wrote his poem in conjunction with his plans for the founding of a college in Bermuda, aimed at the conversion and education of natives. In his view, they still had their natural place in an image of the New World as a pastoral Garden of Eden, as "the seat of innocence, Where nature guides and virtue rules . . . , Not such as Europe breeds in her decay" (Truettner, 1991: 100). It is ironic that in fact Berkeley's name has become linked to an institution of learning, one that fittingly lies at the utmost western rim of the continent.

Following Hector St. John de Crèvecoeur's enthusiastic readings of "the American, this New Man," in the early nineteenth century, Goethe would claim that

> America, You have it better
> Than our Continent, the Old,
> You have no ruined castles
> No basalt.
>
> Your inner self is not perturbed
> At the present time
> By useless remembrance
> And futile fights.[3]

In Goethe's words, Europe appears as a place of frozen forms (*Basalte*), useless remembrance, vain struggle, a prey to forces of decay. America is free from all this. It "has it better." It is empty. In the early twentieth century another European, H. G. Wells, in *The Future in America*, again paraphrased this recurrent view: "There is no territorial aristocracy, no aristocracy at all, no throne, no legitimate and acknowledged representative of that upper social structure of leisure, power, State responsibility" (Wells, 1907: 85).

Yet, in counterbalance, it was never below the Europeans to remind America of its permanent cultural inferiority in comparison to Europe. As early as the second half of the eighteenth century, certain ideas had gained currency in Europe that testify to a cultural anti-Americanism and echo Prospero's scorn toward Caliban. With the added semblance of scientific argument, French authors in particular (e.g., Buffon, De Pauw, and Raynal) proffered theories concerning the climate and geography of America that would doom all cultural transplants from Europe to wilt on arrival. Just as humans were of stunted growth in the American clime, likewise culture would never come to full bloom there. Against the cocky nationalism of the young American republic, Europeans smirkingly pointed out the absence to date of the likes of Shakespeare, Homer, or Dante. Abbé Raynal for instance wrote in 1770: "It is a cause of amazement, but until today America has not produced one good poet, not one skilled mathematician, not a single genius in any art or science" (Echeverria, 1957: 32–33). A trap was thereby set into which the Americans naively walked.

Thus, an early cultural nationalist, one of the so-called "Connecticut Wits," John Trumbull, prophesied the advent of an American Shakespeare, in fact holding up a European standard for Americans to emulate. And until the present day this compelling European standard of cultural success has maintained its discouraging sway in America. Each time Americans have wondered whether their national culture really measures up, they have to admit to lagging behind Europe. In 1917 Theodore Dreiser, already an established novelist, wrote in the cultural journal *The Seven Arts*: "it is a thing for laughter, if not for tears: one hundred million Americans, rich . . . beyond the dreams of avarice, and scarcely a sculptor, a poet, a singer, a novelist, an actor, a musician, worthy of the name" (Dreiser, 1917: 363). We encounter the same complaint in Sinclair Lewis's 1930 Nobel Prize address. And as late as 1981, with facetious glee, George Steiner reiterated the complaint in *Salmagundi*.

"Europe" as the counterimage to "America" may have burdened Americans with a lingering sense of inferiority, yet they also had sufficient ingenuity to compare themselves to Europe in a more positive light. After all, the European repertoire of phantasies about America consists not only of images of darkness and decline. As we have seen before, there is another gallery of images glowingly depicting the land in the West. The ingenuity of Americans vis-à-vis these latter views has always consisted of casting themselves in the role of historical expediters of positive dreams. More than that: they have successfully managed to appropriate the more general dreams concerning "the Americas" and to redefine them as uniquely applying to the United States. The very word "Americans" as we are using it here testifies to this act of appropriation. Whenever the inhabitants of the United States refer to Americans, they are referring to themselves. And Europeans—with the possible exception of inhabitants of the Iberian peninsula—follow their example. It is in fact an act of linguistic arrogation as well as of arrogance, indicative of the extent to which "Americans" deem themselves to be the rightful and exclusive heirs of all those European dreams that see America as the "Land of the Free" and the "Promised Land."

METAPHORICAL DIMENSIONS OF THE EUROPEAN CRITIQUE OF AMERICAN CULTURE

So far we have considered America as a tabula rasa, as a blank projection screen, that both the European and the American imagination have filled at will and whim. Its emptiness was a potent metaphorical ingredient in the production and projection of images from outside. One version of this is the new beginning, the clean slate. It is the hopeful version that sees America as offering the possibility of renewal, rejuvenation, to a European culture that is old, weary, and decadent. A different version sees the emptiness in a negative light, as the denial of Europe's rich cultural heritage. This latter perspective is current in Europe as well as in America. We shall consider below a number of recurrent metaphors that Europeans, in their critique of America, have connected with the central image of America as an emptiness.

First, much of the European imagery about America is in fact a matter of a comparison, often made tacitly, between Europe and America. Whenever Europeans call Americans shallow or superficial—arguably the most common stereotype about Americans—in one and the same breath they are also saying that Europeans are neither. A second dimension is a temporal axis. Statements referring to America as "young" or "new"—irrespective of whether they are meant to disparage or praise—or referring to it as a country lacking history or historical awareness, conjure up a contrast to Europe in terms of time as a sociocultural variable. A third yardstick measures a contrast in mentality; according to this measure, Americans lack the European sense of organic cohesion, of a cultural gestalt. This contrast normally translates into European languages as a contrast between quality and quantity. Whenever Europeans blame Americans for being obsessed with dollars and the price of material goods, they in fact blame Americans for ignoring the intrinsic qualities of objects that Europeans value for their uniqueness while ruthlessly reducing them to the one-dimensional standard of their exchange value in dollars. Americans "value" things differently, and more literally, than do Europeans. The American approach to the heritage of Western civilization displays a literally analytic touch that dissolves the context and cohesion of individual objects and that leaves Europeans wringing their hands in dismay and disgust. In the eyes of Europeans, Americans rush in where the initiated fear to tread.

All these examples show that Europeans, in their views and conceptions of America, use the imagery of metaphors. In these metaphors there is both a quintessential "otherness" and a recognition of their own European future in the current features of America. At times the country assumes the tonic quality of a beckoning horizon—for instance, when it is seen as the harbinger of a world of democracy, freedom, and equality. Many, in both Europe and America, have chosen to regard the country in this light, as a guide and promise. Even when Europeans have seen cultural erosion and the demise of values and norms in America, they have often related this to processes of social change that were also at work in Europe.

We should, therefore, keep two things separate. Sometimes, in their metaphors about America, Europeans try to express what strikes them as peculiarly American, as a cultural modus operandi with its own logic, distinct from Europe. The venture does not reflect back on Europe and therefore can be done in a spirit of intellectual curiosity. This is not the case when America is seen as foreshadowing Europe's future. Inevitably these findings are measured in terms of European anticipations. Different as these two forms of discourse concerning America and American culture are, in fact they often tend to mingle. Then the metaphorical image of America takes place in a European context of cultural concern and discontent. "America" becomes a figure of speech, a code word that stands for decay and corruption in Europe, even in the absence of an empirical link or parallel. Ironically, though, even in such cases where America is wrongly seen as the root of a particular evil in Europe, it may well be that people have correctly sensed some of the inner workings of American culture.

LIFE ON THE SURFACE

Many metaphors about America present the country as a place of cultural erosion, leveling the contours of the cultural landscape as Europeans know and appreciate it. Here particular European observers show the duality we have just described. Only rarely do they, in intellectual detachment, state the transatlantic difference; more commonly there is a tone of unease, as if people have the ominous sense of America being the harbinger of Europe's future. America then appears as the country that corrupts and perverts European values and cultural standards, eroding the complex outline of Europe's cultural landscape. Not only does America have this effect on cultural transplants from Europe, it similarly affects culture in its European setting. The *locus classicus* of this view is Alexis de Tocqueville's analysis of cultural life under conditions of social equality, *Democracy in America* (1850). He develops this argument in the second part of his study of democracy in America, the more somber part in which America serves as no more than the illustration of Tocqueville's more general reflections about equality as the main organizing principle of social life. In a remarkable foreshadowing of much later work by others in the cultural and political critique of mass democracy comes his famous exposé concerning *individualisme*—a word that he invented— as a form of hide-bound conformism, political apathy. Tocqueville's "equality" begins to resemble the later French sociologist Emile Durkheim's *anomie*. It is an erosive force that leads to the complete leveling and flattening of the political and cultural landscape. As Tocqueville put it: "The greater the extent of equality, the more insatiable the taste for it becomes." It is not so much that the range of human desire has widened, but that the desire itself has changed in shape and essence. "When people have become roughly similar and follow the same route, it is hard for any single one among them to walk fast and to leave behind the uniform crowd that surrounds and presses him on all sides." Not only is there a collective force that works to obstruct individual distinction, but the very concept of distinction has been reduced to a narrow range of marginal differentiation. "No matter how democratic the social state and the political constitution of a people, one can be sure that every single citizen will always see near himself some points that rise above him. One may expect that he will fix his gaze on precisely those points."[4]

He will do this—we may add—with a view to leveling such differences as have caught his attention. People may still have an eye for distinction as well as an urge to distinguish themselves, yet the very impulse has become self-defeating. Not only do people no longer aspire to rise above the multitudes; worse, they no longer aspire to rise above themselves. People have become thoroughly socialized animals, meekly following the marching order of the crowd around them.

Similarly, such leveling can be observed in matters of cultural taste and cultural standards. As Tocqueville argues, the production of literary work no longer follows the traditional rules of composition and form. Literary tradition or a sense of the historical genesis of other forms of art no longer play a role. History has contracted into the ephemeral "Here and Now." Surface effects have taken the place of depth. The leveling proceeds from both sides—heights are eroded, depths are filled in. All that remains is the emptiness of horizontal space as the last haunt for the unstoppable leveling spirit.

In his critique of America, seen as the ideal type of egalitarian democracy, Tocqueville ushered in a range of familiar metaphors that would recur in later critical writings about mass society and mass culture. In their evocation of pairs of logical opposites—flatness versus height or depth, constraint versus boundlessness, an expanse of time versus the single moment, the group versus the individual—the underlying antithesis is always between the ways of Europe and those of America, or, in more historical terms, between societies of an aristocratic mold and the emerging type of democratic society.

Not until the traumatic advent of mass democracy in Europe, in the turmoil of the immediate post–World War I period, did these rhetorical motifs gain currency among a generation of conservative critics of culture in Europe. Once again, America provided them with material for their case. Once again, they looked toward America with the ominous sense of watching Europe's future. People such as Oswald Spengler in Germany, Georges Duhamel in France, and Johan Huizinga in the Netherlands are among the better-known examples of this era of cultural pessimism in Europe. Theirs was an anguished awareness of the erosion of cultural standards ushered in by the age of mass consumption and mass culture. To the extent that America was the harbinger of this modern world, the country inspired in them mostly a sense of decline and loss. Interestingly, at the same time, others in Europe welcomed the modernity of America. These were mainly on the political left, in the trade union movement or left-wing political parties; or they were leading intellectuals, such as Antonio Gramsci in Italy or Hendrik de Man in Belgium. What intrigued them was not so much the culture of mass consumption as the power of mass production. America, to them, represented a breakthrough from the realm of scarcity and poverty toward the realm of affluence, with consumption open to everyone. Gramsci was the first to use the word "Fordism" to describe this quantitative leap in society's production potential.

Yet whatever the precise tone of European reflections on America in this period, whether a cultural pessimism or an anticipation of progress, both groups looked toward America as representing Europe's future. Few chose any other light. One was a man whose name is usually mentioned as one of the leading cultural pessimists in the interbellum, the Spanish philosopher José Ortega y Gasset. He had no use for America in his critique of cultural trends in Europe. To him, America did not foreshadow Europe's future. As he saw it, America had only just entered history and Europe could learn nothing from its experience. America was still at a primitive stage, albeit in the camouflage of the latest inventions. In a "Preface to French Readers," which in 1937 he added to his *Revolt of the Masses* (1929), he expressed the satisfaction of having been proved right by history. America was mired in economic depression. Against all those that in the 1920s, from a stagnant Europe, had looked hopefully toward an America wallowing in prosperity, he maintained that America, far from holding out the prospect of the future, was in fact a distant past, a primitivism. But he was an exception.

An interesting case from the Netherlands in the 1920s was Menno ter Braak. In 1928 he published an essay entitled "Why I Reject 'America.' " At the time of writing, the author was a budding intellectual just 26 years old. One should not misread the title, or for that matter the entire piece. Indeed, the America that is so curtly dismissed is really an America in quotation marks: "America," a construct of the mind, a composite image based on the perception of ominous trends that are linked to America as the country and the culture characteristically—but not uniquely—displaying them. Nor is it uniquely for outsiders to be struck by them and reject them. Indeed, as ter Braak himself admits, he is willing to acknowledge as a European anyone sharing his particular sensibility and intellectual detachment, "even if he happens to live on Main Street." This attitude ter Braak illustrates with the striking parable of a young newspaper vendor whom he saw one day standing on the balcony of a prewar Amsterdam streetcar, surrounded by the pandemonium of traffic noise, yet enclosed in a private sphere of silence. Amid the pointless energy and meaningless noise the boy stood immersed in the reading of a musical score, deciphering the secret code that admitted entrance to a hidden inner world. This immersion, this loyal devotion to the probing of meaning and sense, to a heritage of signs and significance are, to ter Braak, the ingredients of Europeanism. To him, they constitute the quintessentially European reflex of survival against the onslaught of a world increasingly organized around the tenets of rationality, utility, mechanization, and instrumentality, yet utterly devoid of meaning and prey to the forces of entropy. The European reaction pays tribute to what is useless and unproductive, defending a quasi-monastic sphere of silence and reflexiveness amid the whirl of secular motion.

This reflex of survival through self-assertion was prevalent in Europe during the interbellum, a time when Europe was in ruins not only materially but spiritually as well. Amid society's disorganization and the cacophony of demands accompanying the advent of the masses into the political agora, Americanism as a concept came to focus the diagnosis of Europe's plight. The impulse toward reassertion—toward the concentrated retrieval of meaning from the fragmented score of European history—was therefore mainly cultural and conservative as much as it was simultaneously an act of protest and defiance.

Huizinga provides another expression of conservative apologetics. Following his only visit to the United States, at about the time that ter Braak wrote his defense of Europeanism (the late 1920s), Huizinga expressed himself thus:

Strange: among us Europeans who were travelling together in America . . . there rose up repeatedly this pharisaical feeling: we all have something that you lack; we admire your strength but we do not envy you. Your instrument of civilization and progress, your big cities and your perfect organization, only make us nostalgic for what is old and quiet, and sometimes your life seems hardly to be worth living, not to speak of your future. (Huizinga, 1972: 312)

In this statement we hear resonating the ominous foreboding that "your future" might well be "our future." For indeed, what was only implied here came out more clearly in Huizinga's more pessimistic later writings, when America became a mere piece of evidence in his case against contemporary history losing form. Thus, in his 1935 book *The Shadows of Tomorrow*, there is the following sweeping indictment:

The number, so it was said, washed across the individual; the mass dragged the individual along, defenceless, and lowered him to a level that always was the largest common denominator of the more simple and coarser features, while levelling and washing away the more complex and 'higher' expressions of the individual. New regimes could stimulate these coarsening trends and use for their own purposes such negative feelings like rancour, vengefulness and cruelty. (Huizinga, 1950: 313)

Huizinga and ter Braak may have inveighed against an obnoxious Americanism, against an "America" in quotation marks, but neither could be mistaken as a mouthpiece for vulgar anti-Americanism. Both were too subtle for that, being aware of the counterargument, of ambiguity; both were also too open to the real America, as a historical given, to relinquish the mental reserve of the quotation mark. Thus ter Braak concluded as follows: " 'America' I reject. Now we can turn to the problem of America." And Huizinga, in his book of travel observations (which already was full of ambivalence), continued: "And yet, it is we that have to be the Pharisees, for theirs is the love and the confidence. Things must be different than we think." With both authors what strikes us in their rejection of what Europe was wont to call Americanism is their intellectual sense of wonder, of admiration even, and—especially in Huizinga's case—of an affinity with and appreciation of that other variety of Americanism, the heritage of high-minded ideals that had inspired so much of American history.

To the extent that Huizinga and ter Braak do reject "America" and Americanism, it is of interest to note that Americans are second to none in their anti-Americanism. It is almost a constant of American culture, much as it tends to escape European critics. At regular intervals American intellectuals indulge in self-criticism and self-rejection that neither in sharpness nor in use of metaphors differs greatly from the critique by Europeans. In one such period, at the time of World War I, James Oppenheim, editor of *The Seven Arts*, wrote: "For some time we have seen our own shallowness, our complacency, our commercialism, our thin self-indulgent kindliness, our lack of purpose, our fads and advertising and empty politics."[5] The statement is characteristic of a renewed and acute sense of the barrenness of America's cultural landscape. Van Wyck Brooks, one of the leading cultural critics of the time, referred to the concept of Americanism as it had gained currency in Europe: "For two generations the most sensitive minds in Europe—Renan, Ruskin, Nietzsche, to name none more recent—have summed up their mistrust of the future in that one word; and it is because, altogether externalized ourselves, we have typified the universally externalizing influences of modern industrialism."[6] Here we have an early, concise version of ter Braak's and Huizinga's later indictments of Americanism, of "America" as the early version of what the universal forces of industrialism threatened to bring elsewhere as well.

Yet in spite of these similarities, European cultural critics seem to have argued a different case: their main concern was the defense of a European culture that was threatened from without, as much as in fact the actual threat may have been endemic to their own society and culture. Rallying to the defense they chose to take the offensive, rejecting "America." In that sense, Europe's alleged cultural superiority was the ultimate offense vis-à-vis an America that militarily and economically so clearly had the upper hand. Oswald Spengler, in *Jahre der Entscheidung* [Years of Decision], really rubs it in: "Life [in America] revolves solely around its economy and is lacking in depth, the more so as the element of true historical tragedy, of true fate, is absent, which has deepened and educated the souls of European nations."[7] In a 1941 essay about contemporary history losing form, Huizinga made much the same point, yet Spengler's choice of words is more telling. Emphasizing depth and souls, Spengler illustrates the more general tendency toward cultural self-elevation in societies that have seen themselves forced into a defensive posture by stronger rivals. The latter, for all their strength and dominance, are seen as cold and shallow cultures, the very antithesis of the cultures under threat, which are warm, have depth, have soul.

The European and American critics that we have mentioned so far related their critique of America to technical and industrial developments. If America had surfaced as the nation that advanced farthest on the road toward a culture of mass consumption, it had surfaced in a highly metaphorical sense. Not only had it reached the surface, it had become mere surface. It had produced a national culture whose main vectors were all horizontal. Huizinga, unwittingly echoing Van Wyck Brooks, spoke of an "exteriorized culture." In its conformism, in its peer-group emulation, in its consuming quest for ever-changing thrills and satisfactions, it presented a picture of all drift and no mastery. In the great Tocquevillean tradition, Georges Duhamel described the Americans as slaves, subjected to the social dictates of a consumption society in spite of their hallowed rhetoric of freedom and individualism. He saw film, the new form of mass entertainment, "the most potent instrument of moral, aesthetic, and political conformism," as a wave of destruction from America hurling itself across the intellectual landscape of France. Yes, film had the power to entertain, even at times to move an audience; but never, like any true form of art, did it incite the individual consumer to rise above himself (Duhamel, 1931: 61). Never did American culture challenge the individual to pause and reflect, to find coherence and meaning, to consummate rather than consume.

In much the same vein Marnix Gijzen, a young Flemish poet and novelist born in 1899, wrote a preface to his 1927 collection of travel impressions *Ontdek Amerika* [Discover America]:

Almost to a man we undergo the levelling influence of the American film *de quatrième zone* [fourth-rate]: its adaptation to every conceivable audience has been pushed so far as to eliminate its inner meaning . . . . Yet the American film exerts its influence on our think-ing and behavior: by systematically ignoring anything problematic it creates an atmosphere of intellectual indifference, it is a factor dissolving our stabilized popular life. (Gijzen, 1927: 8)

Film was not the only carrier of such harmful influences:

The cheap car and the mobility it provides, are slowly changing our society in ways that we cannot always fathom precisely, but whose advanced state I had every opportunity to study in America. The car as a commodity rather than a luxury object is an American conception: it left its imprint on a society that almost in its very essence could be called nomadic. In this nomadicism, in the extreme mobility that characterizes America, the car is the main element. It plays a main role in public indecency, it further weakens the already fragile ties of family life, it allows youngsters a freedom that without exaggeration we may deem too great. The time that the car helps save in certain respects, it otherwise causes to be lost in pure feverishness: it contributes to 'superficializing' life, it exteriorizes it in large measure. (Gijzen, 1927: 9)

Gijzen also looked on America as a country preceding Europe on the road toward cultural decline and social decomposition. To present his case, he employed the same metaphors of surface, of horizontal motion, of a loss of depth and meaning.

More often than not, people come up with variations on the theme of a vertical dimension missing in America. Whether they see America as cold, efficient, con-formist, or unstoppably energetic, they always refer to a national mentality that operates on the surface, never probing the depths of its innermost stirrings, never rising above the immediate Here and Now. Tocqueville sought the central expla-nation of this life on the surface in the prevailing egalitarianism of the culture. Many later critics tended rather to blame the new culture of consumption. But the two cannot be seen in separation. In fact, many of Tocqueville's observations suggest an interconnection that later authors—such as Thorstein Veblen (*Theory of the Leisure Class*, 1899), W. Lloyd Warner (*Social Class in America*, 1948) and David Riesman (*The Lonely Crowd*, 1950)—would further develop. If competition was the motivating force in the area of production, "invidious distinction" and "marginal differentiation" (to use Veblen's words) would become the engines of a consumptive frenzy. Freud referred to it as the "narcissism of marginal distinc-tion."[8] The role played by rules of etiquette as markers of social distinction in Europe's stratified societies would in the context of America's more egalitarian ethos be played by the socialized dictates of "good" taste, which determined the social game of marginal distinction in a larger setting of overall conformism. Taste had become the marker in a game of reference-group behavior indicating which groups people wanted to be associated with and which they wanted to be differentiated from. As a result "taste communities" arose—or "consumption communities," as Daniel Boorstin called them. Their order is more a horizontal criss-cross than a hierarchy of high versus low.

Thus, the "horizontalization" and leveling that Tocqueville had related to the American ideal of equality was later seen as characteristic of the consumer society. The behavior of individual consumers in mass society now formed the new terrain for the hidebound conformism that Tocqueville had already observed. Individualism in the sense of distinction behavior still occurred, but it had undergone a transformation as compared to Europe, where good and bad taste had long been seen in connection with the socially high and low. Culture there was vertically differentiated into high and low forms. In America the sociocultural distinctions fanned out horizontally, linked to the variety of peer groups that had a keen sense of mutual difference.

When Tocqueville reduced the contrast between Europe and America to one between a proud and self-reliant individualism, loathing social dictates, and a hidebound conformism that took its cues from its social environment, he was overstating his case. Traditional European distinction behavior always betrays elements of social conformism, of a conformation to standards of behavior set by social strata that were hierarchically ordered. Yet the contrast, particularly in its overstated version, has tempted many later observers and has become a staple of the European critique of American mass culture. Even in the work done by Americans (e.g., Riesman's *The Lonely Crowd*) we recognize the contrast, as in Riesman's opposition of two forms of reference-group behavior, reminiscent of the antithesis of individualism and conformism. In the consumption society of postwar America he observed the emergence of "other-directed man" who was forcing out his historical predecessor: "inner-directed man." The latter character type had thrived in the relatively stable social hierarchy of stratified societies in which people at an early stage in their lives were equipped by their parents with a sense of social bearings that would be their compass for the rest of their lives. Rapidly changing American society made this character type obsolete. Like an anachronistic Rip van Winkle, inner-directed man would wander aimlessly in a world utterly beyond his grasp and comprehension. Rather than a compass, people now needed radar in order to catch the constantly changing signals emitting from their surroundings.

Many non-American critics of mass culture see things differently. Their inspiration came from Marx and Freud rather than Tocqueville. Their astute sense of the erosive impact of capitalism on such central pillars of the liberal worldview as self-interest, individual needs, and the rationality of individual behavior, made them explore the massive false consciousness—or as Herbert Marcuse put it, the repressive tolerance—of capitalism. A striking example of this, once again from France, is Simone de Beauvoir's travel report *America Day by Day*. Traveling in America a few years after World War II, she felt torn between excitement and rejection. Repeatedly she found herself carried away in raptures by the pace and variety of American life; yet always there was a reprimanding voice reminiscent of both Marx and Tocqueville:

In this profusion of dresses, blouses, skirts, and coats, a French woman would be hard put to make a choice and not offend her taste. And then one begins to notice that underneath their multi-colored wrappers all chocolates have the same taste of peanut, all bestsellers the same story. And why choose one toothpaste rather than another? There is an aftertaste of mystification in all this useless profusion. A thousand possibilities are open: yet they are all the same. A thousand choices allowed: all equivalent. Thus the American citizen will be able to consume his liberty inside the life that is imposed on him without so much as noticing that such a life itself is not free. (1952: 27)

We recognize the reference of this indictment: taste in its refined European form versus its false imitation in America, European elitism versus an uncouth American egalitarianism, hierarchy versus flatness, and above all the European recognition of the aspect of slavery in the vaunted rhetoric of American freedom.

This same idea emerged again in the liberationist rhetoric of the counterculture of the late 1960s. Other contributions to such relatively short-lived international consensus came from the neo-Marxist Frankfurt School in Germany, or from Marxist sociologists such as Jean Baudrillard in France. And again we recognize the pattern: capitalism was the main theoretical target, but for all intents and purposes the critical arrows were mostly aimed at America as the tangible embodiment of everything that was wrong with capitalism. In both the European and the American varieties of the counterculture, anticapitalism and anti-Americanism seamlessly blended into one another. The critique of what was seen as the leveling and shallowness in American culture derived from the more general critique of the culture of capitalism. What capitalism had done to America, it would in due course do to cultures elsewhere. In this critical context America once again emerged as the harbinger of Europe's future. In this critical onslaught, no one paused to consider whether or not American culture might have a logic all its own, whether or not Huizinga was right to muse that "Things must be different than we think."

In conclusion to this section on metaphors that express the contrast between Europe and America as a matter of a missing vertical dimension in America, let us once again quote from Huizinga. During his only journey to the United States, he kept a diary that was not published until 1993. In an entry for Thursday, April 29, he noted:

In the morning from Philadelphia to Baltimore. The landscape has something light, something *ingénu, sans conséquence* [ingenuous, inconsequential], lacking depth, as if one dimension were missing [sic]. At times everything here makes that impression. As if, orbiting in a sphere around the essence of things, one is suddenly moved out to a more distant, wider sphere, at higher speed but more remote.

THE METAPHORS OF TIME AND COHESION

In the metaphorical space where America is imagined, metaphors in terms of high/low or depth/flatness form only one dimension. Other images refer to time, the sense of time, and the passing of time; they could be grouped along a second dimension. A third, closely related dimension encompasses what we may call the combined effects of space and time, producing the historically unique and organically coherent. Let us now analyze these metaphors in greater depth.

It is an old American claim to be beyond European history. The American Republic constituted a new beginning. Or, as the American National Seal has it, a *Novus Ordo Seclorum*. Long before President Bush, Americans spoke of a new world order. Americans love historical watersheds; they love to proclaim the end of historical periods and the beginning of new ones. If there is not a "New Era" to be proclaimed, there is instead a "New Deal," a "New Frontier," a "New Nixon"; there are always books appearing with titles such as "The End of Ideology" or even "The End of History." How to be a proper historian in a country that likes to conceive of itself as outside of history is certainly problematic.

This remarkable attitude has not escaped Europeans. If they want to be congratulatory, they patronizingly call the country "young" even if this is essentially incorrect. In many respects America is old, or even old-fashioned. Its Constitution and its political parties are among the oldest in the world. County lines were originally drawn at such distance from the county seat that people could reach the center of their government in one day with a horse-and-buggy. But of course in most cases, Europeans have something different in mind.

Again Tocqueville is a good, early observer. As he explained it, public discourse in a mass democracy focuses on the immediately appealing. If politicians want to address the citizenry across all lines of social and regional difference, they would be ill-advised, in the clamor of rival voices, to read a well-crafted historical essay. On the contemporary political stage, dominated by a medium such as television, the political message has reached ultimate condensation into what is known as the sound bite, the catchy, quotable slogan that one hopes will linger in the heads of the zealously zapping TV audience. Yet this is not a new phenomenon. Tocqueville already mentioned the loss of tradition and historical depth in favor of special effects and cheap thrills. The metaphors, in his observations on the topic, get mixed, perhaps unavoidably so. His analysis of the shallowness and loss of depth could not but imply the loss of a sense of history and historical depth.

Huizinga, as we have seen, made similar observations. When in America he longed for things peaceful and quiet, he added in the same breath: "things old." What he must have meant was a sense of the presence in the past, an awareness of historical growth and continuity. What struck him in America was the opposite attitude, tending to fetishize the news. He had this to say about American journalism:

The great newspapers, even if their number is legion, can actually be seen as one, as one loud call that is repeated daily across the land . . . . [The European traveler] hates this daily flood of loud stories, telling of crimes, political scandals, marriage break-ups and weddings, those colored and fragmented bits of political news, that lack of information about what is truly happening in the world. (Huizinga, 1972: 31)

He really means the Old World, forgetting he finds himself in the New World. The word "fragmented" is crucial here. In Huizinga's view the news has broken into disparate tidbits without line, continuity, or context. Of course, there was nothing particularly "new" or "American" about this. Consider the well-known anecdote of Frederick the Great of Prussia, who one day ran into the philosopher Immanuel Kant and asked: "Well, Mister Kant, what's new?" To which Kant responded: "I assume, Sire, that you know the old already?" It is this need for news for its own sake, clearly not unknown in Europe, that in the view of many Europeans has assumed excessive proportions in America. Even Huizinga, in spite of his mental reserve and open appreciation, is led to conclude that the journalist in America aims at reducing the intellectual challenge to his readers while simply trying to catch their attention. Longer articles are printed in fragmented form ("continued on page 4"), which, according to Huizinga, prevents the reader from looking up the sequel to even the most thrilling paragraph. The newspaper aims at the reader simply "picking up a few bits here and there." The approach tends to reduce printed matter to the lowest form of equivalence: the small news, the big news, the advertisements, all have been taken out of context and cohesion and have become mere morsels of information, miscellaneous messages.

The question today, of course, is whether these observations about America can still make outsiders frown. We have all become used to the techniques as described by Huizinga, in our contemporary media, the press, radio, and television, wherever we live; our own European countries offer daily illustrations of an attitude and approach that could strike Huizinga as peculiarly American. What remains of interest, though, is that these trends did strike Huizinga as American, that apparently in his day and age there was a more marked difference between Europe and America than today. If so, it would illustrate a more general phenomenon: what people see as crucially different in America, if not as "typically American," is only a matter of different phases in developments otherwise parallel. The question then is, even if indigenous trends occurred in Europe later than in America, could these still have received a prior American "coloring"?

The fragmenting of the news, the separation of current events from their historical context, the reduction of the news to, as Huizinga put it, "Slogan, the brief, catchy phrase," all constituted "a regression of culture." They all resulted from America's status as a mass democracy and would therefore, in due course, come to other mass democracies as well—clearly a case of parallel developments, with Europe following closely on the heels of America. Yet Huizinga also related these general trends to a strictly American background factor, the "anti-metaphysical cast of mind" in America. This mentality was the lasting heritage of an Enlightenment rationalism that had entrenched itself more firmly in America than any-where else. "Do we not feel as if placed back in the eighteenth century?" Huizinga wondered. And, he continued, "the anti-metaphysical cast of mind naturally im-plies an anti-historical one. In spite of a flourishing and superbly organized prac-tice of history [as an academic endeavor], America's mind is thoroughly anti-historical. A historiography that in the march of humankind wants to see purely the theodicee of progress, is not the true kind." Or, as he commented elsewhere, the American is directed too much toward the present and the future to be open to the mystery of the past (Huizinga, 1972: 175).

Many others have tried to put into words this aspect of American culture. Time and again they tried to evoke the image of a nation that lacked the European sense of history, that was without memory, cut adrift from the passage of time, bobbing along with shifting tides and currents. Spengler pointed to the lacking element of true historical tragedy, *das große Schicksal* [the great destiny]. He too mixed two metaphorical dimensions: lacking a sense of historical tragedy, the American soul had never had a chance to deepen. The superficiality of American life Spengler related to the lack of "real" history. To Ortega y Gasset, America had only just entered into history; it was at a primitive stage, it was primitivism itself.

These metaphors have continued to retain their currency. In 1986 Jean Baud-rillard published a thin volume entitled *Amérique*. America's lack of a history is one of the many contrasts between America and Europe that Baudrillard apho-ristically conjures up for us. Like Ortega, Baudrillard calls America primitive, unburdened by Europe's historical heritage. In America he finds the triumph of oblivion over remembrance. America, to him, is "the only primitive society of the future . . . a society that is totally metasocial, with unforeseeable consequences, whose immanence delights us, but which has no past to reflect it—a society, therefore, that is quintessentially primitive." It is a society that never pauses to reflect upon itself, "beautiful in its superficial diversity." Complex and diverse, yes, but superficially so. Therefore the true immanence of America, "the truth of America," can only be fathomed by Europeans; only they tend toward reflection. Only for their eyes can the surface come to reflect deeper layers, hidden from direct view. They are able to envision what is not there to be seen. Therefore, only Europeans can conceive of life at the surface in America as a "perfect sim-ulacrum," the mere reflection of deeper meanings. This perception will always escape Americans. Engaged in forming the ghost images of their collective exis-tence, they are like bathing beauties in a 1950s Esther Williams movie, unable themselves to see the figurations they form. Baudrillard puts it thus: "The Amer-icans themselves have no sense at all of the simulation. They are its perfect con-figuration, but they are unable to describe it, because they themselves constitute the model." Europeans know the raptures of analytic thought. They are the excited audience watching from the side. Americans lack this reflective attitude. They live in "perpetual actuality of all signs," a continuing story without history. Americans have no sense of historic roots; they are uprooted (all quotations from Baudrillard, 1986: 58).

Whoever lives in the present has no sense of historic meaning and context. Nor will such a person have a sense of organic cohesion. For indeed, anything that can be conceived of in terms of internal coherence has a historical dimension. This leads us to a third metaphorical motif that Europeans have used to give expression to American cultural defects, as they saw them. Once again Huizinga provides us with a telling example. When introduced to the Dewey Decimal System, used for the systematic filing of library holdings in America, he recognized a quintessentially American impulse at work. As he saw it, time and again the living organic connections in the body of human knowledge were sacrificed to the need for classification. The human mind had been made subservient to the tyranny of the decimal system. This confirmed Huizinga's intimations concerning the antimetaphysical bent of the Americans and their inclination to subject the spiritual realm to the dictates of technical organization.

Many are the areas in which Americans were seen to display this lack of reverence for the organic cohesion of things. If in Europe Marx, in his early writings about the alienation of industrial work, had had in mind the pre-industrial craftsman who could express his individuality in the products he made, then America offered a more radical illustration of these ominous trends than did Europe. In America, about the time Marx was writing, a transformation of industrial production was taking place that would become known as the "American System of Manufactures." It centered around the idea of "replaceable parts" that would henceforth conceive of industrial products as a set of components, separately produced and separately replaceable. The idea had first taken hold in the manufacture of arms and had been introduced there by Samuel Colt. In his case there would be no Marxian alienation: his name would become synonymous with the guns leaving his factory. Yet his productive innovation would spell the end of the individual craftsman. Henceforth, no finished product would display the individual craftsmanship of its maker. Individuality as a unique, organically coherent whole of characteristics had fallen prey to America's antimetaphysical spirit.

Americans themselves would probably call it good old Yankee ingenuity, thinking of the slightly eccentric spirit of nonconventionality deemed characteristic of New England but found elsewhere in America as well. It is a spirit that thrives on the assumption that cultural entities will reveal their inner secrets if you disassemble them into their component parts. Once you have taken that liberty, why not be as irreverent when re-assembling the parts? Consider the example of Charles Ives, successful businessman and composer, one of the great innovators of the musical idiom of our age. As he remembered it, his father, "half in fun and half seriously," let him form chords by piling thirds—one major, one minor—on top of one another. As if seeing himself through his father's eyes, Ives continues: "This boy's way—of feeling, if you can have two 3ds, major or minor, in a chord, why can't you have another one or two on top of it, etc.—[is] as natural to a boy as thinking, if three bases in baseball, why not four or five . . . —it's an obvious and natural way of having a little fun!" *Having a little fun*—the fun of the craftsman who has just invented a new contraption. Ives must have been aware of the comparison. He mentions a concert of his music at which young Sally Whitney was present, and he goes on to say: "Sally's grandpa, Eli, invented the cotton gin, so Sal was used to invention!" (Kirkpatrick, 1972: 120).

America's attitude toward Europe's cultural heritage has always shown this spirit. When faced with the aura of holiness, historicity, individuality, and local setting that envelops European culture, Americans characteristically have displayed the happy irreverence of the uninitiated. They did not find themselves inside European history, but facing it from the outside, like tourists in a museum. An entire historical heritage presented itself to them in the light of contemporaneousness. Henry James, another famous son of New England, had this to say: "It seems to me that we are ahead of the European races in the fact that more than either of them we can deal freely with forms of civilization not our own, can pick and choose and assimilate."[9] Americans, according to James, have an eclectic freedom that allows them to select elements from European culture at their own will and whim and in the same spirit to rearrange them. The American modernist Ezra Pound is another, more extreme case in point; he showed how the American imagination, free from European traditions, could make something new from its separate elements, something that could appeal equally to Americans and Europeans.

Ives, Pound, and James are highbrow examples. They all followed a high artistic calling. But we can find this fragmenting, anti-organic attitude of the Americans on a more everyday level as well. If, for instance, the skyscraper is a uniquely American contribution to international architecture, that is not due only to its sheer size but mostly to its sovereign infringement of traditional rules of stylistic unity, proportion, measure, and scale. The skyscraper lacks all the ingredients of organic closure. Another story can always be added, in any style. It represents an architecture that is quintessentially composite, lacking any compelling logic of cohesion or closure. In *The Future in America*, H. G. Wells had already addressed this issue. Entering New York harbor, he saw the skyscrapers of Manhattan rise up before him, "the strangest crown that ever a city wore." He went on to say: "They have an effect of immense incompleteness; each one seems to await some needed terminal." Comparisons with St. Peter's in Rome or St. Paul's in London force themselves on him: "These are efforts that have accomplished their ends. . . . But New York's achievement is a threatening promise, growth going on under a pressure that increases." "Mechanical, inhuman growth," he termed it in the next line (Wells, 1907: 42).

The skyscraper might be called the middlebrow illustration of what we have in mind. It illustrates the anti-organic spirit of Americans as it affects the realms of the engineer and of technical design. When we turn to the area of lowbrow mass culture, examples abound. Umberto Eco, in his *Travels in Hyperreality* (1987), has described America tongue-in-cheek as "the last beach of European culture." Whereas cultural heritage is slowly crumbling in Europe, in America we can find the complete collection, copied a thousand times over, enlarged or reduced, in every material conceivable. If America is a land without castles, no problem: America will buy them in Europe, take them apart, and reassemble them in random order. Hearst Castle in California, with its many rooms, offers the visitor a tour through European periods and styles. When the French protest the opening of a Euro Disney on their hallowed ground, Disney's director, Michael Eisner, is truly amazed (or feigns to be). How can people say that Disney would have no eye for older cultures? There is an entire section at Euro Disney devoted to the discoveries and fantasies of Leonardo da Vinci and Jules Verne. "Culture?" Eisner asked. "Sleeping Beauty is culture, and that's French; Peter Pan is English, Pinocchio Italian, Snow White German."[10] What are these Europeans complaining about?

We could go on in this vein. Clearly, in their way with history, tradition, and organic closure, the Americans show a characteristic talent for cultural dissolution, mixed with an ingenuous nonconventionality, which together strike many a European observer as a cultural deficiency. Europeans can never simply take American culture as an intriguing variant of Western culture in its own right and explore its unique characteristics; they always want to sit in judgment. More often than not the judgment is negative, cast in words that testify to a virulent anti-Americanism. A striking case in point is Sigmund Freud. In Peter Gay's biography of Freud, the latter appears as a rabid anti-American—"Yes, America is gigantic, but a gigantic mistake"—full of scorn for the dull, coarse, and gullible American who is able to understand only one language, that of money. In endless variation Freud expounded the "dollaromania" of the Americans. As Gay points out, Freud was far from original in this. He was using clichés that were a century or more old. In *Martin Chuzzlewit*, Charles Dickens had already produced a biting caricature of the Americans using essentially the same ingredients. The Americans (or so we are told in Dickens's novel) preach freedom but live in fear of public opinion; they talk about equality yet own slaves. They are snobs and money-grabbers. Conversations with Americans "may be summed up in one word—dollars. All their cares, joys, hopes, affections, virtues, and associations, seemed to be melted down into dollars" (Gay, 1988: 569).[11]

Many others in Europe have used similar language in their descriptions of Americans. The language is highly telling; the reference in the Dickens quotation to "melted down into dollars" is perhaps the central metaphor for America's anti-organic, decomposing cast of mind. For indeed, what has a greater dissolving effect on the nature and identity of things than money? Money is the central instrument for the reduction of the endless variety of the intrinsic value of things to the one thing they have in common: their exchange value. Everything has its price; everything can be bought and sold. Money is the ideal instrument for what Freud called "the American pattern of replacing quality with quantity" (Gay, 1988: 563–64). And many Europeans do picture the American as the one who, checkbook in hand, has reduced European culture to a garage sale, who has dissolved its context and discarded its aura.

THE ATTRACTION OF THE VOID

Europeans have created their own imaginative space for America. They have filled this space with images and metaphors expressing the conviction that America, in contrast to Europe, has been found lacking. As Huizinga put it: "We all have something that you lack." Sometimes, as in the case of Crèvecoeur and Goethe, the lack was viewed positively. But most often the evaluation is negative and the implication is a critique, if not a rejection, of American culture. At times, as we have seen, the criticism is delivered dispassionately, when observers are able to see American culture as a separate entity, unrelated to Europe. But more often America is seen as a threat, as a force of corruption affecting cultures elsewhere.

Yet there are exceptions. This same metaphorical repertoire has sometimes been used to describe America as a rapturous counterpoint to European civilization. In much European resistance to American culture there is often a submerged fascination, a repressed Freudian pleasure principle, that works to make the public discourse more vituperative, if not abusive. But sometimes temptation wins out. Then, suddenly, Europeans are able publicly to appreciate forms of American culture, at times even sooner than their American counterparts. Jazz, the "hard-boiled" detective novel, and the Hollywood B-movie were first discovered by Europeans as an act of cultural rebellion. Younger generations rebelled against the entrenched cultural order and turned values upside down, embracing American forms of culture not for what they lacked but for what they offered in terms of vitality and energy.

A good recent example of this can be found in Jean Baudrillard's *Amérique*. Although the author was no longer a young man when he wrote it, the book has all the aspects of a cultural revolt that one tends to associate with the young. As in the case of so many Frenchmen before him, America becomes the central expression of this revolt. French intellectuals have a collective history of infatuation, secret or not so secret, with America. I remember watching a film years ago—it must have been about 1960—made by a young French director, François Reichenbach, entitled *L'Amérique insolite*.[12] I was reminded of it by Baudrillard, who mentions the title in the course of his argument. Reichenbach gave us a view of America as a sustained theatrical effect, as a case of Brechtian alienation; his film is like a report on life on a distant planet—alien yet strangely seductive. Baudrillard undertakes a similar voyage through space, traveling a universe of pure and absolute freedom, in a successful escape from the gravitational pull of Europe—Europe that has become mired in its heritage of intellectual rituals, caught in rigid conceptual frames, decadent, incapable of an unmediated, direct confrontation with reality. America, to him, offers liberation from that conceptual imprisonment:

What we lack is the inspiration and courage for what one might call the zero degree of culture, for the power of non-culture . . . . We will always remain nostalgic utopians, torn between the ideal and our reluctance to realize it. We declare everything to be possible while never proclaiming its realization. Precisely the latter is what America claims to have achieved . . . . It is us who think that everything culminates in its transcendence and that nothing exists without first having been thought through as concept. Not only do they [the Americans] hardly care for that at all, they rather see the relationship in reverse. They don't care to conceptualize reality, but to realize the concept and to implement the ideas. (Baudrillard, 1986: 167)

We cannot but hear old echoes resounding in this statement. Baudrillard is not the first to hold that America has had the audacity to implement what had been thought out and dreamed up in Europe. It has shed the old Europe, burdened by history and caught up in unreal structures of thought. Thus, America could have become the authentic expression of Modernity, whereas Europe, in Baudrillard's words, will never be more than its dubbed or subtitled version. But there is more to Baudrillard's argument than this. He seems to return to the 1960s, hankering for the libertarian rapture, the sense of instant gratification, unmediated by the intellect, that to so many at the time was the appeal of the counterculture. Yet much as he was on the Left himself, challenging the established order, as an ideologue in the French manner who was looking to China and the Soviet Union for conceptual guidance rather than to America, he missed out on the excitement of the moment. It took the disenchantment of the French Left during the 1970s and 1980s, and their sense of ideological bankruptcy, for Baudrillard to become susceptible to the lure of American culture.

Once again, before our eyes a romance unfolds, a game of cultural adultery in which many French intellectuals have indulged. They have a keen eye for all that is banal and vulgar in America, yet at the same time more than anyone else they are tempted by the *élan vital*, the shameless authenticity of American culture. These romances always have one basic plot. It is always a case of a tired, elderly European turning toward America in the hope of regeneration, if not rejuvenation. America is unspoiled, primitive, youthful. It is unaware of itself. It is Eden before the fall. Europeans have tasted the forbidden fruit—they are obsessed by knowledge and reflection—yet hope to lose themselves in America. Baudrillard is in a sense a twentieth-century Crèvecoeur, reaffirming America's regenerative potential.

In Baudrillard's *Amérique* and Eco's *Travels in Hyperreality*, a remarkable twist is given to the familiar arguments of so many critics, American or European, of American mass culture. Where from Henry Adams on critics have deplored America's forsaking of its historical spirituality, where they have seen the signs of a fall from grace precisely in the mindless entropy of consumerism, Baudrillard and Eco testify to a sense of exhilaration. Cities, highways, traffic—all are as meaningless as America's deserts, but the impact is at the same time liberating. It is all utterly devoid of significance. It is just there, but in a rather complex way. Both Baudrillard and Eco speak of hyperreality. Reality has spawned its own replicas. Surrounded by phantom images of itself, one can no longer tell which is the real thing. America becomes Disneyland. Whether it is vulgar or sublime matters no longer. Those are European categories better left behind. One should experience America as it presents itself, the only truly primitive society of our age, a utopia become reality.

In Eco's view of America as "the last beach of European culture," everything will still be there when the real heritage has crumbled to dust in its countries of origin. For America to fulfill its salvage mission, it has to treat Europe's culture in a highly modernist, if not postmodernist, fashion—treating all of it as one large *objet trouvé*, recasting, duplicating, multiplying, cross-breeding, mass-marketing it. On the whole, Eco's tone and choice of words is slightly more critical, quoting Louis Marin on Disneyland as a degenerate utopia. In this world of the fake, "what is falsified is our will to buy, which we take as real, and in this sense Disneyland is really the quintessence of consumer ideology" (Eco, 1987: 43). Baudrillard is well beyond such criticism and seems to revel in alienation. Floating freely through America's universe, an escapee from European gravity, he offers a reader's guide to America's phantom images. With great metaphorical virtuosity he moves from image to image. At one point he calls America a "special effect." It leaves the reader slightly puzzled. Who is behind the effect? The French book cover doesn't help. It gives us two names: "Amérique" and "Jean Baudrillard." Is it Baudrillard who allows us to perceive America in its many phantom images, or is it the other way around? I tend toward the latter option. America becomes one wide projection screen for Baudrillard's fantasies of self-liberation. In one ongoing stream of aphoristic, often highly imaginative but totally noncommittal snippets, he takes us on his psychological journey. But strangely, he still seems entrapped in habits he pretends to have abandoned. With all his metaphors and associations, he is still busy weaving America into an argument and a structure of concepts. He is still quintessentially the European, taking America into the world of European intellectual preoccupations. Enjoying life "on the surface," sucked along in the slipstream of American life, Baudrillard also testifies to the European sense, expressed by Huizinga and others, that "we have something that you lack." But Baudrillard's point is precisely that Europeans cannot be too sure they should cherish that "something."

"L'AMERIQUE, MAIS C'EST LA DECONSTRUCTION!"

Europeans have woven America into a web of images of their own making. Meanings have become attached to "America" that truly belong to a European history of critical self-reflection. America has become a constituent element of the history of European ideas. Rarely therefore are Europeans able to approach America free of all preconceived ideas. It is always themselves they are likely to see reflected there. They are apt to see the country as an unsettling counterpoint to their own cultural conventions and to translate the "otherness" of America into contrasts that tend to reflect America in much the same way a distorting mirror would. We can all produce our own lists of such contrasts. Europe values quality;

America only knows quantity. Europe has a keen sense of authenticity; America adores the fake and phoney. Europe appreciates things old and quiet, it has "depth"; America dissipates its energies in shallow pursuits. Europe experiences itself as meaningful and finds in America what is pointless. Europe knows and appreciates individuality; America subjects it to ruthless standardization. There individuality turns into spurious diversity, producing ten breakfast cereals that all taste like cardboard. These are contrasts that can be reduced to the metaphorical dimensions explored above. Always America is molded and made subservient to the purposes of a European discourse, to European categories and preoccupations. America becomes a construct of the European mind.

Yet one intriguing question remains. Could it be that in this rich collection of images about America there is more than prejudice and stereotype? Could there be kernels of truth and astute perception? In every image that we have reviewed, there is always a mixture of evaluation—mostly negative—and of observation. When could we say the balance between the two is such that observation prevails over evaluation and the image can truly be seen as an intimation of the real inner working of American culture? I am inclined to say that the imagery representing America in terms of spatial and temporal metaphors does not really teach us much about America. The element of evaluation far outweighs observation. Rarely are such images more than the ready stereotypes that travelers take along as part of their luggage.

The balance is different in the case of all those images that see an anti-organic streak in the American cast of mind. The deep structure, or matrix, of American culture listens to a number of transformation rules that work to dissolve into its constituent elements everything that Europeans perceive as an integral whole, only to be appreciated in its entirety and integrity. This is a cultural inclination that may have to do with America's historical eccentricity. The country has long been at the margin of the older, European cultures. Everything crossing the Atlantic to come to its shores—immigrants from every European country, cultures from every European country and cultural period—always suffered a loss of historical context and meaning. Europe has never existed in America in any form other than disassembled into its constituent elements. That perhaps is what has allowed American culture its remarkable freedom at rearranging that which had undergone historical gestation and growth in Europe.

We can find one ironic illustration of this in the recent intellectual fashion of deconstructionism in the United States. Transplanted from France and derived from theoretical views developed by Lacan, Derrida, Foucault, and other French philosophers, deconstructionism in America proved a wonderfully apposite instrument for giving intellectual shape to the militant emancipation of minorities that had been going on since the late 1960s. In this emancipation—of women, blacks, gays, natives—a new awareness arose of one particular instrument of oppression: entrenched forms of hegemonic discourse. The inferiority of minority groups had been encoded into linguistic conventions and had thus been made to appear as part of a natural order of things. Once cast in this light, emancipation came to be seen as a battle for linguistic control. Every construction that language allowed people to give to reality, all conceptual conventions that had entrenched themselves in everyday language, served to perpetuate established views of minority positions. Emancipation movements therefore must squarely confront such linguistic conventions and aim to deconstruct them. Thus, language and linguistic conventions, as tools of oppression, were ruthlessly taken apart into their component elements and rearranged as so many tools to give voice to those that had been ignored by the reigning discourse. Although the philosophical insights inspiring this approach were novel and fashionable—which to a certain extent could account for their intellectual snob appeal—they could effortlessly blend into a game long familiar to Americans. Derrida for one must have sensed some of this when he pondered why his views had gained such fashionable currency in America. In 1986, with a facetious little smile, he proffered the following hypothesis: "L'Amérique, mais c'est la déconstruction!" (Derrida, 1986: 18).

NOTES

1. *Paris au XXème siècle* [Paris in the twentieth century], a manuscript from the early 1860s, was discovered by a descendant of Jules Verne in the late 1980s and eventually published in 1994. [Editors' note]
2. Restrictions of space allow but a list of the earliest examples: the early cartography of a tripartite *Orbis Terrarum*, an *Oecumene* with an inaccessible West screened off by the unfathomable river Oceanus; Plato's myth of Atlantis from his *Timaeus* and *Critias*; the biblical tales from Genesis of a lost paradise, of Noah and an all-engulfing flood resulting in a cleansed, rejuvenated Earth; the composite Celtic hero Saint Brendan, who sailed to a land in the West without sorrow or death (*Navigatio Sancti Brendani*); Seneca's remark in *Medea* about a future time when the most distant land of Thule "will no longer be ultimate Thule"; and Dante's character Ulysses in the *Divina Commedia*, who transgresses the bounds of the self-enclosed medieval world and glimpses the island of Purgatory itself before he and his shipmates are drowned.
3. Translated from *Goethes Werke vol. 1 Gedichte und Epen* (Hamburg: Christian Wegner Verlag, 1948) 333.
4. Translated from Alexis de Tocqueville, *De la Démocratie en Amérique* vol. III (Paris: Librairie de Charles Grosselin, 1839–1840) 277, 278.
5. James Oppenheim, "Editorial," *Seven Arts*, June 1917: 201.
6. Van Wyck Brooks, "Toward a National Culture," *Seven Arts*, March 1917: 547.
7. Translated from Oswald Spengler, *Jahre der Entscheidung* (München: Beck, 1933) 48.
8. David Riesman, Nathan Glazer, Reuel Denney, *The Lonely Crowd* (New York: Doubleday Anchor, 1950, 1953) 64–65.
9. T. S. Eliot wrote about Henry James: "It is the final perfection, the consummation of an American to become, not an Englishman, but a European—something which no born European, no person of any European nationality can become." Quoted in M. J. Laski, "America and Europe: Transatlantic Images," in A. M. Schlesinger, Jr., and M. White (eds.), *Paths of American Thought* (London: Chatto and Windus, 1964).
10. Quoted in the *Guardian*, 14 October 1991.

11. Much later, Freud's daughter Anna wrote to Ernest Jones: "I quite agree that one should avoid publishing adverse remarks of my father about America" (Archive, British Psychoanalytical Institute, London). Thanks to Dr. Han Israels for bringing this to my attention.

12. *L'Amérique insolite* [Uncanny America], dir. François Reichenbach, 1960, documentary, 1 h 24 mins. [Editors' note]

REFERENCES

Baudrillard, Jean (1986). *Amérique*. Paris: Grasset. Trans. as *America* (London: Verso, 1988).

Beauvoir, Simone de (1952). *L'Amérique au jour le jour*. Paris: Gallimard. Trans. as *America Day by Day* (London, 1952).

Berkeley, George (1735). *On the Prospects of Planting Arts & Learning in America* in *Essays, Principles, Dialogues: With Selections from Other Writings*, edited by Mary Whiton Calkins (New York: Scribner, 1957).

Derrida, Jacques (1986). *Memoirs for Paul de Man*. New York: Columbia University Press.

Dreiser, Theodor (1917). "Life, Art and America." *Seven Arts* 1 (February).

Duhamel, Georges (1931). *America the Menace: Scenes from Life of the Future*. Boston: Houghton Mifflin.

Echeverria, D. (1957). *Mirage in the West: A History of the French Image of American Society to 1815*. Princeton: Princeton University Press.

Eco, Umberto (1987). *Travels in Hyperreality*. London: Picador.

Gay, Peter (1988). *Freud: A Life for Our Time*. New York: Norton.

Gijzen, Marnix (1927). *Ontdek Amerika*. Brussels: N.V. Standaard Boekhandel.

Huizinga, Johan H. (1950). *In de schaduwen van morgen* [1935]. Haarlem: H.D. Tjeenk Willink. Collected Works, Vol. VII, 313–424.

——— (1972). *America: A Dutch Historian's Vision, from Afar and Near*. New York: Harper and Row. Trans. of *Amerika levend en denkend: Losse opmerkingen* (Haarlem: H.D. Tjeenk Willink, 1927).

Kirkpatrick, J. (ed.) (1972). *Charles E. Ives Memos*. New York: Norton.

Ortega y Gasset, José. *The Revolt of the Masses*. New York: W. W. Norton & Co., Inc., 1957. [Spanish original *La Rebellión de las Masas*, 1929.]

André Siegfried, *America Comes of Age: A French Analysis*. New York: Harcourt, Brace and Company, 1927, translated by H. H. Hemming and Doris Hemming [Originally: *Les Etats-Unis d'aujourd'hui*, 1927].

Steiner, Georges (1981). "The Archives of Eden." *Salmagundi* 50/51 (Fall 1980/Winter 1981): 57–89.

Ter Braak, Menno (1928). "Waarom ik 'Amerika' afwijs." *De vrije bladen* 3.

Tocqueville, Alexis de. *Democracy in America*, edited by J. P. Mayer, translated by George Lawrence. New York: Anchor-Doubleday, 1969. [Final French edition of *Democracy in America* in Tocqueville's lifetime, 1850.]

Truettner, William H. (ed.) (1991). *The West as America: Reinterpreting Images of the Frontier, 1820–1920*. Washington and London: Smithsonian Institution Press.

Wells, Herbert Georges (1907). *The Future in America: A Search after Realities*. Leipzig: Bernhard Tauchnitz.

Part I

The Image

1 Blackface Minstrels and *Buffalo Bill's Wild West*: Nineteenth-Century Entertainment Forms as Cultural Exports

John G. Blair

The first impulse of many practitioners of American Studies is to concentrate on the media because they are so powerfully present both within the United States and elsewhere. By turning back the clock to nineteenth-century entertainment forms, we can analyze relevant cultural issues before film, radio, records and tapes, television, compact discs, and e-mail came into existence. One may play down technology in favor of underlying cultural factors and see that what matters most is not the new technologies but the spirit in which they are exploited.

I concentrate here on the two outstanding American entertainment innovations of the nineteenth century, both of which were taken up abroad very rapidly. First, blackface minstrels were that time's single most popular genre of American stage entertainment, starting from individual blackface acts in the 1830s and expanding from the 1840s to the end of the century as full-evening entertainment. These shows spread quickly throughout the English-speaking world,[1] especially the British Isles and Australia and to a lesser extent to South Africa and other outposts of the British Empire (for Australia, compare Waterhouse, 1990). Second, *Buffalo Bill's Wild West*, the Western world's greatest traveling attraction for three decades starting in 1883, skillfully blended rodeo competitions, historical reenactments, and ethnographic authenticity for a total of some 50 million spectators in more than 1,000 cities in 12 countries (Blackstone, 1986: 92). The appeal of this kind of spectacle reached all over the Western world, its availability enhanced by concentrating on action over verbiage. Performances could reach even the illiterate with images of the triumph of Western Civilization.

The differences between these two entertainment forms are not negligible, but I leave them aside for now to highlight the similarities, which carry over from stage to fair grounds, from mid-century to late, and from one importing culture to another. For expository convenience I divide these factors into four categories: subject matter, marketing, performance values, and messages of the medium.

SUBJECT MATTER

Whether we focus on blacks or natives, these American entertainment forms play on exoticism. What was unfamiliar to American urban audiences seemed doubly exotic to Europeans. The early minstrel acts purported to represent plantation life (Jumping Jim Crow) or flashily dressed urban blacks (Zip Coon or Jim Dandy). It bothered no one that the portraiture was flagrantly satirical in conception, the outlines crudely drawn, the movements as exaggerated as a clown's, the sentiments unrefined. The cultural work of minstrelsy in the American context provided northern audiences with entertaining reassurances of the inherent inferiority of blacks wherever they might be found, a message that met no resistance among the primary working-class audiences in New York and comparable American cities. The less the spectators knew of or thought about actual blacks, the better. The cultural stereotypes were deeply absorbed and driven home with the irrefutable argument of laughter.

In England the portraiture was basically the same, but the local sponsorship was dramatically different. In the 1840s, early American performers and songs were received in Britain as exotic artifacts that happened also to confirm the cultural rightness of British imperialism in Africa. British ethnocentrism could be doubly served by reading these "blacks" as embodying African origins plus American mediation. The initial appeal in 1843 is clear from a *Times* review:

The spectators and auditors of the wonders exhibited at this theatre have during the week been amused by what is called an Ethiopian concert, by four Virginian minstrels, in which some of the aboriginal airs of the interior of Africa, modernized if not humanized in the slave states of the Unions and adapted to ears polite, have been introduced by the musical conductor of the theatre. (Nathan, 1977: 137–138)

This contextualization of minstrelsy could not be imagined in the United States, where Africa was of no concern whatsoever. Ethnocentrism controlled cultural importations so thoroughly that these audiences responded only in terms of what they were inclined to see. Each culture assimilated the genre to its own ends and preoccupations. The British had it both ways; America was merely a halfway station from Africa, and civilization was defined by Britain's superior "spectators and auditors." The reference to "slave states of the Union" was, of course, total fantasy, because the minstrels had only the most distant and stereotypical ties with plantations and the life of slaves.[2]

Exoticism in the case of *Buffalo Bill's Wild West* is all the more obvious because there were no noticeable populations of Native Americans in any of the cities where the *Wild West* played. Indians elicited still more fascination than blacks because of the centuries of reports and speculations on "savages" as "nature's noblemen." The basic material was the myth-charged narrative of the American West: the cowboys-and-Indians melodrama acted out for spectators even as the historical process of white domination was still being completed. Above all, the *Wild West* reenacted the triumphant drama of Western civilization, which spread not only in the United States but throughout the Western world as well.

In addition, *Buffalo Bill's Wild West* brought to ordinary people in urban surroundings a simulated vision of the manly outdoor "strenuous life" that was being mythologized during the same period by Theodore Roosevelt, Owen Wister, and Frederick Remington (counted an especially close friend by Cody). The intense and violent encounter of a bronco and a masterful rider epitomized an ideology of individual heroism. This mythology was American in flavor, but it spoke to fantasy lives all over the industrializing world. The success of Marlboro advertising over the last few decades has been an extension of this same appeal. Moreover, the *Wild West* established the way in which people distant from the scene should view Native Americans. Although William F. Cody may not have intended it this way, the show demonstrated wherever it went that the Sioux were the prototypical Indian nation, that their teepees and long-feathered headdresses represented universal Indian practice—and that whites should dominate Indians. The "authenticity" of *Buffalo Bill's Wild West* could not be impugned.

MARKETING

Blackface minstrels entered the British world with an aristocratic sponsorship totally unprecedented in its American origins. What had been designed originally to appeal to the lower classes in U.S. cities was taken up by the high and mighty. That the appeal was from the top down is clear from the marketing techniques employed. Minstrel shows became the darlings of the aristocracy for a time in the mid-1840s, especially once Queen Victoria and Prince Albert requested a command performance. An extraordinary document survives in the Harvard Theatre Collection that details just which notables honored performances of the Ethiopian Serenaders at St. James Theatre with their patronage: Duchesses, Marchionnesses, Countesses, Viscountesses, Ladies, and Misses—132 names in carefully graduated lists according to descending order of status (*List*: 6–8). These are followed by more pages listing 168 names of Princes, Ambassadors, Ministers, Dukes, Marquises, Earls, Viscounts, Counts, Barons, Lords, Honorables, Sirs, Colonels, Captains, and Esquires (8–10). There follow seven nearly identical programs of private entertainments sponsored by members of the royal family.

In London the St. James Theatre quickly became specialized in minstrelsy, a calling it maintained for Londoners until it was torn down in the early twentieth century. As proof of the acceptance of blackface minstrelsy in polite society, one old performer recalled seeing many clergymen in the audience (Reynolds, 1928: 104). In short, minstrelsy's rollicking farces with occasional tear-jerking sentimental ballads could please people from any class, and the initial aristocratic sponsorship gave permission for anyone who could afford it to attend.

In the case of *Buffalo Bill's Wild West*, the marketing genius of Nate Salsbury deserves much credit, but the enthusiasm of European nobility for the drama of the Great Plains clearly precedes his work. William F. Cody knew of it firsthand because he had served as organizer and guide for hunting trips that turned into command performances on their own. In 1872 General Philip Sheridan assigned him the job of organizing a buffalo hunt for Grand Duke Alexis of Russia. Cody arranged with a band of Sioux to put on a demonstration of their group hunting techniques and to stage a "war dance." In another foreshadowing of *Buffalo Bill's Wild West*, the Second Cavalry band took part in the festivities (Yost, 1979: 52–54). Other wealthy Europeans, led by the Earl of Dunraven, came forward seeking similar safari-spectacles. The step into show business was not complicated: basically, it meant taking the performance to the spectators rather than the other way around.

In England, once *Buffalo Bill's Wild West* arrived in 1887, royalty and other public figures were skillfully exploited by Salsbury and Cody. The greatest triumph was a command performance for Queen Victoria, who had not attended public entertainments for a quarter of a century since the death of Prince Albert. Her evident pleasure led to another command performance on June 20, 1887, for royalty from all over Europe who had assembled for Victoria's Golden Jubilee; this success in turn ensured bookings in major continental countries. The Deadwood Stage was driven by Buffalo Bill himself that day because it held "four kings": those of Denmark, Greece, Belgium, and Saxony (Russell, 1960: 331).

Having found the ideal marketing ploy in associating its own presence with grand-scale public events, the *Wild West* worked the same strategy wherever possible. Its next European swing began with a long stay near Paris during the International Exposition of 1889 that gave the world the Eiffel Tower. The World's Columbian Exposition of 1893 brought the *Wild West* to Chicago for similar reasons. Indians off-duty from their roles themselves became highly visible tourists at such affairs, thereby attracting still more paying customers of their own.[3]

On tour in Rome when Don Onorto Herzog of Sermoneta challenged the *Wild West* cowboys to master his Cajetan stallions, reputed to be the wildest and meanest in Europe, the Prime Minister of Italy headed the aristocrats on hand. Although the owner claimed "no cow-boy in the world could ride" these horses, in fact it was an affair of minutes, an impressive addition to the plaudits being accumulated by the American horsemen.[4]

Blackface minstrels and Buffalo Bill were not the last exotic American entertainments to attract Europe's finest. At the end of the century the upper classes took up yet another import in the form of ragtime music and associated dances such as the cakewalk, much to the profit of James Weldon Johnson and others.

PERFORMANCE VALUES

The third category of influential entertainment values involves performance style. The very physicality of the imported American entertainment forms (their vulgarity, some might say) gave them what seemed to Europeans a primitive vigor that fit well with their mythologized imagery of the New World. One gain was in sheer spectacle. Before minstrel incorporation, the folklore of Mike Fink and Davy Crockett was primarily limited to songs and story-telling. The same verses, transformed on stage as words sung by a "Jim Crow" figure in tatters and blackface, not only revivified a rollicking ballad but attached it to a startling dance unprecedented among familiar square dance figures. Hans Nathan summarizes the dance itself:

Rice, according to his own words, wheeled, turned, and jumped. In windmill fashion, he rolled his body lazily from one side to the other, throwing his weight alternately on the heel of one foot and on the toes of the other. Gradually, he must have turned away from his audience, and, on the words "jis so," jumped high up and back into his initial position. (Nathan, 1977: 52)

This was a spectacular act, the first of many. Physically vigorous dances were indeed an impressive part of the initial appeal. "Juba," a black dancer named William Henry Lane, so extraordinarily talented that he was the only known black performer permitted onstage in antebellum minstrels, epitomized the athletic side of this dancing—according to one of his stage bills of 1845:

The entertainment to conclude with the Imitation Dance, by Mast. Juba, in which he will give correct Imitation Dances of all the principal Ethiopian Dancers in the United States. After which he will give an imitation of himself—and then you will see the vast difference between those that have heretofore attempted dancing and this WONDERFUL YOUNG MAN. (Nathan 1977: 115)

The vigor of blackface performance can best be suggested to twentieth-century people by associating them with more recent performance genres, say the Marx Brothers (who worked in a vaudeville tradition directly influenced by minstrelsy), or more recently on American television with *Hee Haw* (1969–1971). British audiences believed blackface performances were above all good for the continuous belly laughter appropriate to farce.

An additional performance factor that encouraged British adoption of blackface minstrelsy was its portability. From the outset, minstrel performances incorporated a good deal of improvization in their acts. This was not jazz improvization elaborating variations on a theme, but the quick recombination of familiar elements in a flow of one-liners or selecting verses of a song in response to audience moods. This flexibility made it easy to include local references that were sure to elicit laughter from the audience. As early as 1837 the *Times* printed new local verses for "Jim Crow's Trip to Downing Street" (March 9, 1837).

In the case of *Buffalo Bill's Wild West*, the sheer spectacle was overwhelming. When William F. Cody launched his outdoor traveling show, rodeo shenanigans and simulated battles with blank ammunition invited large-scale gestures. Buffalo Bill was up to the task. The *Hartford Courant* evaluated the first season in 1883 as the "best open-air show ever seen. . . . The real sight of the whole thing is, after all, Buffalo Bill. . . . Cody was an extraordinary figure, and sits on a horse as if he was born in the saddle. His feats of shooting are perfectly wonderful. . . . He has, in this exhibition, out-Barnumed Barnum" (Russell, 1960: 297). This last was the highest compliment possible in the business of attracting public attention, for P. T. Barnum, as he vaunted in his 1869 autobiography, was the inventor and master of every aspect of advertising and show biz. Besides the sheer spectacle, hard work as well went into the *Wild West*: Cody reportedly missed only nine performances in the first 26 years (Blackstone, 1986: 92).

Bonafide Indians and authentic paraphernalia continued to prove their worth as Cody invested in one of the original Deadwood stagecoaches and proudly advertised it year after year (see sample program for 1893 in Russell, 1960: 376–377). Wherever the *Wild West* went, the Deadwood Stage served to transport local dignitaries in inaugural parades, thereby affirming their local importance in trade for their implied endorsement and patronage. The same principles applied to hiring participants with reputations. With the box office in mind, Bill was willing to pay Sitting Bull more than the going rate because this Indian, identified in popular fantasy as "the killer of Custer," could be given top billing under the slogan "Foes in '76—Friends in '85" (Russell, 1960: 316). These features of advertising and showmanship were just as applicable in Europe as they were in the United States. The combination of authentic and exotic proved unbeatable.

The contemporary appeal of "authenticity" in Britain is well expressed in a commentary in the *Manchester Guardian* of December 19, 1887:

It is the conjunction of scenery . . . with people who have lived the phases of life it represents that gives its peculiar interest and value to the "Wild West" Show. We are told that everything about it is real. The emigrant waggons [sic] the audience sees crossing the prairie have . . . been there. So with the Deadwood stagecoach, and about the buffaloes, the Indians, and the cowboys there is of course no doubt. In short the show is realism as close as it can be managed. (quoted in Brasmer, 1977: 150)

"Realism" becomes a justification for investment in something more than mere amusement, a key to the middle-class patronage that kept *Buffalo Bill's Wild West* prospering wherever it went.

Middle-class customers could feel that they were purchasing not just entertainment but also education, because the whole family could see "authentic" natives. The ethnographic appeal paralleled the late nineteenth-century expositions in Europe and the United States exhibiting "primitive" peoples in simulated "native" circumstances. The *Wild West* capitalized on this interest by charging separate admission during off-hours to watch the Indians in their encampment, which was complete with tepees and other Sioux accoutrements.[5] Family life was carried on as "normally" as possible, and for some racially mixed couples—mostly white men with Indian wives—it might have proved easier to raise mixed-blood children with the *Wild West* than in many communities back home. Journalists throughout Europe were fascinated with such native commonplaces as replacing clothing with body paint. For example, the London *Daily News* of May 10, 1887, remarked: "Some of them [Indians encamped at Earl's Court] had little else about them except paint; but the yellow, or blue, or black and blue pigments took the edge off an effect which might otherwise have shocked the anti-nudists of modern times."[6] The ethnographic-exotic appeal of Indians, although hardly an invention of *Buffalo Bill's Wild West*, would be hard to overestimate.

MESSAGES OF THE MEDIUM

In the preceding sections I have identified reception factors such as social class that go far beyond the ostensible contents of these entertainments, but here I seek something more ephemeral: prefigurations of practices and conceptions that only in this century would be identified as "modern." In part these are technological, implying the readiness of the American performers to make use of new or unexpected technologies and ultimately to make them a source of appeal.

The first stage involves the representation of machines—for example, the imitation of a steam locomotive by the Ethiopian Serenaders in their 1846 program (*List:* 11). The British press spoke of this act in uniformly glowing terms (here the *Times* of January 20, 1846):

The best of the evening, however, was the Railroad Overture, in which the starting, rattling along, and stopping of a train is admirably imitated, all the players imitating some mechanical action of the engine. The effect is wonderfully striking; Germon's legs, arms and tambourine, violently agitated like so many cranks and levers, swelling into the most rapid motion, and gradually subsiding into lazy action, and at last, repose, presented the very type of a railway engine. (*List:* 21)

No echo here of a Luddite hostility to machinery; instead, the performers (in blackface) are praised for their ability to adjust human performance to a perfectly convincing imitation of the mechanical.

A further step involves the incorporation of technology as part of the spectacle. In 1858, Christy's minstrels ran for several months in New York with a moving diorama of the Broadway skyline as the backdrop of the skit that made up their "Sleigh Ride" (see the rare full description printed in the *New York Picayune*, a text that has not before been called to scholarly attention). Normally such a diorama would have been presented elsewhere in the city for an admission fee aiming at middle-class spectators, a group overlapping only in part with the minstrel audience.[7]

Although the minstrels were never hostile to mechanicity as such, later in the century, in *Buffalo Bill's Wild West*, technology played a more central role in the performance itself. The *Wild West* was originally designed for outdoor presentation as a kind of traveling rodeo, but that meant losing any hope of winter audiences at precisely the season when urban boredom was high. By the winter of 1886–87, however, the show for the first time set up for the winter in Madison Square Garden, where it played its two performances a day before a house usually filled to the 15,000-seat capacity. In its London tour starting the following year, its installation at Earl's Court was on a still larger scale: 20,000 in seats and boxes, plus 10,000 more in covered stands, plus standing room for another 10,000—making a total of 40,000 per performance. In London *Buffalo Bill's Wild West* also gave its first night performance under electric lights (Cody, 1908: 700–715). By 1899 in Boston, the program advertised the lighting itself as worth seeing: "The enormous double electric dynamos used to illuminate the *Wild West* performances are well worth inspecting, as a scientific and mechanical triumph. They are the largest portable ones ever made, with a combined 250,000 candle power."[8] This pitch is roughly parallel to throwing in for the regular admission price a level of technological appeal comparable to a Universal Studios tour in Los Angeles.

Wherever the *Wild West* went in its mature days, the basic company comprised approximately 700 people, 500 horses, and 15–20 buffalo, not counting mules and lesser animals (Blackstone, 1986: 39). Implicit in such a scale lies an additional message of the medium—that bigness itself is worthy of attention. Even though blackface minstrels began with small troupes, after the Civil War they grew to appeal to spectators by the 1880s as "mammoth minstrels," that is, doubling up of every defined role within the minstrel panoply of character types. There could be upwards of 80 performers on stage, often in elaborate costumes that prefigure the dress-up spectacle of later Broadway revues. Admittedly these were minstrelsy's last-ditch efforts to hold audiences for a whole evening in blackface; but they also reflect an emerging American valuation of *size as such*, which impressed Europeans as well.

By 1900 the United States and its cultural exports were not yet identified by spectators on either side of the Atlantic as the epitome of the "modern." This linkage would have to wait until after World War II. But trends show that the Americans were comfortable with technological change and bigness, and were increasingly ready to exploit their entertainment value.

This survey of how and why two American entertainment innovations found a ready audience in Europe emphasizes cultural factors that continue to play a role in later European reception of American cultural products. Europeans were ready to accept the vigor if not the vulgarity of American performances as appropriate to the ruder state of civilization in the New World. But that very rudeness carried with it physically and imaginatively exciting possibilities that readily caught up audiences accustomed to more controlled and polite performances. American skills at inventing and marketing such performative vigor have obviously continued to grow over time, helping to promote ever-increasing exports of American cultural artifacts.

NOTES

1. The Continent did not take to minstrelsy. In Germany the few attempts to import American minstrels were loudly refused once audiences found these were not "real" blacks. Only after the Civil War did some all-black companies make their way to Germany. Thus, the very performance premise (white actors in blackface) that made the genre acceptable in the United States made it unacceptable in Germany. In France importation also failed, but for language reasons: the elaborate puns and word-play on which minstrel humor depended proved untranslatable.

2. The reminiscences of minstrel performers who claimed otherwise were strongly influenced by the postbellum importance of *authenticity* as a justification for entertainment.

3. See, for example, Rita G. Napier, "Across the Big Water: American Indians' Perceptions of Europe and Europeans, 1887–1906," in Feest, 1987: 383–401.

4. The account offered in the 1899 New York Program includes the following:

The anxiety and enthusiasm were great. Over 2,000 carriages were ranged round the field, and more than 20,000 people lined the spacious barriers. Lord Dufferin and many other diplomatists were on the Terrace, and amongst Romans were presently seen the consort of the Prime Minister Crispi, the Prince of Torlonia, Madame Depretis, Princess Colonna, Gravina Antonelli, the Baronness Reugis, Princess Brancaccia, Grave Giannotti, and critics from amongst the highest aristocracy. In five minutes the horse were tamed. (39)

5. Charles Griffin, for example, cites the first birth in England, on June 7, 1903, of "squaw papoose" to Chief Standing Bear and his wife Laura; the girl was named Alexandra-Pearl-Olive-Birmingham-England-Standing Bear. Two days later the family was on exhibit in the annex, "where they proved a potent attraction" (Griffin, 1908: 28–29). Their "potency" was clearly monetary.

6. As quoted by Danielle Fiorentino, " 'Those Red-Brick Faces': European Press Reactions to the Indians of Buffalo Bill's Wild West Show" (Feest, 1987: 405).

7. Similarly, Christy's in the 1850s advertised a new diorama of the Hudson River Valley, which could easily be unrolled behind a boat containing minstrel performers instead of a canvas sleigh. Such sources of spectacle were typically available to urban viewers at large, although for a higher price.

8. *Buffalo Bill's Wild West and Congress of Rough Riders of the World*, 1899: 14 (Boston).

REFERENCES

Blackstone, Sarah J. (1986). *Buckskins, Bullets, and Business: A History of Buffalo Bill's Wild West*. Westport, CT: Greenwood Press.

Brasmer, William (1977). "The Wild West Exhibition and the Drama of Civilization." *Western Popular Theatre*, eds. David Mayer and Kenneth Richards. London: Methuen, 133–156.

Buffalo Bill's Wild West and Congress of Rough Riders of the World (1899). Boston: Huntington Avenue Grounds.

Buffalo Bill's Wild West and Congress of Rough Riders of the World (1899). Greater New York: Fless & Ridge Printing.

Cody, William F. (Buffalo Bill) (1908). *Story of the Wild West* [1888]. Chicago: Thompson & Thomas.

Feest, Christian F. (ed.) (1987). *Indians and Europe: An Interdisciplinary Collection of Essays.* Aachen: Edition Herodot, Rader Verlag.

Griffin, Charles Eldridge (1908). *Four Years in Europe with Buffalo Bill.* Albia, IA: Stage Publishing.

A List of the Royal Family, Nobility & Gentry, who have honoured the Ethiopian Serenaders, Germon, Stanwood, Harrington, Fell & White, with their patronage at the St. James's Theatre, London, Together with the Opinions of the London Press [1846]. W. S. Johnson, "Nassau Stream Press."

Lott, Eric (1993). *Love and Theft: Blackface Minstrelsy and the American Working Class.* New York: Oxford University Press.

Nathan, Hans (1977). *Dan Emmett and the Rise of Early Negro Minstrelsy.* Norman: University of Oklahoma Press.

Reynolds, Harry (1928). *Minstrel Memories: The Story of Burnt Cork Minstrelsy in Great Britain from 1836 to 1927.* London: Alston Rivers.

Russell, Don (1960). *The Lives and Legends of Buffalo Bill.* Norman: University of Oklahoma Press.

Waterhouse, Richard (1990). *From Minstrel Show to Vaudeville: The Australian Popular Stage 1788–1914.* Kensington: New South Wales University Press.

Yost, Nellie Snyder (1979). *Buffalo Bill: His Family, Friends, Fame, Failures, and Fortunes.* Chicago: Swallow Press.

2 Creative Chiasmus: Comparative Evolution of U.S. Television and Cinema Products in the 1980s

Francis Bordat

My purpose is to carry out a critical review of the parallel evolutions of movies and television products in the United States since the early 1980s. The key idea that underlies this chapter will probably sound like a sweeping statement, for want of room for nuances. My contention is that even though the U.S. cinema and television industries followed parallel courses in many respects throughout the 1980s, they also inverted their respective positions in terms of dynamism and cultural creativity. I consequently take the opposite view of the common discourse, which holds that motion pictures form the last bulwark against television's quantitative invasion and qualitative decline in recent times.

The 1970s witnessed "Hollywood's Renaissance." The U.S. film industry revived the tradition of box-office hits (*The Godfather*, 1971; *The Sting*, 1973; *The Exorcist*, 1973; *Jaws*, 1975) by returning to classical genres and trying to combine them in order to maximize audiences. *Star Wars* (George Lucas, 1977) blended the world of the western and the ancient epic/spectacular in a simultaneously archaic and futuristic screenplay. Besides, increasing importance was attached to often brilliant special effects (the potential of which had been revealed since 1968 by Stanley Kubrick's *2001: A Space Odyssey*), such as in *Close Encounters of the Third Kind* (Steven Spielberg, 1977) or *Alien* (Ridley Scott, 1979). Special effects soon became the American cinema's New Frontier, improved consistently over 15 years, stimulated by the penetration of fantasy into almost all genres. Thanks to them, directors such as Terry Gilliam, Ridley Scott, Tim Burton, or Canada's David Cronenberg endowed their imaginary worlds with novel dimensions. Unfortunately, by appearing too frequently and taking increasing importance in screenplays and budgets, they became predatory elements to filmmaking in the early 1980s. Like *Alien's* monster, they ate the cinema's belly from inside, only to leave a hollowed-out husk.

U.S. cinema of the 1970s was also *auteur* filmmaking. Even the new "movie brat" generation (Francis Ford Coppola, George Lucas, Steven Spielberg, Brian De Palma, Martin Scorsese) imposed personal styles. Although these young Turks' movies dominated the market as of 1975, they did not actually corner it. Rather, they made room for a number of other directors, who took advantage of the Hollywood recovery to create intense and original works: Jerry Shatzberg, Arthur Penn, Sydney Pollack, Alan J. Pakula, Roman Polanski, Terence Mallick, Stanley Kubrick, Richard Lester, Sidney Lumet, Milos Forman, Michael Cimino, John Boorman, Robert Altman, Sam Peckinpah, Mike Nichols, and a host of more or less direct heirs to 1960s counterculture. It should also be noted that the big ancients of the "theater generation" (Elia Kazan, Joseph L. Mankiewicz, Billy Wilder) had not yet been excluded from that decade's cinema, although they were shamefully ostracized in the 1980s—when neither their age nor their skills justified such a rejection.

Finally, although it was still firmly grounded in Hollywood's entertainment tradition, U.S. cinema in the 1970s remained in close contact with the realities of its time. Even Spielberg's films prove to be interesting documents about suburban America. Besides, many others tapped into topical issues to touch off controversy: *Little Big Man, One Flew Over the Cuckoo's Nest, Network, The Deer Hunter, Apocalypse Now.*

In opposition, 1970s television retrospectively appears as a medium for soft entertainment. A few exceptions can of course be pointed out: the live coverage of great events, the interesting ideological rupture initiated by the sitcom *All in the Family* in 1971, the timely success of *Roots* in 1976–1977, a few clever detective series such as *Starsky and Hutch* or *Columbo*, and the famous (although programmed on PBS) *Sesame Street*. Nevertheless, most television output of the 1970s was mediocre in terms of form as well as content; despite their high ratings, *Happy Days* (1974), *Kojak* (1973), *The Little House on the Prairie* (1974), *The Waltons* (1972), and even *The Mary Tyler Moore Show* (1970) and *M*A*S*H* (1972) seem rather dull next to the period's cinematographic works (which the latter shows consistently plagiarize), or even next to the previous decade's television products, such as *The Untouchables, The Invaders, The Beverly Hillbillies, Rowan and Martin's Laugh-In,* or *Gunsmoke* (which introduced "adult" themes into television westerns). The worst examples from the 1970s are probably Harve Bennett's ABC series *The Six Million Dollar Man* (1973) and *Bionic Woman* (1976), insofar as they epitomized a process of psychological leveling that, according to David Buxton, stems from the ideology and esthetics of advertising.[1] More than at any other period, although its droning seemed about to be disrupted by the introduction of new technologies, commercial television of the late 1970s seemed to be content with the humdrum utilization of formulas and stereotypes.

Despite its good commercial standing in the United States and its increasing influence in the rest of the world, the U.S. cinema entered a phase of creative decline during the 1980s. One word summarizes the cause of this process: globalization. For ten years, Hollywood has seen an unprecedented increase in budgets. A full-length film costs an average of $29 million—yet *Terminator II*'s budget reached $94 million and *Jurassic Park*'s $100 million. Such investments can no longer be recouped on the domestic market alone; at least 40 percent of a film's income is expected to be provided by the international market. The double upshot of this process is American testiness toward all forms of "cultural exceptions" and what many observers have described as the reduction to the "smallest" common denominator of taste and intelligence. To unify the world audiences, the U.S. cinema must erase all original form or content likely to unnerve or upset the global teenager community, which has become its main public. Charles-Albert Michalet refers to the big Hollywood movies making up the core of the film industry today as "world cinema" (*cinéma-monde*)[2] rather than "U.S. cinema."

As a matter of fact, current blockbusters seem to be drifting away from America's social and cultural reality and falling back instead on the most dully consensual archetypes of the Western world. According to Jacques Goimard, "dodging certain screenplay implications is enough to make you accepted by all publics. You are totally free, as long as you have nothing to say."[3] Until the 1970s, although Hollywood decision makers frequently claimed the opposite, American movies commonly used to defend ideas transcending the dominant ideology—American "dream" or "way of life"—shared by nearly everyone. In terms of messages De Mille and Mankiewicz were miles apart, even though both loved Cleopatra. More recently, such visions of Vietnam as Michael Cimino's, Francis Ford Coppola's, Oliver Stone's, or Barry Levinson's stand out clearly. Nevertheless—although exceptions can be found—it is becoming increasingly difficult to identify a stance in the majors' current output. The problem is not that U.S. films no longer convey an ideology, but that the ideology more and more coincides with its own repression.

One of Hollywood's strengths is its consistency in relying on the zeitgeist and availing itself of the epoch's fads and phobias (this has been Adrian Lyne's specialty through *Fatal Attraction* and *Indecent Proposal*); characters, themes, symbols, and discourses all blend into a playful logic in which references and stakes tend to phase out: everything is worth everything else, or becomes a citation, a pastiche, a simulacrum. Warfare becomes war games. Films are no longer about life, but about films. Pictures do not refer so much to reality as to previous pictures, thereby epitomizing a video clip syndrome or Disney effect. In *Positif* (January 1993), Jean-Loup Bourget asked a fundamental question about Coppola's *Dracula*: "Is postmodern cinema so substanceless that it needs to suck substance out of its own past as a vampire?" Even a movie "with a message" like *A Few Good Men* was called "embarrassingly derivative" by David Denby (*New York*, April 6, 1993). Yet Bourget's question nowadays concerns two out of every three films, including those made by young independent creators such as *El Mariachi* (Robert Rodriguez, 1992) or *True Romance* (Tony Scott, 1993). Another significant symptom of Hollywood's "inspirational crisis" is the continuous quest for ideas abroad and the increasing number of U.S.-made versions of European movies.

The three *Rambo* films, which uphold blue-collar values, are not the only factor prompting Asian or South American spectators to interpret them as propaganda for the Third World even though the films seemed to further the Great Communicator's crusade so adequately. The other key factor is the deliberate policy of ideological neutralization, as visible in the screenplay as borne out by the performance itself. It is indeed obvious that today's U.S. cinema is better off saying nothing, thus leaving itself open to any reappropriation. As for ostensible exceptions, they are in fact half-exceptions: insofar as *JFK* and *Malcolm X* were also made with a view to becoming global box office hits, their commitment is accompanied by a creative stiffness that testifies to their compromised nature.

The increasing number of R-rated films shows that Hollywood more and more ensures the "universality" of its output through violence and sex. Its movies are no longer genuinely "adult." The best examples are *Basic Instinct* or even *The Silence of the Lambs*, whose overstated gruesomeness poorly conceals an evident lack of substance. On the other hand, G- and PG-rated features, which make up the majority of releases, clearly exemplify growing infantilization. Although *Honey, I Shrunk the Kids, Home Alone*, or *Kindergarten Cop* are not examples of shameful entertainment per se, they fail to satisfy any filmgoer over 15 years of age. In fact, a serious problem at the moment is that under current conditions of distribution (by glutting the market), such movies leave less room for other types of films.

One can retort that such criticism has been voiced ever since Hollywood was born. Back in 1951, Joseph L. Mankiewicz pointed out that "the secret of U.S. films' universality lies in their being targeted to an audience with a mental age of 12."[4] Yet his own movies (e.g., *People Will Talk*, 1951) testified to the contrary. But do they have any contemporary counterparts?

I will readily agree that a certain feeling of freedom and friendliness, even a sort of euphoria, are occasionally conveyed by Hollywood's new playfulness. The contemporary U.S. cinema allegedly derives from a postmodern esthetic of parodic distance and ironic citation, which, for instance, is well exemplified by David Lynch's or the Coen brothers' style (or stylistic exercises). However, postmodern virtuosity is instrumental in erasing references and impoverishing meaning,[5] two adverse effects that its decorative brilliance does not necessarily succeed in offsetting. Characters lacking in density, a prerequisite of this leveling, are typical of the current output. This trait shows blatantly in *Basic Instinct*, parodically in *Jurassic Park*.

In comparison to this new orthodoxy, out of which even independent filmmakers fail to break, the television industry has assumed the function of a creative laboratory. One would be narrow-minded to overlook the vistas that new media such as cable, satellite transmission, and video have opened up for U.S. viewers over the past decade. Of course, one is still free to choose not to choose, but the first attempt at channel-surfing or browsing at a Blockbuster Video outlet will pique one's curiosity. Consider basic cable: in addition to the four (soon to be five) networks' programs, public channels, free-access channels, CNN, Court TV, C Span 1 and 2, televangelists, Bravo, American Movie Classics (AMC) and many more offer a hitherto unheard-of package of information and entertainment, under the evident condition that you seek some and have personal preferences. AMC shows black-and-white films on a 24-hour basis, although American television viewers allegedly no longer care for them. Americans reportedly loathe foreign films, especially in their original languages with English subtitles; yet such movies make up Bravo's daily fare.

Probably stimulated by new competition and still essentially dependent on specifically American audiences (unlike the movie industry), television filmmaking seems to have undergone a positive evolution over the 1980s. *Dallas* and *Dynasty* were still hot sellers in foreign countries at the end of the decade even though they had long lost their appeal in the United States, where products better adapted to the period's sociocultural background had taken over.

First, a "kinder, gentler" America (as President Bush later called it) appeared in new prime-time hits such as *The Cosby Show* (NBC, 1984). During the heyday of Reaganism, when blacks were featured on television only as drug addicts, fools, or prostitutes, the Huxtable family skillfully reasserted values of intelligence, public spirit, and tolerance, as well as paid renewed attention to minorities.

However, the ensuing emergence of a new wave of series and sitcoms, which conveyed nothing kind or gentle, gave Bush and Quayle reason to be alarmed. A show born at the time of Reagan's reelection, *Miami Vice*, presented a genuine caricature of Reaganism. A baroque eulogy of luxury and spending, the series emphasized the liberal system's violence and corruption (for instance, through the show's glamorization of criminals). That is why it was perhaps ideologically less "passive" than was noted at the time. Along different lines, other mid-1980s shows—*Family Ties, Thirtysomething, L.A. Law, Moonlighting, Cagney and Lacey,* and *Hill Street Blues*—lent more sustance to their respective genres and shed a more critical light on contemporary society.

Television filmmaking seems to have crossed another boundary with shows featuring vivid depictions of the late 80s social reality. *Roseanne* first exemplified this new trend—although in a still moderate vein, close to *The Cosby Show*'s. Its female protagonist is neither pretty nor young nor wealthy; she works in a plastic factory for obnoxious employers and finds it hard to make both ends meet at the end of the month. This show is a long shot from *Dallas*. *Murphy Brown* stirred up an outcry when the protagonist, a divorced fortysomething played by Candice Bergen, decided to have a child out of wedlock. Her head-on confrontation with the Bush administration was one of 1992's great television moments. HBO's *Dream On* (produced by John Landis) displayed startling political and sexual outspokenness on the small screen. However, the most abrasive series were offered by Fox, with *The Simpsons, Married with Children*, or *Beverly Hills 90210*. If *Roseanne* is a twisted response to *Dallas, Married with Children* is unmistakably the same for *The Cosby Show*: its corrosive naturalism has been emphasized, with a family made up of a father who is a failure, a mother who is a fool, where the television set is always on and the fridge perenially empty. It is almost an understatement to say that *this* television "relies on proximity instead of escapism, on daily life instead of adventure."[6]

Realism has been intensified in what are now called "reality shows." These programs have already originated a considerable amount of literature and generally negative comments. However, I believe it is a mistake to equate them with "trash TV" of the late 1980s, which is only one form of the phenomenon. There is ample reason to take a dim view of talk shows such as Geraldo Rivera's or Mort Downey's. One may as well be rightfully shocked by violent or humiliating game shows, such as *American Gladiators* or *Rollergames* (Fox), or reenactments of sordid crimes, as in *Crime of Passion* or *Missing Reward*. Critics have associated such excesses with the decaying of Reaganism and the collapsing social order of the late 1980s. But the TV-truth trend generated its most unsavory avatars recently with complacent interviews of criminals and hastily produced television films based on gutter press stories.

An overall look at the wave of "true stories" on U.S. television (with shows such as *Studs, American Detectives, Unsolved Mysteries, Rescue 911, Street Stories, Cops, America's Most Wanted*, talk shows such as Oprah Winfrey's, or programs tapping into home-made taping such as *A Current Affair* or *America's Funniest Home Video*) reveals a significant trend that must be assessed in an unbiased manner. An essay recently published in *Esprit*[7] pointed out that reality shows respond to a very strong demand for communication from viewers isolated by modern life; such programs fill a void that institutions, incapable of understanding and unable to cope with these individuals' problems, have failed to handle adequately. Reality shows renew the viewers' modes of participation and identification by installing them inside the pictures. At best, one comes close to the ideal of Jean-Jacques Rousseau, who hated shows as a rule but imagined a new form thereof in his *Letter to d'Alembert*: "Put the spectators into a spectacle; make them actors; let every one of them see himself and love himself through the others so that they all be better united."[8] One is fairly close to a European or American documentary tradition. Is there a clear-cut fault-line between reality shows and certain documentaries that are allegedly above any suspicion, such as François Reichenbach's, Raymond Depardon's, the Maysles brothers' or Frederick Wiseman's?

Reality shows testify to a new taste for the authentic side of daily life, even if they often reformat reality to meet the dramatic norms of the spectacle. They also testify to the public's boredom toward the imaginary, possibly to a slump in the desire for fiction. To this extent, the televisual mode runs counter to Hollywood's policies. Whereas mainstream cinema follows an escapist creed, the television industry takes over neighborhood life, whether banal or astonishing, by way of response. The trend is deep-rooted and concerns all genres—including pornography, whose contemporary blockbusters are "amateur" performances.

It should be noted here that whereas contemporary moving pictures are characterized by an accelerating pace, shows that are taped live are increasing in number and almost epitomize the zero degree of camerawork and editing. This is found not only in news and talk shows aired on networks and cable but also on a number of specialized outlets such as C Span, Court TV, or public-access channels. Willy-nilly, these shows cater to a new type of viewer, rather active if not interactive, differing from drug-TV's dazed zombie. Of course, voyeuristic urges are pandered to, as when lawyers and witnesses on Court TV give a detailed description of the way in which serial killer Jeffrey Dahmer (successively) murdered, sodomized, cut up, partially ate, and dissolved in acid the body parts of 17 young homosexuals. But are these urges not pandered to just as much in supposedly more dignified areas of our culture? Besides, I believe that such static-shot, real-time slices of unadulterated visual plainness give one access to the most direct and comprehensive coverage of a case, however gruesome, and I am under the impression that one can take advantage of it to make up one's own opinion.[9]

New realism is taking over the television just as new playfulness is overwhelming the cinema. Film lovers are right to dread this evolution and worry that the seventh art is turning its back on what French novelist Hervé Bazin called its driving force: the progress of realism—even though, as Leroi-Gourhan pointed out, realism is always "a disturbing form of maturity in the life of arts."[10] Jean Douchet recently bemoaned the current evolution of cinema's style, which he described as a ceaseless build-up of appearances. According to him, the cinema is losing its soul, that is, the link with reality.[11] However, 20 years ago Roger Tailleur also singled out the real (le réel) as what had always given impulse to the western genre's evolution.[12] As entertainment-cinema is eluding any contact with reality, the task of the new television realism may be to upset and destabilize clichés.

A second chapter would be necessary to outline the limits of this destabilization. It is not inconceivable, for instance, to find a relation between the film industry's neo-playfulness and the television industry's neo-realism by demonstrating how they borrow elements from the same rhetoric. As a matter of fact, a comparison between the last few years' fantasy films and, say, the dozen weekly Manhattan Cable shows whose raw material is reality will show that the real and the supernatural are treated in fairly similar ways. In both cases, the *effect*, whether special or not, tends to bypass the symbol; and the image shifts from representation to presence, conceptualization to sensation, evocation to simulation, distancing to fascination. Again, to quote Jean Baudrillard, "events shift from a human level, where a grasp of events was still possible and significant, 'made sense,' to an inhuman level, which is that of pure immanence, of things in their detail, in their eccentricity"; "things continue to function, although . . . severed from their idea, their value, their referent, their destination."[13] In other words, truth-TV and special effects are relevant to the selfsame sphere of "the visual"[14] that has been analyzed by Serge Daney and Régis Debray, even to the virtual reality fantasy that haunts the modern imagination.

Nonetheless, I believe that a form of revitalizing realism capable of giving a new impulse to audiovisual creativeness has appeared in today's U.S. television. This new trend cannot possibly characterize all television products: everyone remembers the "clean," Hollywood-ish pictures of the Gulf War. However, Serge Daney already had an inkling of this potential in 1986, when he distinguished three audiovisual languages: a universal language (a kind of Esperanto), a cultural language (a sort of Latin), and a popular (*vulgaire*) language (a sort of dialect). The universal language is Hollywood and its mythology. The cultural language is the one spoken by the world's *auteurs*, who try to touch the general by conjuring up the particular. As for the dialect,

it is what I would call basic TV language. Not the cinema's segment which has "moved" into television to be cited, plundered, transformed into hybrid made-for-TV films or educational programs, but the properly visual, "village" dimension to which McLuhan referred: news, games, entertainment, sports, series. There, the point is no longer to draw something universal from the local (it used to be the cinema's aspiration), but to rescue a local intonation (an "accent") out of hopelessly standardized mechanisms.[15]

However standardized its formats, the new U.S. television is returning to its dialects, as to some substance long repressed by mannerisms. It is thereby less exportable; *Dallas* brought *Rambo* and *E.T.* in its wake—what contemporary series is following Arnold Schwarzenegger? Yet it is not inconceivable that Hollywood decides to draw inspiration from television. It did so once before, in 1953 (a "watershed year" according to Alain Bergala), when filmmakers upset by television "put their characters and spectators to the test of a documentary reality impossible to turn into screenplays,"[16] or in the 1960s, when a new generation of TV-trained directors (John Frankenheimer, Sidney Lumet, Robert Mulligan, Martin Ritt, Arthur Penn) started working for movie studios. Those still disturbed by the vulgarity of realism ought to be reminded that all the esthetic revolutions of motion pictures—the invention of the cinema itself, soundtracks, color, television, the large screen, THX sound, video—were all first judged as inroads into vulgar realism and consequently dismissed by the intelligentsia . . . until the latter succeeded in recycling its own intelligence.

Is a new process of reinvigoration taking place? Whereas Louis Malle, at the 1992 Cannes Festival, emphasized the articulation of fiction and reality as central to his own works, Steven Spielberg, who had just completed *Jurassic Park*, chose a black-and-white, semi-documentary approach for *Schindler's List*.

NOTES

1. David Buxton, *From The Avengers to Miami Vice. Form and Ideology in Television Series* (Manchester: Manchester University Press, 1990).

2. Charles-Albert Michalet, *Le Drôle de drame du cinéma mondial* (Paris: La Découverte; Centre fédéral FEN, 1987).

3. *Le Cinéma en l'an 2000, Revue d'esthétique* 6 (1984): 134.

4. Quoted by Pascal Mérigeau, "Contre Hollywood, tout contre," *Cahiers du cinéma* 465 (March 1993): 46.

5. Cf. Vivian Sobchack, "Postmodern Modes of Ethnicity," in *Unspeakable Images*, ed. Lester D. Friedman (Urbana and Chicago: University of Illinois Press, 1991) 329.

6. Serge Halimi, "Les séries américaines dépriment M. Bush," *Le Monde diplomatique*, August 1992.

7. "Les *Reality shows*, un nouvel âge télévisuel?" *Esprit*, January 1993.

8. *Lettre à d'Alembert sur les spectacles*, quoted by Pierre Chambat, "La place du spectateur, de Rousseau aux *reality shows*," *Esprit*, January 1993: 56.

9. *Le Monde diplomatique* also pointed it out for C Span:

Throughout the primaries, only C Span enables the citizen/TV viewer to follow every single candidate—a long lyrical discourse delivered by Jesse Jackson to an emotional New York audience, a debate on agriculture among Republican candidates in Iowa, a protracted handshake session in a coffee shop, somewhere in a backwater state . . . . Sometimes, one of these moments will leave a much more vivid imprint in the viewers' minds than the conventional comments of journalists who self-righteously analyze opinion polls or are satisfied to run the gamut of commonplaces.

Translated from Serge Halimi, "C Span, une chaîne anti-bêtise: montrer la démocratie au travail," *Le Monde diplomatique*, August 1990.

10. Quoted by Régis Debray, *Vie et mort de l'image* (Paris: Gallimard, 1992) 172.

11. *L'Armateur* 6 (March 1993).

12.

In this case, as often in other cases, each return to realism, to "real life," to the historical accuracy of facts and costumes, etc. triggers off a reaction and gives the genre a second breath. It so happened with Ince, Hart, *The Covered Wagon*, the epics of 1940, and TV's *Gunsmoke*. There have always been people to subvert clichés: the likes of Tom Mix and Roy Rogers, the circus-western performers, the perfect, useless, standardized, spotless, emasculated singing cowboys.

Translated from Roger Tailleur, "L'Ouest et ses miroirs," *Le Western* (Paris: 10/18, 1966) 39.

13. *Libération*, 15 February 1990.

14. Cf. note 10 above.

15. Serge Daney, "Cinéma européen, un déclin irrésistible?" *30 jours d'Europe*, March–April 1986.

16. Alain Bergala, Programme of the *cinémathèque française* (April 28–June 28, 1993).

3 A Comics Interlude

Jean-Paul Gabilliet

THE U.S. IMPACT ON FRANCO-BELGIAN COMIC STRIPS: A FEW LANDMARKS

Throughout this century, comic strip art has been an outstanding propagator in Europe of popular American images. Although such early syndicated strips as Winsor McCay's "Little Sammy Sneezes" and Richard Felton Outcault's "Buster Brown" were translated and published in book form in France at the very beginning of the century, it was not before the 1930s that U.S. comics significantly broke into the European market. This movement was initiated by the marketing of Walt Disney comic products in hardbound collections and weekly magazines as of the early to mid-1930s. In the second half of the decade, U.S. funnies literally flooded the European comics market. This paralleled a North American phenomenon, the emergence of the so-called "comic magazine"—today's "comic book"— as a new commodity developed thanks to the seemingly inexhaustible supply of cheap syndicated strip reprints (Gabilliet, 1994). Likewise, European publishers readily tapped into the cornucopia of American funnies; such features as Hal Foster's "Prince Valiant," George McManus's "Bringing Up Father," Phil Davis's "Mandrake the Magician," Ray Moore's "The Phantom," and Alex Raymond's "Flash Gordon" became household names for many European kids in the pre–World War II years.[1]

However, this was not an all-European phenomenon. In the late 1930s, the governments and authorities of many countries did not take kindly to the influx of U.S. comic strips. In fact, the only countries where their popularity and visibility grew to a large extent were Great Britain and France, as Germany, Italy, and

Spain were going through politically "difficult" periods. Meanwhile, the Catholic Church maintained a strict control over juvenile entertainment in Belgium and the Netherlands and thereby took a dim view of those violent, garish pictures propagating Protestant, "American" values. Only in France were U.S. comics fairly widely enjoyed by a juvenile readership undergoing less stringent parental and institutional control than in the rest of Europe.

Yet these discrepancies in the penetration of U.S. material between European countries proved beneficial in the long run; they allowed for the emergence of specifically European comic-making traditions in all these countries,[2] except Germany.[3] The phenomenon was most brilliantly exemplified in Belgium, where in 1929 the Brussels-born cartoonist Hergé (Georges Rémi) created the juvenile reporter "Tintin," arguably the most famous comic strip character ever. The post–World War II years saw the rise of comics publishers Casterman (based in Tournai) and Dupuis (based in Marcinelle), whose respective flagship titles were the weekly magazines *Tintin* (launched in 1944) and *Spirou* (launched in 1938). *Spirou* is a good example of how national comics production took off in the late 1940s; when it first came out, it used to contain both Belgian and U.S. material (e.g., "Superman" and Fred Harman's "Red Ryder"), a characteristic necessary to compete with French magazines featuring only U.S. strips, such as *Robinson* or *Junior*. The supply of U.S. comics was interrupted during the war years. When *Spirou* resumed publication in 1944, it offered a similar mix until a French law passed on July 16, 1949, started regulating the publication and diffusion of material for children's magazines, particularly by forbidding the printing of strips featuring too much action and violence. Sponsored by Communist representatives and a French government going through an overtly anti-American phase, the 1949 law obviously targeted U.S.-made strips for both ideological and protectionist reasons. The move was efficient; the drastic reduction of the U.S. comics influx made for more room in the pages of national comic magazines, and the renewed demand was subsequently filled by the local production.[4] As far as Belgium was concerned, the strong Catholic influence had anticipated this political development by a few years; when *Tintin* started in 1944, it only contained Francophone material.

U.S. comics did not disappear from these countries' newsstands overnight, however. Although mostly abandoned by big publishers, they remained available through smaller businesses putting out inexpensive black-and-white pamphlets printed on very cheap paper, very close in format to their U.S. counterparts. By the 1950s, however, Franco-Belgian comics had begun a process that, after a couple of decades, would establish the credibility of the medium. Stories previously serialized in comics magazines were collected in at first thin, paper-bound volumes sold on newsstands and in general bookstores. By the late 1970s the so-called "albums" had become mostly hardbound books carried by bookstores and supermarkets.

In this context, reprints of U.S. material have been marginalized; they have never made it into the bookstore-friendly album form but remained newsstand fare because of their format. Their overwhelmingly young urban male readers regard them as disposable commodities. This readership can be roughly divided into two categories—on the one hand, reasonably well-read bourgeois children value booklike albums and national comic periodicals but consider U.S. reprints as second-rate material, even while occasionally reading them for their entertainment value; on the other, lower middle/working class readers are socially and economically prone to value only the U.S.-made comics' potential for quick, on-the-spot consumption.[5]

This explains why U.S. comic output has failed to be much of an influence on European comics since the postwar years. However, the local production has not evolved ex nihilo. Paradoxical though it may seem, the most significant area of U.S. influence on European comics has been movies and popular literature, particularly science fiction. This has not always been the case. When early French comics characters would go to America, their gaze was mostly one of social criticism; when Louis Forton's anarchistic trio Les Pieds Nickelés[6] traveled to the United States in 1921, the cartoonist took "pot shots at prohibition, racial segregation, the electoral process, Hollywood and President Harding" (Horn, 1976: 554). Ten years later, the Casterman album Tintin en Amérique (1932) contained a handful of film noir clichés (very mild ones, as "Tintin" then appeared in a periodical edited by Catholic priests) but weaved a more consistently critical discourse on natives, machinism, and U.S.-type modernity. The same applied in 1930 to the French bestselling Zig et Puce à New-York,[7] although with less sophistication in storytelling.

The vision of America mostly came from cinema and the images printed in the popular press. "Charlot," an adaptation of Charles Chaplin's screen character, was published in hardbound volumes drawn by French cartoonist Thomen as of 1926. Likewise, the French Catholic weekly Coeurs Vaillants offered a low-key western (at least by contemporary standards), Marijac's "Jim Boum," from 1931 on. Before the en masse coming of syndicated strips in the late 1930s, America's appeal as an alien land had to compete with the "local" exoticism fueled by images from European colonies. In the popular mind, Europe's "elsewhere" was still primarily in Asia and Africa, not across the Atlantic. It is one of the reasons why science fiction motifs were largely absent from European strips until the late 1940s. Except for René Pellos's futuristic strip Futuropolis (published in Junior in 1937–38), a visually stunning mix of Flash Gordon-ish design and science fiction à la Jules Verne, pre–World War II France and Belgium did not take to U.S.-type science fiction. By the time they developed a taste for it, the war had broken out. In 1942, E. P. Jacobs was asked by Bravo to draw a "Flash Gordon" takeoff entitled Le Rayon U, after it turned out that his style was almost indistinguishable from that of Alex Raymond.

Nonetheless, U.S.-type science fiction visuals were never extremely successful in Europe after World War II. As the appendix to this chapter shows, the major source of U.S. content for Franco-Belgian comics was western movies,[8] which reached their apogee in the United States and Europe in the 1940s and 1950s. Their impact was tremendous on European moviegoers, who had been weaned

Cover of the 1964 album *La Caravane* © Morris

off U.S. cinematic material for five years; the national film industries were in no way capable of meeting the public's demand. The visibility of westerns was so considerable that it had a lasting influence on the European comics output, notably by originating "Lucky Luke," the third all-time bestselling European comic series (after "Tintin" and "Astérix") created by Morris (Maurice de Bevère) for *Spirou* in 1946. The congenial, soft-spoken, trouble-shooting cowboy and his talking horse Jolly Jumper were initially the protagonists of a straight take-off of contemporary westerns. In 1948, Morris left for the United States and spent six years there; he perfected his knowledge of U.S. civilization and worked increasing substance and relevance into his strip, which he continued to mail to *Spirou* across the Atlantic. In New York City, Morris met budding French script-writer René Goscinny. The two men subsequently sailed home and went on to collaborate on the strip; although both stressed historical authenticity in the feature, Goscinny successfully infused it with the kind of wit—hitherto unheard of in Europe—that he had developed in contact with the *Mad* crowd (Harvey Kurtzman, Jack Davis, etc.), whom he had befriended in New York.

Besides the protagonist, the only recurring characters are the fictitious quartet of the Dalton brothers and the slow-witted, unlucky, cowardly dog Ran-Tan-Plan. This reduced cast has allowed the creators to involve Lucky Luke in a number of authentic historical developments of the West's conquest and make him meet such famed Far-West figures as Billy the Kid, Jesse James, Calamity Jane, Judge Roy Bean, Horace Greeley, and the like—even though the adventures they share with Luke generally fall short of historical accuracy. If chronological verisimilitude has also suffered in the process (unless one believes Lucky Luke looked 30 years old throughout the nineteenth century), the strip's consistency and enduring success mostly stem from the interplay between spirited plots, striking one-liners, carefully cultivated clichés, Morris's unmatched skills for caricaturing celebrities,[9] a pertinent historical grounding, and above all a potential to appeal to readers in all age brackets—"For the young from 7 to 77," as *Tintin* used to boast on its cover. All these elements are responsible for the strip's particular flavor; it responds in a very personal and entertaining fashion to the widespread interest and concern for the preservation and reappropriation of the past—no matter how alien to one's own civilization—so characteristic of European cultures and foreign to the American mind.

No western strip has ever surpassed Lucky Luke's long-term success. Yet in order to cash in on the success of Morris's character and the publisher Dupuis's subsequent release of several "Red Ryder" albums as of 1949, several popular competitors emerged in mainstream comic weeklies in the early 1950s and quite a few regular "national" characters traveled to the United States (e.g., Spirou himself in the then extremely well-received western story "Les Chapeaux noirs" [The Black Hats] published in album in 1952). Tibet's (Gilbert Gascard's) "Chick Bill"—published in *Junior*, then *Tintin*—and Jijé's (Joseph Gillain's) "Jerry Spring"—in *Spirou*—epitomized different approaches. Created in 1953, "Chick Bill" was initially an animal strip in a western setting aimed at younger readers;

after a while the main characters became human, and the congenial young sheriff Chick Bill has since gone through several dozen light-toned and humorous adventures. In contrast, "Jerry Spring" was created in 1954 to exploit a "real-life" vein, to come as close as restrictions on violence would allow to a movie western in comic-strip form. This high-quality but often humorless strip is most important because it introduced realism in a western strip published in a mainstream comic magazine and opened the way for the next decade's best example of this approach, Gir's (Jean Giraud's) 1963 "Lieutenant Blueberry" series for the French weekly *Pilote*. A former student of Jijé, Giraud created a Civil War strip whose protagonist initially looked like *Nouvelle Vague* actor Jean-Paul Belmondo—his face changed gradually afterwards. With the Belgian script-writer Jean-Michel Charlier, Giraud proceeded to push even further into graphic realism than Jijé had done. This ambition gave birth to a critically acclaimed strip that craftily cashed in on the spaghetti western fad in the late 1960s while gradually improving the characterization of a very colorful cast.[10]

Created in *Tintin* in 1969, "Comanche" followed in the wake of "Lieutenant Blueberry," although the Belgian creative team of Greg and Hermann never succeeded in developing a dramatic dimension equivalent to Gir's and Charlier's. The series is named after the "Triple Six" ranch's female owner, in fact a secondary character next to her right hand, the tough, Irish-born cowboy Red Dust. Despite excellent scenarios and artwork, "Comanche" has a "sedentary," poised quality that fails to match Blueberry's unpredictable and colorful action, plots, character interplay, and overall inventiveness.

To close this quick overview, the "fourth generation" in Franco-Belgian western strips is best exemplified by Michel Blanc-Dumont's 1974 series "Jonathan Cartland" and Swiss cartoonist Derib's anthropologically oriented strip on natives entitled "Celui qui est né deux fois." Such strips seem atypical at first glance; "Jonathan Cartland" is written by a woman (Laurence Harlé), and both series have introduced politically correct concerns such as ethnic issues and environmentalism into a genre hitherto (and still) appreciated for violence, action, and gunfights. In a certain way it shows that European western strips have followed the evolution of the U.S. western genre and shifted from slam-bang gunfights to more sedate and socially conscious themes.[11]

The western is the only genre with properly U.S. contents that has left its mark on Franco-Belgian comics. Except for strips such as *Spirou*'s overly militaristic "Buck Danny," which featured U.S. Air Force pilots, the American influence on the rest of the output has been largely dominated by themes rather than contents. All in all, American characters and settings were not that common in Franco-Belgian comics and by a long shot never outnumbered "local" protagonists and locales. Conversely, a number of themes originally developed and popularized by U.S. popular culture, although not specifically American in origin or content, have made their way into the Franco-Belgian comic production to be reappropriated by it. Post–World War II comics featured a number of spies, jungle ad-

A typical sample of "Lieutenant Blueberry" from *Marshal Blueberry: The Lost Dutchman's Mine*

venturers, space adventurers, air fighters, private eyes, costumed heroes, and secret agents first brought to Europe by U.S. films, comics, and popular fiction.

A good example is the *Tintin* strip "Luc Orient," created in 1967 by writer Greg and cartoonist Eddy Paape. Although the strip's background and characters were obviously "Francophone," the design of furniture, cars, architecture, and clothes was utterly modern, even futuristic, and the plots were laden with fantasy and sci-fi elements. Still, in no way can "Luc Orient" be remotely considered an exemplar of U.S. influence. Its specificity is more easily explicable in terms of cultural diffusion—namely, the futuristic streak in visuals, graphics, and design that permeated Belgium in the wake of the 1958 Brussels World Exhibition and whose pervasive influence was perceptible to various degrees in almost every Belgian comic strip of the late 1950s to early 1960s.

Another telling example is *Tintin*'s "Bruno Brazil," a strip created in 1967 to cash in on the secret agent fad. The latter started with the first James Bond film in 1963. It subsequently contaminated U.S. popular culture, mostly in the form of popular television series (*The Man from UNCLE, Mission: Impossible*)—which also proved very successful when they were imported to Europe. Yet the only tangible and unquestionable sign of Americanization in "Bruno Brazil" was the Anglophone consonance of many characters' names. For the rest, such strips simply attested to the global appropriation of and reliance on popular culture formats, genres, and narratives—of which the U.S. cultural industry was the most dynamic marketer and propagator. To all intents and purposes it was only another manifestation of the old transatlantic intercultural chiasmus: in order to seem desirable, a product has to sound or look "American" to a majority of European consumers, and any nontechnological commodity has to sound or look "European" to be perceived as sophisticated by North Americans.

However, too much of an American overtone is not necessarily an asset. A majority of European comics readers are indifferent to or even thoroughly dislike costumed, super-powered characters, which they dismiss as an irremediably unexportable American concept and an assembly line–produced, immature, and ideologically dubious epitome of escapist adolescent male power fantasies. Moreover, the packaging of superhero comics as newsstand products that never reach bookstores' shelves has been fatal to their development as competitors for national products.[12] In fact, the super-powered superhero is perceived as such a nontransposable U.S. stereotype that the only successful exemplar of it in France has been the caustic spoof "Superdupont," created in 1972 by cartoonist Marcel Gotlib. This is practically a unique instance of French appropriation of a U.S. motif exclusively for parodic purposes; Superdupont is the secret identity of a stereotyped, narrow-minded, chauvinistic Frenchman with a paunch who becomes a superhero whenever his country is threatened by the secret organization "L'Anti-France" or by various foreign villains (such as a Bruce Lee–like karate type who eventually defeats the French superman by drinking red wine with ice cubes in front of him). Gotlib's caustic wit is at its best in Superdupont stories, but the really interesting characteristic of this strip is that it is more a subversion of the

French stereotyped self-image than of any U.S. super-character. Here the U.S.-born superhero paradigm is used only as a filter to convey scathing derision about French chauvinism through the discrepancy between a béret-wearing, baguette- and camembert-eating, red wine–drinking character and the exclusively American format of the flying, caped superhero.

"Superdupont" may be said to epitomize the disruption of and clash between usually compartmentalized cultural signs. Some would probably call this use of ironical pastiche a "postmodern" strategy to subvert popular cultural motifs. However, pastiche (such as it is defined in Jameson, 1984: 65) is at work, although with no such humorous purposes, in a contemporary trend that appropriates U.S. contents with a distinctively Franco-Belgian style. Both French cartoonist Ted Benoît and Belgian Philippe Berthet draw in the *ligne claire*[13] style. Ted Benoît's artwork is self-consciously reminiscent of Hergé-ish visuals; his character Ray Banana is a hapless private eye whose stories take place in moody 1950s U.S. settings where Raymond Loewy design has pride of place. Although not so close to Hergé's own style, Philippe Berthet's artwork has an unmistakably Belgian flavor, which he puts to use to tell film noir–like stories set in 1930s and 1940s America.[14]

In the same vein, although relying much more on gritty realism and far less on *ligne claire*, one could also mention the French team of Raives and Warn's; their character Lou Cale (now published by Humanoïdes Associés) is a reporter-photographer in postwar America who gets involved in whodunits interspersed with authentic anecdotes enabling the protagonist to constantly come across celebrities of the period. Likewise, Michel Blanc-Dumont's "Colby" series (published by Dargaud) features private eyes in a carefully reproduced 1940s America.

These four strips hint at a striking phenomenon in contemporary Franco-Belgian comics. The reliance on U.S. themes and contents with a nostalgic twist is a clear sign of postmodern appropriation of foreign popular narratives through a local means of expression. By imposing self-consciously Franco-Belgian types of artwork on postwar, U.S.-set narratives, these cartoonists actually express a deep-seated current in their own culture, the reactivation of old genres and themes through established graphic traditions that initially developed their specificity by rejecting U.S.-made products. Fredric Jameson's "nostalgia mode" (Jameson, 1984: 66–68) is clearly discernible in these contemporary Franco-Belgian strips, where a medium eventually legitimized on a local scale is utilized to tell stories that tap into the foreign imagination of the past. America has been so ubiquitous in European daily life and popular culture since World War II that the new "exoticism" thereby developed is no longer deployed in space, but in time. The reader is not taken to present-time foreign lands but to the *imaginary* America of the pre- and postwar periods, the America whose images (and not reality) initiated the great American pipedream of so many Europeans in the 1950s.

Such strips actually *remind* one of U.S. popular culture's imaginary universe. Nonetheless, their decidedly European narrative style and flavor emphasize that what matters here is less what is perceived than the perception thereof. The United

States of contemporary comic strips in France and Belgium is not America per se but Europe's America—the very same one that Morris originated when he invented Lucky Luke, and that French comic strip artist Jean-Claude Mézières discovered as a kid.

JEAN-CLAUDE MEZIERES

Jean-Claude Mézières was born in Paris in 1938.[15] From a very young age he developed a passion for drawing, comic strips, and America. At age 15 he joined an art school, where he met Jean "Gir" Giraud, who became a lifelong friend. There he also perfected his draftsmanship, which allowed him to get his first assignments—western comic stories published in *Coeurs Vaillants* under the pseudonym "Mézi." Like all French male citizens, he was drafted into the army at age 20; there he served for 26 months, including a full year in Algeria, in the last throes of this country's violent process of liberation from French colonization. After being discharged he worked for an advertising agency and the publisher Hachette, for which he illustrated encyclopedias. Meanwhile his friend from art school, Jean Giraud, had joined the studio run by Jijé, Jerry Spring's creator, and started a promising career at *Pilote* in 1963 with the successful "Lieutenant Blueberry" strip. Mézières was becoming fed up with his routine work and daily life. Thanks to Jijé and Gir, he succeeded in securing a temporary work visa for a draftsman's position with a company in Houston, Texas. In the first days of 1965, Mézières left for America.

He never went to Houston, though. Instead he spent almost two years traveling across the United States and making a livelihood from odd jobs and cowboy work on ranches. In the process he perfected his knowledge of a country that was mythical to him, to which he had been exposed since his childhood through movies, comics, music, and popular literature. In late 1966 he found Pierre Christin, then a French literature teacher in Salt Lake City, Utah; he was another childhood friend whom Mézières had met in underground shelters during the war, when they were five. Spurred on by Christin's offer to make comic strips together and by his own increasingly difficult relationship with U.S. immigration services, Mézières returned to France in the last days of 1966. The two men's first strips were published in *Pilote* after Gir presented them to editor René Goscinny (of "Lucky Luke" and "Astérix" fame), but their collaboration really took off when the 30-page story "Les mauvais rêves" [The Bad Dreams] was serialized in *Pilote* in 1967–68. Set in the year 2720 in a galactic empire whose capital was the Earth city "Galaxity," the strip featured an unusual protagonist: Valérian was a flippant, good-natured "space-time agent" whose first assignment was to track down Xombul, a renegade Galaxity technocrat who had fled to the Middle Ages after disrupting the dream-generating equipment on which the whole Galaxity population relied to survive. After arriving in the eleventh century, Valérian came across Laureline, a gorgeous, fearless, sword-wielding woman who helped him find

Xombul and defeat him after the entire cast traveled back to the twenty-eighth century.

Pilote's readers responded warmly to the new strip. Many wrote to praise Christin's witty script, Mézières's artwork, the generally "different" tone of the strip, and the thoroughly novel concept embodied by the Valérian-Laureline interplay. Although the male was no muscle-bound macho brainlessly punching his way into the story, but rather a good-humored and occasionally blundering adventurer, the story's woman was a free, initiative-taking, totally unsubmissive character with both charm and brains. A female protagonist was still a rarity in French comic strips, but one of this ilk was simply mind-boggling to most readers.

Goscinny gave the successful creative team the green light for another "Valérian" story. "La Cité des eaux mouvantes" [The City of Moving Waters] was thus serialized in Pilote in 1968, "Terres en flammes" [Blazing Land] in 1969. In the following year the first "Valérian" album was published; La Cité des eaux mouvantes contained the 1968 and 1969 stories.[16] Nowadays, with 15 titles,[17] it has become Dargaud's fourth best-selling series (behind such leading lights as "Astérix" and "Lieutenant Blueberry") and has been successfully translated into eight foreign languages—except English.[18] Unfortunately, Dargaud's ambition proved a commercial failure after a couple of years, because of poor reception and very bad marketing, at a time when specialty comic-bookstores were still very few and overwhelmingly promoted the stapled four-color booklet format.

Another reason may have been Valérian's very unusual outlook for U.S. comics readers. One of the strip's numerous initial assets was Mézières's rendition of the space-opera atmosphere stemming from his and Christin's longtime passion for U.S. science fiction literature. Valérian lives adventures set against visually stunning backgrounds: complex architectural inventions, futuristic machines, otherworldly landscapes, and odd-looking aliens are staples of Mézières's seemingly boundless visual inventiveness. There is no reason why this characteristic would not have appealed to U.S. readers. However, what might have unsettled them has been Christin's approach to script-writing; "Valérian" is a self-conscious strip teeming with references to science fiction and mainstream literature,[19] cinema, and canonical European and U.S. comics. Its most unnerving trait for U.S. comics readers is probably Christin's constant reliance on social commentary; a liberal himself (like Mézières), he writes stories with particular emphasis on dictators, outcasts, haves and have-nots, and as a rule works political, environmental, and feminist concerns into his narratives—thereby showing that social ills are universal, no matter on which planet you land. The two protagonists exemplify this commitment; whereas Valérian is very much an anti-hero, occasionally cowardly, weak, and indecisive, Laureline is a willful person who cares and is ready to fight for ideals of social justice and individual liberation. Just like "Lucky Luke" and "Astérix," "Valérian" is therefore one of those Franco-Belgian comics that is extremely palatable and entertaining for a wide range of European readers thanks to its various levels of reading. On the other hand, it has proved unattractive to North American comics readers seeking standardized formula entertainment and

being generally unprepared to respond positively to a "different," literate, and ideologically committed comic strip.

Despite this commercial failure in the United States, the two creators know that their strip's influence has spread much farther than one could expect. Many Americans would indeed be surprised to discover how much Mézières's drawings have inspired sci-fi movie designers and comic artists all over the world. The community of graphic and visual artists crosses genres, mediums, and national boundaries; and Mézières has lastingly impressed a number of designers whose own creations have subsequently received worldwide critical acclaim. Yet Mézières has not given birth to any heirs; his style, a very personal blend of various influences (including those of Jijé, Gir-Moebius, and U.S. cartoonist Jack Davis), has never been imitated or plagiarized. It is in fact so personal that Mézières has never been able to hire an assistant for very long—he is never satisfied with their attempts to match his style. His creative individuality has earned him the most prestigious European prize to which a comic-strip artist can aspire; in 1984, he was awarded the Grand Prix of the Angoulême, France, International Comics Festival, a distinction granted to an outstanding comics creator once every year since 1974.

Although "Valérian" is the outcome of a collaboration between two childhood buddies sharing common tastes and ideas, the piece reproduced here as Chapter 4 is a one-man product. Since the mid-1960s, Goscinny had encouraged regular and occasional contributors to offer "personal" fillers to be published next to the usual columns and serialized strips of *Pilote*. "My Very Own America" is one such piece, an eight-page story first published in 1974, recounting Mézières's 1965–1966 stay in the United States. Beyond the narrative's autobiographical dimension, the story's interest has increased with time as it expresses how a Frenchman glanced back at mid-1960s America a decade later and we the readers consider it another two decades later.

When he returned to France penniless in late 1966, Mézières left behind a young woman, one of Christin's students. After he sent her a ticket a few weeks later, she came to France and they have been together since. In the following years, Mézières's passion for America never let up; he would cross the Atlantic at least every six months and spend a few weeks or months in the United States to gather material and work on ranches. But America continued to change, faster indeed than his own perception of it. Since the mid-1980s he has ceased to go frequently to the United States, for professional and family reasons. The kind of fascination that he, Christin, and many Europeans of their generation experienced in the 1950s, 1960s, and 1970s is no longer possible simply because, as he puts it, "for ten, fifteen, twenty years, America has crossed the Atlantic." When he made "My Very Own America" in the mid-1970s, his goal was "to talk of America, to go beyond anecdotes," and convey to *Pilote* readers the significance of America in his personal evolution. This is the first English publication of the story. The editors have translated it, and Jean-Claude Mézières very kindly took care of the

English lettering.

One final note: the story's last panel pastiches the final panel of many "Lucky Luke" albums. It shows Luke riding Jolly Jumper into the sunset while singing "I'm a poor lonesome cowboy and a long way from home." The allusion is obvious for European readers, but not so much for their American counterparts.

NOTES

1. For the most recent short bibliography on comic art criticism, see Sabin, 1993: 293–306.

2. For a historical survey of European comics' development, cf. Sabin, 1993: 184–199. A quick overview of contemporary European comics is found in the catalog of the exhibition "The Comic Strip in Europe" held at the Brussels Belgian Centre for Comic Strip Art in 1992–1993 (Dierick, 1992).

3. Germany has never really developed a substantial corpus of national comics. Until the late 1980s the *only* comic strips available in bookstores were translations of Franco-Belgian material and a few Spanish and Italian features. The situation has slightly evolved nowadays; a few German-made strips are available in bookstores, but their visibility and popularity do not compare with those of translated Franco-Belgian fare. Finally, comics sales figures in Germany are much lower than in other European countries. The reasons why the Germans read few comics these days are probably historical and demographic; whereas the generation that slowly and gradually promoted comics-reading in other European countries as of the early 1960s was born in the 1930s, their German counterparts grew up under the Nazi regime, which strictly forbade U.S. and foreign funnies and never relied widely on comics as a means of propaganda. Although comics-reading has remained a fairly outlandish activity in Germany, the country never had the opportunity to develop a comics-making tradition relying on national products because the Americans flooded the existing market with their own products after World War II. Whatever evolution has been going on for a few years is therefore currently based on the reading of contemporary rising stars from the rest of Europe.

4. For an exhaustive presentation of Franco-Belgian comics to the early 1980s, see Filippini et al., 1984.

5. U.S. comics regained visibility by the late 1960s–early 1970s, with the first translations of Marvel material. However, they were not turned into albums before the late 1970s; and even since then, their availability on newsstands but not in bookstores has prevented them from developing any specific legitimacy with the "dominant" album-reading readership. Even album editions of outstanding U.S. material (e.g., DC's 1986 groundbreaking limited series *Batman: The Dark Knight Returns* and *Watchmen*) have failed to attract the vast bourgeois readership of their European counterparts.

6. Created in 1908, *Les Pieds Nickelés* is the oldest European strip still in existence.

7. "Zig et Puce" was created in 1925 by Alain Saint-Ogan. It was the first "modern" French comic strip; Saint-Ogan was the first French cartoonist who systematically used balloons instead of under-panel captions.

8. The same characteristic then applied to Italy. Italian-made western comic strips rode this wave as well; they were also very popular with Belgian and French readers then, less for their quality than for their inexpensive format.

9. Wallace Beery, W. C. Fields, David Niven, Lee Marvin, Jack Palance, Jean Gabin, and so on.

10. Giraud subsequently became famous under the pseudonym Moebius for his extensive illustration work and participation in the design of various films, particularly Ridley Scott's *Alien* and the early 1980s Disney-produced experimental computer-graphics movie *Tron*.

11. For a detailed study of western motifs in comics in the early 1980s, see Herman, 1982.

12. Cf. note 5 above.

13. *Ligne claire* (clear line) is the generic name given to the graphic style based on Hergé's artwork, which used to be the main form of comic-strip graphics among *Tintin* collaborators after World War II. The *ligne claire* style has gone through a revival since Hergé's death in 1983.

14. Cf. the Dupuis series "*Le privé d'Hollywood*" and "*Pin-up.*"

15. Much of the material found in the following text comes from an interview with Jean-Claude Mézières in his Paris studio on May 19, 1995.

16. The very first one was not reprinted in album form before 1983 because, by comparison with subsequent stories, the characters' interplay in it was fairly sketchy and Mézières's artwork was judged a bit too rough and cartoony.

17. Cf. references at the end of this chapter.

18. Only four titles were published as paperbound albums by Dargaud Publishing International (Greenwich, Conn.) between 1982 and 1984, in connection with the French publisher's early 1980s attempt to break into the U.S. comics market. *Ambassador of the Shadows, World without Stars, Welcome to Alflolol*, and *Heroes of the Equinox* are still available from some comics mail-order dealers.

19. For example, *L'Empire des mille planètes* takes place in a city called Syrte, clearly based on French writer Julien Gracq's classic novel *Le Rivage des Syrtes*.

REFERENCES

Dierick, Charles (ed.) (1992). *The European Comic Strip*. Brussels: Belgian Centre for Comic Strip Art.

Filippini, Henri (1990). *Dictionnaire de la bande dessinée*. Paris: Bordas.

Filippini, Henri, Jacques Glénat, Numa Sadoul, and Yves Varende (1984). *Histoire de la bande dessinée en France et en Belgique*, 2nd ed., rev. & enl. Grenoble: Glénat.

Gabilliet, Jean-Paul (1994). "Le *Comic book*, objet culturel nord-américain." Unpublished doctoral thesis. Bordeaux: Université Michel de Montaigne.

Herman, Paul (1982). *Épopée et mythes du western dans la bande dessinée*. Grenoble: Glénat.

Horn, Maurice (ed.) (1976). *The World Encyclopedia of Comics*. New York: Chelsea House.

Jameson, Fredric (1984). "Postmodernism or the Cultural Logic of Late Capitalism." *New Left Review* 146 (July–August): 53–92.

Reitberger, Reinhold, and Wolfgang Fuchs (1972). *Comics: Anatomy of a Mass Medium*. London: Studio Vista. First published in German as *COMICS Anatomie eines Massenmediums* (Munich: Heinz Moos Verlag, 1971).

Sabin, Roger (1993). *Adult Comics: An Introduction*. New York: Routledge.

Sadoul, Jacques (1989). *93 ans de BD*. Paris: J'ai Lu.

J.-C. MEZIERES: A SHORT BIBLIOGRAPHY

Unless otherwise stated, all Mézières comics material is published by the Paris-based publisher Dargaud. Mézières has also produced an extensive body of illustration work (book covers, posters, advertising art, etc.), which is not listed here.

There are 15 "Valérian" albums written by Pierre Christin and drawn by Jean-Claude Mézières:

La Cité des eaux mouvantes (1970)
L'Empire des mille planètes (1971)
Le Pays sans étoile (1972)
Bienvenue sur Alflolol (1972)
Les Oiseaux du maître (1973)
L'Ambassadeur des ombres (1975)
Sur les terres truquées (1977)
Les Héros de l'équinoxe (1978)
Métro Châtelet direction Cassiopée (1980)
Brooklyn Station terminus cosmos (1981)
Les Spectres d'Inverloch (1984)
Les Foudres d'Hypsis (1985)
Sur les frontières (1988)
Les Armes vivantes (1990)
Les Cercles du pouvoir (1994)

All stories were serialized in Pilote before publication in album form until 1988. Afterwards the magazine disappeared.

Other books are listed below:

Sur les chemins d l'espace (1979; out-of-print collection of short "Valérian" stories).
Mézières et Christin . . . (1983; out-of-print collection of various Mézières and Christin pieces, including the very first "Valérian" story).
Lady Polaris (Paris: Autrement, 1983; Mézières and Christin's illustrated narrative of a quest across Europe for an enigmatic woman).
Les Habitants du ciel (1991; drawings of the creatures and settings appearing in "Valérian").
Les Extras de Mézières (1995; collection of Mézières artwork).

APPENDIX

This table is largely based on information found in Henri Filippini's *Dictionaire de la bande dessinée* (Paris: Bordas, 1990). It is a representative sample of Francophone comics with significant American content and/or influence since the 1920s. The "Title" column lists each strip's title and the magazine in which it was first published. The "Author(s)" column indicates each strip's first artist; when two names are given separated by a slash, the first name is that of the writer. Exceptionally popular strips are highlighted in bold type. The three countries concerned are Belgium (B), France (F), and Switzerland (CH).

Date	Title	Author(s)		Commentary
1926-1972	Charlot (*L'As*)	Thomen	F	Based on Charles Chaplin's famous comedy character.
1931-1950	Jim Boum (*Coeurs vaillants*)	Marijac	F	First a scout in 19th century Western America; later a World War II air fighter as the former's grandson.
1939-on	Zorro			Various French, Italian, and Dutch adaptations since 1939.
1942	Le Rayon U (*Bravo*)	Edgar-Pierre Jacobs	B	"Flash Gordon" take-off drawn in a style almost indistinguishable from Alex Raymond's.
1944-1948	Poncho Libertas (*Coq hardi*)	Le Rallic	F	A very European-looking Mexican crimefighter near the US border in the 19th century.
1945-1949	Fantax (*Fantax*)	JK Melwyn Nash (Marcel Navarro)/Chott	F	British superhero in the United States after World War II.
1946-on	**Lucky Luke** (*Spirou*)	René Goscinny (on a few albums)/Morris	B	The most popular Franco-Belgian western comic strip.
1946-1948	Kaza le martien (*OK*)	Kline	F	Another "Flash Gordon" take-off.
1946-1964	Buffalo Bill (*Tarzan, L'Intrépide*)	Various writers/ René Giffey	F	Adventures of the legendary Far-West hero.
1947-on	**Buck Danny** (*Spirou*)	Jean-Michel Charlier/ Victor Hubinon	B	US Air Force stories with strong militaristic undertones.
1947-1974	Lynx (*Vaillant*)	Roger Lecureux/ Bob Sim	F	"Jungle Jim" take-off.
1948-1952	Sitting Bull (*Coq hardi*)	Marijac/ Pierre Duteurtre	F	Pro-Indian biography of Sitting Bull featuring French-born immigrants.
1948-1986	Garry (*Garry*)	Félix Molinari	F	A war hero turned secret agent.
1949-1962	Sam Billie Bill (*Vaillant*)	Jean Ollivier/ Lucien Nortier	F	Straightforward western.
1952-1986	Vigor (*Vigor*)	Raoul and Robert Giordan	F	Adventurer whose stories take place wherever the United States was at war in the 1940s and 1950s.
1953-on	**Chick Bill** (*Junior*)	Tibet	B	An extremely popular western for children.
1953-1956	Le Chat (*Heroïc-Albums*)	Michel Denys (Greg)	B	Costumed hero working for Scotland Yard, in fact a Batman take-off.
1953-1956	Kim Devil (*Spirou*)	Jean-Michel Charlier/ Gérald Forton	B	Another "Jungle Jim" take-off.
1953-1968	Lucky Bold (*Zorro*)	Marcel Radenen	F	Comedy western.
1954-on	Dan Cooper (various titles)	Albert Weinberg	B	"Steve Canyon" take-off.

1972-on	**Superdupont** (*Pilote, Fluide Glacial*)	Marcel Gotlib	F	A caustic parody featuring a béret-wearing, camembert- and baguette-eating French superhero with a paunch and nationalistic narrowmindedness.
1974-on	**Jonathan Cartland** (*Lucky Luke, Pilote*)	Laurence Harlé/ Michel Blanc-Dumont	F	Realistic western with an environmental slant.
1974-on	Mac Coy (*Lucky Luke*)	Jean-Pierre Gourmelen/ Antonio Hernandez Palacios	F	Realistic strip with a strong psychological dimension featuring a former Southern soldier serving in the US army after the Civil War.
1975-on	Capitaine Apache (*Pif Gadget*)	Roger Lecureux/ Norma	F	Whites and Indians in a Civil War setting.
1976-1977	Al Crane (*Pilote*)	Alexis	F	Extremely tongue-in-cheek western spoof.
1977-on	L'Indien français (*Circus*)	René Durand/ Georges Ramaioli	F	A Frenchman among Indians in a late 19th century fantasy setting.
1977-on	Les Inoxydables (*Charlie*)	Victor Mora/ Antonio Parras	F	Unlucky adventurers in 1920s America.
1977-on	Ray Banana (*Charlie*)	Ted Benoît	F	A private eye in a moody US 1950s setting. Artwork self-consciously reminiscent of "Tintin."
1980-on	Photonik (*Mustang*)	Malcolm Naughton (Marcel Navarro)/Cyrus Tota	F	Take-off of Marvel-type superheroes.
1981-on	Le Chariot de Thespis (*Gomme*)	Christian Rossi	F	Adventure in Civil War setting.
1981-on	Durango	Yves Swolfs	B	Violent spaghetti western à la Clint Eastwood.
1983-on	Le privé d'Hollywood (*Spirou*)	François Rivière and José-Louis Bocquet/ Philippe Berthet	B	Film noir parody set in 1930s Hollywood. Stylish artwork and moody ambiance.
1983-1986	Celui qui est né deux fois	Derib (Claude de Ribaupierre)	CH	Albums on Native Americans with a strong anthropological slant.
1984-on	**XIII** (*Spirou*)	Jean van Hamme/ William Vance	B	An intricate manipulation plot featuring an amnesiac protagonist in an unnamed country looking very much like the United States. A bestselling title in France since the late 1980s.
1986-on	Soda (*Spirou*)	Philippe Tome/ Luc Warnant	B	Humorous, action-packed strip about a police officer living in present-day New York with his elderly mother who believes he is a minister.
1987-on	Lou Cale	Raives/Warn's (Jean-Luc Warnauts)	F	A reporter-photographer in post-World War II America. Gritty realism including allusions and authentic anecdotes about celebrities of the period.
1990-on	Colby	Michel Blanc-Dumont	F	Private eyes in 1940s United States.
1994-1995	Pin-Up	Philippe Berthet	B	Three-album story about a World War II G.I. fighting abroad and his former girlfriend. Homage to Milton Caniff, cheesecake art, and 1940s US design.

1954-1960	Red Canyon (*Red Canyon*)	Guy Forez/ André Gosselin	F	Straightforward western.
1954-1978	**Jerry Spring** (*Spirou*)	Jijé (Joseph Gillain)	B	A United States marshall roaming the Far West with his faithful Mexican sidekick Pancho.
1955-early 1960s	Davy Crockett			Various French and Italian adaptations.
1956-1961	Bill Jourdan (*Bayard*)	Jean Aquaviva/ Loys Pétillot	F	Straightforward western.
1957-1981	Jim et Heppy (*Coeurs vaillants*)	Guy Hempay (Jean-Marie Pélaprat)/Pierre Chery	F	Western strip for children.
1958-1962	Oumpah-Pah (*Tintin*)	René Goscinny/ Albert Uderzo	F	An Indian warrior befriends a French knight in 18th-century America. Authored by the team who subsequently created "Astérix."
1958-1972	Superboy (*Superboy*)	Robert Bagage/ Félix Molinari	F	A straight take-off of the homonymous character.
1963-on	**Lieutenant Blueberry** (*Pilote*)	Jean-Michel Charlier/ Gir (Jean Giraud, Moebius)	F	The best French-made realistic western strip.
1963-1975	Teddy Ted (*Vaillant*)	Roger Lecureux/ Yves Roy	F	Utterly stereotyped western strip taking place in Tombstone.
1966-1973	Lone Sloane (*Pilote*)	Philippe Druillet	F	Baroque space-opera strip initially drawing its inspiration from US 1960s comic books.
1967-on	**Valérian** (*Pilote*)	Linus (Pierre Christin)/ Jean-Claude Mézières	F	The first French quality science-fiction comic-strip.
1967-1983	Bruno Brazil (*Tintin*)	Greg/ William Vance	B	Mid-1960s secret agent fare reminiscent of *The Man from UNCLE* and *Mission: Impossible*.
1968-on	**Les Tuniques bleues** (*Spirou*)	Raoul Cauvin/ Louis Salvérius	B	A very popular Civil War strip featuring Chesterfield and Blutch, two likeable Northern soldiers.
1969-on	**Comanche** (*Tintin*)	Greg/ Hermann (Herman Huppen)	B	A Belgian-made quality western with sophisticated characterization.
1969-1983	Loup Noir (*Pif Gadget*)	Jean Ollivier/ Kline	F	Pro-Indian strip featuring a Sioux hero.
1969-1988	Jess Long (*Spirou*)	Maurice Tillieux/ Arthur Piroton	B	Adventures of an FBI agent.
1970-on	Sammy (*Spirou*)	Raoul Cauvin/ Berck	B	Comic stories of two bodyguards for hire in 1930s gangland America.
1970-on	Yakari (*Tintin*)	André Jobin/Derib (Claude de Ribaupierre)	CH	Successful strip featuring a likeable Sioux child and his horse.
1970-1978	Horace, cheval de l'ouest (*Pif Gadget*)	Jean-Claude Poirier	F	Tongue-in-cheek kids' strip featuring an obnoxious horse and his gullible owner.
1971-on	Archie Cash (*Spirou*)	Jean-Marie Brouyère/ Malik	B	This Charles Bronson look-alike lives violent adventures in exotic locations.
1972-on	Buddy Longway (*Tintin*)	Derib (Claude de Ribaupierre)	CH	Western strip with environmental and multicultural slants. Reminiscent of the movie *Jeremiah Johnson*.

4 My Very Own America

Jean-Claude Mézières

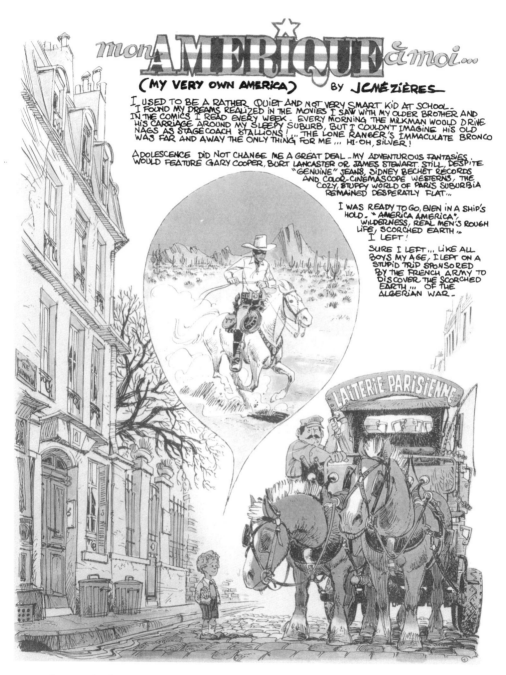

mon AMERIQUE à moi...
(MY VERY OWN AMERICA)   BY JC MÉZIÈRES

I USED TO BE A RATHER QUIET AND NOT VERY SMART KID AT SCHOOL. I FOUND MY DREAMS REALIZED IN THE MOVIES I SAW WITH MY OLDER BROTHER AND IN THE COMICS I READ EVERY WEEK. EVERY MORNING THE MILKMAN WOULD DRIVE HIS CARRIAGE AROUND MY SLEEPY SUBURB, BUT I COULDN'T IMAGINE HIS OLD NAGS AS STAGECOACH STALLIONS! ... THE LONE RANGER'S IMMACULATE BRONCO WAS FAR AND AWAY THE ONLY THING "FOR ME ... HI-OH, SILVER!

ADOLESCENCE DID NOT CHANGE ME A GREAT DEAL. MY ADVENTUROUS FANTASIES WOULD FEATURE GARY COOPER, BURT LANCASTER OR JAMES STEWART. STILL, DESPITE "GENUINE" JEANS, SIDNEY BECHET RECORDS AND COLOR-CINÉMASCOPE WESTERNS, THE COZY, STUFFY WORLD OF PARIS SUBURBIA REMAINED DESPERATELY FLAT...

I WAS READY TO GO, EVEN IN A SHIP'S HOLD. "AMERICA AMERICA", WILDERNESS, REAL MEN'S ROUGH LIFE, SCORCHED EARTH ...
I LEFT!

SURE I LEFT ... LIKE ALL BOYS MY AGE, I LEFT ON A STUPID TRIP SPONSORED BY THE FRENCH ARMY TO DISCOVER THE SCORCHED EARTH ... OF THE ALGERIAN WAR.

HIT THE ROAD, J.C.!

THE ARMY WASN'T MY THING. I WAS STILL FOOL ENOUGH TO ENJOY US WAR MOVIES, BUT NOT TO BUY INTO THE FRENCH FILM THEY CALLED "PACIFICATION". ANYHOW, AFTER I CAME HOME I GOT A JOB IN A SMALL ADVERTISING AGENCY. BUT I STILL HAD MY OLD DREAM...

ONE DAY I LEFT. AND, I'M ASHAMED TO CONFESS IT, YOU CAN'T POSSIBLY KNOW HOW I FELT TO DISCOVER THIS GRAND DUNG-HOLE: I GOT HIGH ON THE CONSUMER SOCIETY.

W 86 ST

DON'T WALK

NEW YORK! AUTOMOBILES AS LONG AS FREIGHT CARS, CRAZY NEON SIGNS, AND MILLING AROUND AT THE BOTTOM OF CONCRETE, GLASS AND STEEL CANYONS WAS THE CROWD— BUMS, COPS, GAYS, FREAKS, WHORES, JERKS AND JUNKIES AS THE BULLSHIT OF OUR FRENCH PAPERS ABOUT " LA VIOLENCE US." HAD WARNED ME BUT I ALSO SAW " THE OTHER SIDE OF THIS SULTRY, SMELLY CITY, WHERE HUMAN RELATIONS ARE MORE OPEN THAN ELSEWHERE... NEW YORK, WHERE THE SKY'S THE LIMIT!

46

I FELT A DUBIOUS THRILL WHEN I FINALLY CAME ACROSS THE AFFLUENT SOCIETY'S POOR! NUMBED BY ITS OWN FILTH **HARLEM** SHOWED ME THE PIONEER'S ADVENTURE GROTESQUE REVERSED ... I WAS ENTRANCED BY THE CAPITALIST FAILURE OF THOSE WHO ARE DOOMED TO NEVER MAKE IT ...

I WAS SUCH A JERK TO LOVE AMERICA ... GONE THE CHEERFUL BROADWAY MUSICALS! GONE THE ELEGANT TIME SQUARE EVENINGS! GONE TRIUMPHANT WESTERNS! ALWAYS YOU COME BACK TO 42nd STREET, TO MINDLESS SLEAZE, THE SEX MARKET, DRIFTERS ... WHAT IF IT WERE THE "MESSAGE OF TODAY'S AMERICA ?

HOT FLESH
ALSO
THE SEXY 7
STARRING RITA BOOBS

HO
ALSO
T
STARR

NEVER SEEN BEFORE

BOOKS

3D MOVIES
for adults
GADGETS
BOOKS

ADULTS
ONLY
2 Smashing big hits

Strictly for a

AND IT'S A FAIRLY HARD MESSAGE TO DECIPHER. BECAUSE THERE'S ALSO FREEDOM, THE JOY THAT OUR STALE EUROPEAN CITIES CAN NO LONGER GENERATE ... BASKING IN THE SUN WHILE LISTENING TO WASHINGTON SQUARE MUSICIANS.

THEN, SOMEWHERE AROUND THE HARBOR, A VOICE THAT CAME MAYBE FROM A JOHN FORD, KING VIDOR OR RAOUL WALSH SAGA WHISPERED INTO MY EAR THE WORDS THAT SO MANY AIMLESS GUYS FROM ALL OVER THE PLACE HAD HEARD BEFORE ME ...

GO WEST YOUNG MAN, GO WEST!

③

GO WEST! AND IT'S SO MUCH EASIER IN THE 20TH CENTURY! I THUMBED MY WAY ACROSS THE FRONTIER TO THE PACIFIC. THE ROAD STRETCHED ENDLESSLY AWAY INTO THE DISTANCE, THE SUN IN MY EYES... GO WEST... BUT MY DREAM STROVE FOR SOMETHING ELSE THAN HILLY SAN FRANCISCO ... SO ...

HIT THE ROAD AGAIN J.C.! TO SEE THE WILD WEST! NOT THE WILD WEST OF SCHEDULED GUNFIGHTS FOR TOURISTS VISITING OK CORRAL, BUT ONE HARDER TO FIND WHERE A COWBOY'S REAL JOB STILL EXISTS. I KNEW OF ITS EXISTENCE AND I WANTED TO EXPERIENCE IT.

CHOTEAU MONTANA, MONTICELLO UTAH. EVANSTON WYOMING LEADVILLE COLORADO OR KINGMAN ARIZONA. SMALL TOWNS CRUSHED BY THE IMMENSE SKY. BRICK AND WOODEN FACADES, SLIM SILHOUETTES OF BOOTED MEN, OF WOMEN WEARING JEANS OR BRIGHT-COLORED DRESSES ... IS IT SO FAR FROM THE CLASSIC WESTERN MOVIE TOWN? OF COURSE HORSES ARE GIVEN LIFTS ON PICKUP TRUCKS WHOSE DOORS SPORT THE RANCH'S BRAND THERE ARE SUPERMARKETS LIKE EVERYWHERE ELSE AND THE SHERIFF GOES ON PATROL IN HIS CAR. BUT THERE IS A PERSISTENT WHIFF OF CLOSE ADVENTURE ...

AND THOSE FACES! HAS HOLLYWOOD PLAGIARIZED COWBOYS OR HAVE THEY SEEN TOO MANY MOVIES? ... STILL, WHAT WAS A GUY LIKE ME - WHO DID NOT EXACTLY LOOK THE PART - SUPPOSED TO DO TO FIND A JOB ON THE RANCH?

IN FACT YOU DON'T HAVE TO BE A ROUGH RIDER TO BE HIRED ... BECAUSE AT THE BEGINNING DRIVING TRACTORS, LAYING MILES-LONG LINES OF POSTS, STRETCHING BARBED WIRE OUT, CLEANING UP STABLES ... YOU FIND OUT IT'S ALL PRETTY MUCH WHAT CONQUERING THE WEST WAS ABOUT, NOW AND IN THE PAST.

AND AFTER THE QUARANTINE-LIKE BREAK-IN YOU START WORKING WITH THE CATTLE ... THEN IT'S BETTER THAN IN MY DREAMS ...

BELIEVE ME — IT'S EVEN GREATER THAN IN THE MOVIES...!

HORSE-RIDING YOUR DAYS AWAY TO WATCH OVER HERDS... ALTHOUGH THE TRADITIONAL BRANDING OF COWS IS NOWADAYS FOLLOWED BY VACCINATION...

ALTHOUGH YOU DRIVE A TRUCK TO THE NEAREST TOWN'S GENERAL STORE FOR GROCERIES AND A NEIGHBORLY CHAT OVER COFFEE...

DAILY LIFE ON THE RANCH STILL FOLLOWS THE PACE OF IMMENSE NATURE...

SOMETIMES, ON THE NAVAJO RESERVATION, TIME FEELS LIKE IT HAS GROUND TO A HALT...

ALTHOUGH THE REFUSE OF THE WHITE MAN'S CIVILIZATION TESTIFIES TO THE "BENEFIT" OF PROGRESS AT THE FOOT OF A HOPI VILLAGE ON TOP OF A SACRED MESA...

EVERYWHERE FACES ASSERT THAT A WORLD SYSTEMATICALLY BETRAYED, FORGOTTEN, DESPISED, HAS REFUSED TO DISAPPEAR. BUT TIMES HAVE CHANGED FOR YESTERDAY'S LOSERS." I AM THE REAL AMERICAN" HAS BECOME THE MOTTO OF THOSE YOUNG NATIVE WHO COMFORT THE MODERN WORLD WITHOUT DISOWNING THEIR LEGACY...

THIS IS MY VERY OWN AMERICA AND IT IS THERE! THESE DRAWINGS DO NOT AFFIRM AN AMATEUR ANTHROPOLOGIST'S PITY FOR A VANISHING OBJECT. THEY OBSERVE A SIMPLE, INCONSPICUOUS AND PERHAPS MORE HUMAN WAY OF LIFE IN ONE OF THE MOST BEAUTIFUL AND WILD AREAS OF THE US, A HUGE TERRITORY TORN APART BY CONTRADICTORY FORCES...

TALK ABOUT CONTRADICTIONS!
THE ROSY AMERICAN DREAM WHICH USED TO BE THE COLOR OF
WILD CANYONS HAS TURNED INTO AN ATROCIOUS NIGHTMARE...
AMERICA'S NEW FEATURES, WHICH ARE ALL OVER THE TV
SCREENS, RELEGATING HOLLYWOOD'S IMAGINARY EPICS
INTO THE BACKGROUND, SOMETIMES CONVEY PURE HORROR.
HOWEVER THE HOPE THAT GREW OUT OF THAT SOIL IS STILL
THERE!
YET HOPE IS NO LONGER FOUND IN THE CONQUEST OF THE WILDER-
NESS, BUT IN RESTLESS CAMPUSES AND BIG CITIES' GHETTOS.

I HAVE STARTED LOVING THIS AMERICA TOO. OBVIOUSLY IT IS
NOT EXACTLY WHAT I USED TO IMAGINE BACK IN MY SLEEPY
FRENCH SUBURB. BUT THERE IN AMERICA I MET SOMEONE
WHOM I NEVER THOUGHT OF WHEN I WAS A KID...

THE WOMAN WHO EVENTUALLY BECAME MY WIFE!...

J.C. MEZIERES - 74-

Translated by John Dean and Jean-Paul Gabilliet

52

Part II

Popular Music

5 Rocking and Rapping in the Dutch Welfare State

Mel van Elteren

The commercial and cultural reality of entertainment industries is more complicated than most people realize. The conventional wisdom about multinationals versus national producers no longer applies. In our new leisure world, global corporations control the publication, transmission, distribution, and licensing of goods (magazines, books, films, television programs, songs, stars, and stories) that emanate from local producers using local facilities (musicians, engineers, designers, writers). In this new model, the major companies do not share a supranational identity, something to be imposed culturally across the globe; rather, they control an information network—so that whatever sells in one country can be mass-marketed in another: the production of local music for the international market, "local" music made from a "global" perspective (Frith, 1991a).

Statistics prove this point and show the way of future developments. In the early 1980s, a world market share of 60 to 70 percent was divided between five transnationals: CBS, WEA, RCA (American all), EMI (British), and Polygram (Dutch-Philips). Then, the German Bertelsmann Group (BMG) absorbed RCA, and Sony (Japanese) took over CBS; this left WEA (now Time-Warner) as the only American giant. At the same time, America's share of the market in world turnover slipped from 45 percent in 1984 to 35 percent in 1990; this was dramatically offset by steady growth in the European market, from 31 percent in 1984 to almost 44 percent in 1990, and in Japan, from 13 percent in 1984 to 16 percent in 1989. Certain crucial factors enter in here. The American market declined due to the devaluation of the U.S. dollar. The European and Japanese markets had higher growth rates (Reniers, 1992: 7–8). But most important, take-over activity meant that the hardware-software relationship changed. Ownership of the software (films and music) has become ever more important as technological change and the electronic goods boom has slowed.

With regard to American rock music amid these developments, one has to recognize that "authenticity" means first of all to be true to the genre's conventions. Attempts to make a rigid distinction between "authentic" (American) and "imitated" (European) rock tend to be ridiculous. The Irish group U2, or even the Dutch rock singer Herman Brood and the Dutch rock group Golden Earring, can very well play first-rate American rock music. More specifically, the conventions of hard rock and heavy metal are now better understood in Germany and Sweden than anywhere else (Frith, 1989: 171). This is similar to what happened earlier in other domains of popular culture. For instance, the spaghetti westerns of the Italian filmmaker Sergio Leone, such as *Once Upon a Time in the West* (1968), paid more tribute to the genre and gave a more truthful depiction of the actual historical background than did many American-made westerns (Frayling, 1981: 121–137).

THE "ANGLO-AMERICANIZATION" OF POPULAR MUSIC IN THE NETHERLANDS

Consider now the Dutch, who take their historical, linguistic, and territorially rooted cultural identity for granted. They are not as anxious about their identity as are, for instance, the Canadians. The Dutch hold a reputation for openness toward both trade and cultural exchange and take pride in the eclectic nature of their culture (Campbell Robinson, Buck, and Cuthbert, 1991: 122). In this context, we shall examine how they have responded to various types of American popular music as cultural imports in their country during the last decade. Were the Dutch eclectic in this domain? Or were they more selective in their musical appropriation? To what extent were homegrown variants at issue? Can some pattern in the development of these processes of exchange be recognized?

Paul Rutten concluded that Anglo-American pop and rock music, Afro-American music, and English-language mainstream vocal music together accounted for an average of 77 percent of the total number of hits on the Dutch national charts in the period 1960–1985 (Rutten, 1992). The Dutch popular genres and the other continental European genres made up only 21 percent of the total number of top hits. During the years 1960–1963, a tendency set in that culminated in the hegemony of Anglo-American genres and of the English language at the center of Dutch pop music. The increase in those years of the significance of Anglo-American music was detrimental to both the Dutch and other continental European genres. From 1966 onward, the share of Anglo-American genres on the Dutch charts remained far above 70 percent. After a modest decline in 1971, the share of Anglo-American genres gradually grew toward the largest one in the studied period: 91 percent in 1985. In that year, nine out of ten hits belonged to the Anglo-American tendencies. This was largely at the expense of the other continental European genres, whose share decreased to almost zero in the course of the 1980s.

The actual share of *American* popular music on the Dutch charts was highest in the years 1960–1963. From 1963 onward, a steady decline occurred. In 1978 and 1979 a temporary upsurge of American music took place, and during the last years of the period Rutten investigated (1984 and 1985) there was again an increase of American dominance. In these years a limited number of American artists became mega-stars. In 1985 four artists/groups shared more than half of all American hit music on the Dutch charts: Madonna, Prince, Bruce Springsteen, and the Talking Heads. This tendency has continued.

British artists made by far the most important contribution to pop/rock music on the Dutch charts. Their share was 49 percent on average, although pop and rock originate from the United States. This might lead to a misunderstanding about the actual impact of "American" pop/rock, however. Below I will return to the complex relationship between British and American pop/rock music, and American popular culture as a whole. American artists performed 25 percent of the rock and pop music; Dutch artists 19 percent; and other continental European artists only 4 percent.

In recent years the dominant Anglo-American influence on the Dutch national charts has continued, according to a small follow-up study (van den Beemt, 1993). The share of Anglo-American performers has been even higher: 70 percent on average in the period 1985–1992 as compared to 55 percent on average in the period 1960–1985. And although the share of British performers did not change much, 27 percent and 31 percent on average in the two successive periods, the share of American artists has clearly increased: from 28 percent to 39 percent.

From these and other quantitative data on hit music in the Netherlands, we may conclude that the symbolic world in which hit music is created and disseminated has a predominantly Anglo-American character. This is even more important when one takes into consideration the fact that the popular musical culture is highly significant for young people. If television culture represents the mainstream culture for Western society as a whole, popular music does so for youth. Popular musical culture is the most significant component of the socialization of youth through mass communication. As such it is a very relevant form of "institutionalized public acculturation" (Gerbner, 1979), along with other agencies of socialization.

The symbols with which this symbolic milieu is constructed concern mostly cultural forms and contents that directly hail from the United States and Great Britain or are variants thereof. The symbolic world of countries other than America—and to some extent even that of the United States itself—is first of all an *imaginary America* (Webster, 1988). A large part of the British contributions to pop and rock music consisted, and still consist today, of British interpretations of music forms borrowed from the American popular cultural heritage, sometimes mixed with typically British elements from the indigenous music hall tradition or older musical cultural forms among the working class.

When English currencies are rejected in British rock music, appeals are frequently made to American cultural models: the heritage of rock 'n' roll in Buddy Holly imitations; U.S. hairstyles such as the D.A. and elephant trunk; images of Cadillacs and Studebakers, Confederate flags, and baseball jackets. Alan Durant writes:

> In other instances (as in strands of punk in the mid-1970s, and in some countercurrents within European jazz and "classical" music), appeals of rejection are made precisely *against* imported or supra-national values, . . . according these images, insignia and idioms a significance or attachment of value which they bring *with* them rather than which they acquire by their new relations with surrounding discourses on arrival. Against such forms and forces are mobilised notions of local activity and autonomy of production and distribution, concerns which run across both the circulation of music and also what elements of genre or idiom will be taken as antecedents and models for future innovation. (Durant, 1984: 178–179)

The process of Anglo-Americanization is to some extent a process of globalization, with American English as the lingua franca of an international, youth-oriented popular culture. However, unlike the baby boomers, teenagers today are a generation without a *musical* lingua franca. Current tastes in music take many directions. Rock in a narrower sense (referring to rock 'n' roll, and rock music of the 1960s and 1970s as well as their successors) has demographic problems. Teenagers still drive the record business, but rock is what their parents listened to, so they buy rap and anything else that connotes independence. Rock has technological problems as well. The electronics revolution gave baby boomers Stratocaster guitars and record players, unifying their musical culture. But it gave the next generation multi-channel cable TV, isolationist Walkman technology, and recordings of popular music from all over the world, thereby encouraging musical eclecticism. Grammy awards are now bestowed in 78 musical categories, up from 28 when the awards began in 1958 (Cox, 1992).

In reviewing these international–local relationships in the world of pop/rock music, one should guard against a prevailing rock ideology that values the authentic above the plastic, the regional above the global, and that pitches creativity against commerce and independence against the major international music corporations. In a highly critical comment on the basic design and conclusions of the international research project on "popular music and global cultural diversity" (see Campbell Robinson, Buck, and Cuthbert, 1991), and more particularly on the way in which world music has recently been interpreted by several of its advocates and fans, Simon Frith has pointed out that the economic internationalization of popular music "has not just meant the opening up of new local markets or the inscription of local popular music audience into new patterns of international consumption. It has also turned local musicians into a particular kind of internationally defined producer" (Frith, 1991b: 285). An interpretation in terms of the battle between the good (the scattered bands of committed musicians) and the evil (the corporate force of Time-Warner, Sony-CBS, Thorn-EMI, and so on) is in his opinion a misleading one: "The music world is not just made up of large companies, creative musicians, and questing fans; it is shaped in fact by a rich variety of go-betweens. After all, the rise of the various 'independent' Western pop musics (R & B, rock 'n' roll, punk, hip-hop) was dependent on their packagers and promoters and hucksters" (Frith, 1991b: 285).

This has everything to do with the complex interplay between processes of globalization and localization that is characteristic of today's world. In this connection a relevant empirical question is how the local entrepreneurs operate in the various countries, how they deal in turn with the international operators. In other words, we need a clear picture of the music worlds in which they live, worlds in which musical practices and values are maintained (and changed) through a variety of institutional relationships. The process of local popular music production does not merely epitomize the tension between economic internationalization and cultural diversity. Local music worlds "now include international players and expectations. And there are many ways in which the resulting local–international tensions can be resolved" (Frith, 1991b: 286).

INTERPLAYS OF CULTURAL LOCALIZATION AND GLOBALIZATION IN POPULAR MUSIC

Since the mid 1980s, diverse bands and singers have been heralding the return of American rock or offering a contemporary country music functioning beyond the stereotypes of rhinestones and rednecks, and expressing a thoughtful sense of place and tradition. Here the so-called back-projection mechanism that is involved in listening to American pop/rock music is of relevance. It is due to the fact that American popular music is often strongly linked to visions of an American landscape or well-known American localities. Almost all the various forms of music produced in Britain in the 1980s were somehow related to an imaginary America (Webster, 1988: 158–163). This crucial element must be taken into account when one tries to gauge the relative impact of pop/rock music from Britain within the Netherlands, as compared to that from America.

For example, of the leading figures in the U.S. movement, Bruce Springsteen was by far the most famous in Holland. His first performance, as early as 1975, was on the RAI podium in Amsterdam. He and his E Street Band returned to Holland in April 1981, when he gave two concerts at the AHOY hall in Rotterdam. In the late 1980s and early 1990s Springsteen topped the charts in Holland; all his performances at Rotterdam's Feyenoord stadium, where he was on tour in Europe, were major successes. Although other American musicians drew less attention among the Dutch, the Chicano group Los Lobos and more recently the rock group R.E.M. from Athens, Georgia, have also been popular. Almost all American New Authenticity[1] bands have given concerts in the Netherlands.

Although the Dutch context was in many respects quite different from the American, we find tendencies toward authenticity in Dutch rock music that bear some resemblance to the New Authenticity movement in American rock music (Frith, 1990). First, there was a new wave of Dutch rock groups in the early 1980s who sang their songs in Dutch, breaking with a prevailing tradition of singing pop/rock songs in English even when the original compositions were by Dutch musicians. The breakthrough of Dutch-language rock groups was reflected in higher audience figures for specialized radio programs, an expanding live performance circuit, and increased record sales. The Dutch-language rock music— played by groups such as Doe Maar [Go on], Toontje Lager [In a Lower Key, or Change of Tune], Het Goede Doel [Charity], Normaal [Naturally, or Of Course]— was primarily the outcome of changes in the structures of the music industry and pop scene in the Netherlands:

- Through the efforts of the Stichting Popmuziek Nederland (SPN), or Dutch Rock Music Foundation, so-called pop-collectives emerged (partly subsidized by the Ministry of Culture, Recreation, and Social Work) that provided practice facilities for unknown, inexperienced musicians. Their promotion of so-called noncommercial pop music provided a strong impetus to Dutch-language rock (van Elderen, 1989).
- This development was enhanced by an alternative circuit of youth centers and social clubs.
- The crisis in the national record industry (declining numbers of record sales) was met by a new business strategy: picking up and promoting the new trend of singing in Dutch.
- The emergence of a few small independent new labels and music magazines (e.g., *Vinyl*) drew attention not only to punk and new wave developments abroad but to native-language rock as well.

In addition, the audiences for the native rock scene were to some extent constituted by the mass media. For example, the disc jockey of a very popular radio program, De Avondspits [The Evening Rush Hour], played a crucial role by heavily promoting Dutch-language rock. Various television stations, which tried to win support by articulating their own identity—a significant event in the pilloried Dutch broadcasting system—featured some of the groups as well (van Elderen, 1984: 99, 102–105). The broadcasting stations VPRO (formerly of a liberal Protestant bent; since 1968 of a broader, liberal humanistic orientation) and VARA (of a social democratic orientation) were especially active in promoting songs that went against the grain.

Also, it was no longer taboo to emphasize one's Dutch identity in playing such music, because leading figures among the "juvenile elders" (i.e., Baby Boomers) of the pop/rock establishment legitimated this stance vis-à-vis the more highly educated, "progressive" aficionados of rock. For the rest the New Authenticity movement concerned as well an alternation of generations, with newcomers taking over the lead from their predecessors.

In this tendency, no direct American influences were involved. Rather, parallel developments occurred that may be explained in terms of counterreactions to broader postmodernization processes in both the United States and the Netherlands. They concern a cultural-ideological problem of modern people longing for a comprehensible worldview—that is, parochialism—in an abstract society (Zijderveld, 1970). In the Dutch case a link with the cultural crisis in the welfare state should be made, which gave these responses to the postmodernization process a specific flavor.

In the few political comments within the Dutch lyrics, an international dimension was completely lacking; thus, the culture of the modern welfare state seems isolationist. This might mesh with an often-quoted explanation of the emergence of Dutch-language rock songs: the welfare state is supposed to have halted (Anglo-) American cultural imperialism, indirectly enabling the native rock tradition to mature. This is not very plausible, though. The continuing influence of American rock was much too strong when the indigenous rock culture remained underdeveloped.

Nevertheless, some Dutch-language rock musicians were inspired by American examples, particularly by rock groups from the Midwest or South. This probably applies most to the rock group Normaal, which plays what might be called "farmers rock" (taking black rock 'n' roll—Chuck Berry and Little Richard—as a starting point, and sometimes mixing it with streetband music). Its music is robust and rhythmic but does not make reference to the aggressive sounds of the city. A regionalistic rural chauvinism is embodied by the band members, who have their roots in the Achterhoek, a region in the east of the Netherlands near the German border that is considered somewhat backward—especially by people from the Randstad, the urban conglomerate in the west. The band members consistently sing in dialect and local slang, and they express opposition to the cultural dominance of the Randstad. Songs such as "Ik-Bun-Maor-Ne-Eenvoudige-Boerenlul" [I Am Just a Simple Yokel] epitomize the Normaal image: "They are about ordinary experiences, the simple things of life as they touch on everybody. And they make jokes about it—simple countryside humour and laughter, in which subtlety and irony are certainly not lacking" (van Elderen, 1984: 107). Their fans mostly come from the countryside, small towns, and villages and tend to share similar rural (i.e., chauvinistic) ideas.

Insofar as geographical differences still exist in the Netherlands today, they are often related to differences in degrees of urbanity. For this Amsterdam fulfills an avant-garde function. Here new cultural expressions and trends catch on most frequently, after which the diffusion to other towns, suburban regions, and the countryside follows rapidly. Insofar as elements of regional cultures are still discernable, these run the risk of disappearing entirely (regional clothes, dialects, folk songs, marriage customs), or—less frequently—they are incorporated into the national culture. For example, the Carnival and the Elfstedentocht (Frisian, eleven towns skating races) have evolved from regional events into national ones (Knippenberg and de Pater, 1988: 206). In the case of Dutch-language rock, however, the new trends began at the periphery and not in Amsterdam.

More recently, another wave of Dutch groups has arisen. These groups not only sing in Dutch, a regional Dutch dialect, or even the Frisian (northern) language, but they also borrow from older musical traditions in the Netherlands (e.g., old sailors' ballads, accordion music, streetband or carnivallike music, brass band music, and polka dancing). A very good example is Rowwen Hèze, a group from a small town called America (sic) in the north of Limburg, the most southern province of the Netherlands. The area is extremely poor, and its culture is marginal vis-à-vis that of the Randstad. The group's members sing in the regional Limburg dialect and play a wild kind of Tex-Mex music, reflecting well-known American groups and individuals in this genre such as Flaco Jimenez. They add their own creative contributions by using the accordion as played at fairs and the trumpet of the brass bands. In a way, their interpretation of Cajun music evolves from playing a fast-tempo version of traditional Dutch accordion music. Their style is partly influenced by the American Chicano group Los Lobos—thus they have been nicknamed Los Limbos (a clear reference to their regional background). The impact of Los Lobos is obvious in their catchy song "Bestel Mar" [Just Order (a drink)] (1987) based on Los Lobos's "Anselma," which is a faithful rendition of a 100-year-old Mexican song.

The Nits are another group clearly trying to express a Dutch identity, although they sing in English. These former art school students gained popularity with songs such as "Nescio" (1983, a joyful play on the words of the Dutch novelist with that name), "In the Dutch Mountains" (1987), and "Adieu Sweet Bahnhof" (1989). They intermingle various kinds of music with waltz-like rhythms and an occasional Brecht/Weill type of song, deliberately trying to shed the Anglo-American musical mold and reaching a distinctively European style. Paradoxically, the lead singer, Henk Hofstede, sings with an American accent; and the album *Ting* even deals with America's landscape: its houses, rivers and large plains, the Greyhound buses (which the Nits consider a very poetic means of transportation). Yet theirs is truly European music, in a direct line with performances of the troubadours and minstrels. Their intellectual lyrics—containing typically Dutch humor—often express recollections of childhood and youth but also refer to highbrow culture in contrast to mainstream pop music. For example, they make references to the sculptor Henry Moore, the Spanish civil war, the Venice of the film *Don't Look Now*, the Bauhaus-style chair of a former girlfriend (Evers, 1989: 23; Steensma, 1992: 251–252; Steinz, 1992).

ISSUES OF AUTHENTICITY

The "local authenticity" involved in the New Authenticity movement in American rock music is not a cultural form that has indigenous roots. It responds to a larger process of global cultural change. In distancing itself from mainstream pop/rock and articulating its own regional-cultural identity against hegemonic musical styles, local authenticity seeks a clear sense of place and community. Paradoxically, the interplay between national and regional culture occurs through national and even global media networks.

The trend is evident in the recent wave of Dutch rock groups that emphasize local cultural identity—within the Netherlands or within Europe—as opposed to the Anglo-American world and the hegemony of Anglo-American pop/rock. In this respect there is no two-way cultural exchange between America and Holland. In some instances Dutch musicians have actively appropriated Anglo-American pop/rock styles and combined them with musical elements from their indigenous culture. However, Dutch popular music that expresses local authenticity has not been exported as a form of ethnic pop or world music to America, nor may we expect this to happen in the future. The contemporary Dutch culture is not exotic enough, and it is too close to American culture. In fact, most of the few Dutch musicians that have achieved a degree of popularity in the United States did so by accommodating the prevailing molds of American pop/rock, in addition to employing good marketing techniques: Shocking Blue and Golden Earring in the late 1960s and early 1970s; recently, the saxophonist Candy Dulfer, the rock groups Bettie Serveert and Loïs Lane (whose glamorous two lead sister singers toured with Prince and made a few records with him), and Sleeze Beez, a hardrock group hardly known in the Netherlands itself (Rutten and Oud, 1991: 137–138). One exception may be house music, which is often produced in home studios, with which Dutch mixers occasionally score an international hit. In this form of do-it-yourself dance music (which is so anonymous that nationality does not make any difference) Holland ranks among the leading nations, along with America and England. Currently there are about 80 house labels and several thousand producers in this genre in the Netherlands (Quint, 1993: 4). In fact, Holland has become an important supplier of a number of house genres, including "gabber house": an extremely fast-tempo house variant akin to heavy metal that is very popular, particularly among gays and among soccer fans in the Randstad.

Rap music, too, constitutes an authentic response in which a sense of community is emphasized—in this case among Afro-American youths, kindred blacks, and other people of color across the Westernized globe. Identification with, and emulation of, the hip-hop subculture in the United States may help blacks in the Netherlands enhance their self-esteem and thus empower them to seek a better quality of life. Rap is about being a witness: talking about what one sees, feels, and experiences. Such intimacy makes hip-hop compelling and gives it great potential for crosscultural communication. In fact, Chuck D. of Public Enemy has described rap as the CNN of young black Americans (Bernard, 1992: 1). Through this secondary orality disseminated by transnational mass media, kindred groups made up of mostly youngsters of color all over the world may develop common cultural identities within a global hip-hop culture. Because of its Carribean connection, rap has an especially strong appeal to members of ethnic groups living in that area or having roots in the Carribean but living elsewhere (e.g., people of color from the West Indies living in the United Kingdom, or from the Netherlands Antilles and Surinam living in the Netherlands).

Several factors point to a positive reception of American rap and the rise of its Dutch counterpart. First, Holland experienced a deep penetration of American popular culture during the postwar period. Second, Holland has an underclass of colored minorities: people from Surinam and the Netherlands Antilles—former Dutch colonies that still have relations with the Netherlands and are part of the Verenigd Koninkrijk der Nederlanden [United Kingdom of the Netherlands], and Moroccan and Turkish groups that are highly concentrated in specific urban settings—the Bijlmermeer, a southern neighborhood of Amsterdam; and parts of the inner city of Amsterdam such as De Pijp, and of Rotterdam, het Oude Westen [the Old West], and the Afrikanerbuurt (all former white working-class districts). For the youth of these groups, the question of identity is often a hot issue. Moreover, a lack of economic opportunities and positive images have hurt their self-esteem.

In the 1950s, Eurasians and Moluccans from the former Dutch colonies in the Indonesian Archipelago introduced rock 'n' roll to the Netherlands. They have always concentrated on American music. After the beat craze of the mid-1960s, in which they took only a minor part, they turned to soul, funk, Latin, and reggae. Traditionally these musical styles are performed in Holland by nonwhites, mainly musicians from former Dutch colonies. Whereas currently people from the Indonesian Archipelago prefer nostalgia, rediscovering their *krontjong* music and drowning themselves in rock 'n' roll revivals, people from Surinam prefer the popular African and Afro-Caribbean sounds (Mutsaers, 1990). The majority of Dutch hip-hoppers have a Creole-Surinam background, and young people of Creole-Dutch origin have set the tone of the indigenous rap culture.

Yet several factors may hinder the reception of rap in the Netherlands. For example, the status of the black underclass in the Netherlands is not as bad as in the United States and several other European countries (especially the United Kingdom and France), partly because the elaborate welfare system with various forms of financial and social support reduces potential friction. In the United States the physical setting of the ghettos has an especially negative impact on members of the underclass. Holland does not have such ghettos; living conditions are relatively better, due to a governmental policy that offers good housing to lower-income groups. Nevertheless, the social security system—by absorbing many unemployed people—is expected to have negative effects on the long-term unemployed and their children, resulting in an economic underclass to which numerous Dutch black youths will belong. Until now, forms of blatant racism have not been an issue, although more subtle forms of racism (e.g., discrimination in application procedures for jobs and in the work place) have been identified in social research studies (Bovenkerk, 1978; Elich and Maso, 1984).

Finally, one must acknowledge that for the Netherlands, a small country fixed in the orbit of American culture, "America" often functions as a projection screen for people's fantasies. The back-projection mechanism at issue when playing or listening to its popular music offers significant degrees of psychological freedom for Dutch youths who experience their own society as restrictive. America's "expressive individualism" can be highly attractive to Europeans who grow up in more communitarian societies. Even though mainstream Dutch and American culture share Protestant strains, expressive individualism outweighs this.

The picaresque component in American popular culture is also highly attractive to Dutch youth. American pop/rock music is strongly influenced by this tradition. Especially in country and western and country blues, the urge to "travel on" is both celebrated and bemoaned. These musical traditions have offered successive generations of American pop/rock musicians a cultural reservoir of picaresque themes, phrases, and images as well as complete songs (Hatch and Millward, 1987: 16–18). In contrast, Holland is still a welfare state with a rather "predictable" way of life and caretaking from cradle to grave. From this perspective, immersing oneself in an imaginary America offers a release from everyday boredom. In the imagined "land of unlimited opportunities" one feels free from everyday worries, from restrictions set by existing social structures. Alluring lyrics suggest images of either a venturesome life in the dangerous and desolate city, or a vital experience of wide open spaces in which one is continually "on the move" by driving or hitchhiking (van Elteren, 1992; 1994: 218–221). We find a clear reflection of these romantic sentiments in the rock music and lyrics of both the well-known Dutch rock group Golden Earring and rock singer-artist Herman Brood and his former band Wild Romance, who reflect the classical American rock tradition (Didden, 1988). In indulging in these rock 'n' roll fantasies, they express a nostalgia for the American youth culture of the past and its associated imaginary community. For instance, in Golden Earring's older hit "Radar Love," which topped the American charts in August 1973, lead singer Barry Hay sings about having driven all night: "My hand's wet on the wheel . . . . The radio's playing some forgotten song. Brenda Lee's 'Coming On Strong.' The road's got me hypnotized. And I'm speeding into a new sunrise."

COSMOPOLITANISM IN POPULAR CULTURE

As collective systems of meanings, cultures belong primarily to social relationships and to networks of such relationships. Only indirectly do they belong to places: "The less people stay put in one place, and also the less dependent their communications are on face-to-face contacts, the more attenuated does the link between culture and territory become. This is a fact we now encounter every day" (Hannerz, 1992: 39). This does not automatically lead to a collective nostalgia, for there are opportunities to become cosmopolitan. "A more genuine cosmopolitanism entails a certain metacultural position. There is, first of all, a willingness to engage with the Other, an intellectual and aesthetic stance of openness toward divergent cultural experiences. There can be no cosmopolitans without locals, representatives of more circumscribed territorial cultures" (Hannerz, 1992: 252). Thus, we find cosmopolitans not only in the domain of high culture but in popular culture—in this case, popular music in the Netherlands. They actively take part in musical cultures from other countries and regions; and they may be eclectic in their musical preferences, trying to do justice to each cultural form. These cosmopolitans may develop shared sociocultural identities with kindred people elsewhere, across national and regional borders, and thereby undermine a still widely prevailing conception of cultural transmission in terms of interactions between inhabitants of separate nation-states. This cultural complexity will become more significant in the future.

Today more than ever, the local is defined by reference not so much to a specific geography or community, but to a shared sense of place—which is itself part of the global picture. In such a mapping process, one's sense of musical (or more generally, cultural) locality depends on both the immediate material circumstances and the reference groups, identities, and fantasies that are themselves globally mediated. Compare, for instance, the participants from various countries in the current, transnational rap culture. Locality is determined as a sense of difference from the global—it is not a spontaneous expression of actual local traditions (Frith, 1991a: 268). I expect the audiovisual language of symbols and fantasies associated with "America" to remain a core element in the global, mass-mediated culture and its pan-European variant. To paraphrase British rock singer Elvis Costello, this will enable both Dutch youth and Dutch juvenile elders to "speak American without tears."

NOTE

1. The term "New Authenticity" stems from Simon Frith's article "Frankie Said. But What Did They Mean?" (1990). Frith understood New Authenticity as a new pop sensibility which was symbolized, in Britain at least, by the contrast between the group Frankie Goes to Hollywood—with their new pop, artificial style—versus Bruce Springsteen, the very icon of authenticity. For more information, see Frith, 1990: 185; and van Elteren, 1994: 175–177, 244 note 7.

REFERENCES

Bernard, James (1992). "A Newcomer Abroad, Rap Speaks Up." New York Times, 23 August, Arts & Leisure, Section 2: 1, 22–23.
Bovenkerk, Frank (ed.) (1978). Omdat Zij Anders Zijn. Meppel: Boom.
Campbell Robinson, Diana, Elizabeth B. Buck, Marlene Cuthberth, and the International Communication and Youth Consortium (1991). Music at the Margins, Popular Music and Global Cultural Diversity, Newbury Park/London/New Delhi: Sage.
Cox, Meg (1992). "Rhythm and Blues. Rock Is Slowly Fading as Tastes in Music Go Off in Many Directions." Wall Street Journal, 26 August: A1, A8.
Didden, Marc (1988). "Het Verschijnsel Herman Brood. 'Ik hoop dat in mijn muziek niets van Nederland zit.' " OOR, 27 February: 20–27.
Durant, Alan (1984). Conditions of Music. Albany: State University of New York Press.
Elich, J. and B. Maso (1984). Discriminatie, Vooroordeel en Racisme in Nederland. Den Haag: Acom, Ministerie van Binnenlandse Zaken.
Evers, Corné (1989). "The Nits in Moskou." OOR, 9 April: 21–25.
Frayling, Christopher (1981). Spaghetti Westerns. Cowboys and Europeans, from Karl May to Sergio Leone. London: Routledge and Kegan Paul.
Frith, Simon (1989). "Euro Pop." Cultural Studies 3.2: 166–172.
———— (1990). "Frankie Said. But What Did They Mean?" Consumption, Identity and Style:

Marketing, Meanings and the Packaging of Pleasure, ed. Alan Tomlinson. London/ New York: Routledge, 172–185.

―――― (1991a). "Anglo-America and Its Discontents." *Cultural Studies* 5.3: 263–269.

―――― (1991b). "Critical Response." *Music at the Margins: Popular Music and Global Culture*, eds. Diana Campbell Robinson et al. Newbury Park/London/New Delhi: Sage, 281– 287.

Gerbner, G. (1979). "Television's Influence on Values and Behaviour." *Massacommunicatie* 7.6: 215–222.

Hannerz, Ulf (1992). *Cultural Complexity: Studies in the Social Organization of Meaning.* New York: Columbia University Press.

Hatch, David, and Stephan Millward (1987). *From Blues to Rock: An Analytical History of Pop Music.* Manchester: Manchester University Press.

Knippenberg, Hans, and Ben de Pater (1988). *De Eenwording van Nederland. Schaalvergroting and Integratie sinds 1800.* Nijmegen: SUN.

Mutsaers, Lutgard (1990). "Indorock: An Early Eurorock Style." *Popular Music* 9.3: 307– 320.

Quint, Erik (1993). "Haalt Quazar het Jaar 2000?" *FRET* 1.0 (May/June): 4–6.

Reniers, Georges (1992). "Anglo-American, and/or, Global, and/or, Local, and/or . . . Music. The Complex Traffic of Musical Sounds in Spain, the Basque Country, Belgium, Flanders . . . and In Between." Unpublished thesis, Programme in European Leisure Studies (PELS).

Rutten, Paul (1992). *Hitmuziek in Nederland: 1960–1985.* Amsterdam: Cramwinckel.

Rutten, Paul, and Gerd Jan Oud (1991). *Nederlandse Popmuziek op de Binnen- en Buitenlandse Markt.* Rijswijk: Ministerie van Welzijn, Volksgezondheid en Cultuur.

Steensma, Frans (ed.) (1992). *OOR's Eerste Nederlandse Pop-Encyclopedie.* Amsterdam: Bonaventura.

Steinz, Pieter (1992). "In Ieder van Ons Schuilt een Sombere Fin. De Aarzelende Anti-Rock van The Nits." *NRC Handelsblad–Cultureel Supplement*, 13 November: 7.

van den Beemt, Antoine (1993). " 'Straight to the Top.' Hitparade-Muziek in Nederland (1985–1992)." Vakgroep Sociologie, Faculteit Sociale Wetenschappen, Katholieke Universiteit Brabant (unpublished paper).

van Elderen, P. Louis (1984). "Music and Meaning behind the Dykes: The New Wave of Dutch Rock Groups and Their Audiences." *Popular Music 4. Performers and Audiences*, eds. Richard Middleton and David Horn. Cambridge: Cambridge University Press, 97–116.

―――― (1989). "Pop and Government Policy in the Netherlands (1985)." *World Music, Politics and Social Change*, ed. Simon Frith. Manchester/New York: Manchester University Press, 190–197.

van Elteren, Mel (1992). " 'Amerika' in de Belevingswereld van Westeuropese Jongeren." *Beeld en Verbeelding van Amerika*, eds. Eugène van Erven and Jan Weerdenburg. Studium Generale reeks 9207, Bureau Studium Generale, University of Utrecht, 73–107.

―――― (1994). *Imagining America: Dutch Youth and Its Sense of Place.* Tilburg: Tilburg University Press.

Webster, Duncan (1988). *Looka Yonder! The Imaginary America of Populist Culture.* London/ New York: Comedia/Routledge.

Zijderveld, Anton C. (1970). *The Abstract Society.* Harmondsworth: Penguin.

6 Here, There, and Everywhere: Rock Music, Mass Culture, and the Counterculture

Claude Chastagner

Rock music has always been at odds with mass culture. For this it is often both admired and criticized. Rock benefits from mass culture's economic framework and, in return, feeds it with its remarkable energy. But musicians and fans alike have repeatedly expressed feelings of uneasiness or even downright rejection at this interdependence. It is precisely such tensions that give rock music its momentum.

The ambivalent nature of rock music in terms of mass culture stems from a well-known dichotomy that permeates most twentieth-century analyses of cultural productions. For Marxian or Veblenian criticism, the ideological contents of rock music derive from its economic status. Being nothing more than a merchandise, it has to abide by manufacturing and marketing principles such as market research, standardization, advertising, and profitability. These imperatives deprive the consumer of his or her free will and turn rock music into an antirevolutionary art, more concerned with profit margins than with the advancement of radical theories or popular causes. Such views were particularly propounded in the 1960s by journalists or academics such as Donald Horton and Paddy Whannel in England, or Jean-François Hirsch in France, but all agreed that rock music defied reductionistic analyses and was a more elusive subject to tackle than other aspects of mass culture. Paradoxically, Marxian perspectives linked up with the harsh comments passed on rock music by numerous conservative scholars (Allan Bloom, Alain Finkielkraut, and the like) who, drawing on—and distorting— Theodor W. Adorno's theories on jazz, described rock as a degrading and stupefying music. For them, it had nothing to offer but an ersatz of individualism, as it in fact standardizes cultural tastes and practices.

But rock music can be seen as more than the stale product of capitalism. Contrary to the early hostile reception, a different and more positive analysis gradually emerged, prompted by F. R. Leavis's works in the 1930s and D. Riesman's in the 1950s. This analysis held that rock is a popular and authentic artistic medium, the spontaneous expression of minority groups (colored people, young people), that was reflected by the change in terminology: the analysis of "teen culture" rock studies became that of "youth culture." The most active representatives of this new trend were found at Birmingham University, at Stuart Hall and Dick Hebdige's Centre for Contemporary Cultural Studies, which conciliated Marxian theories with a positive approach toward rock music, thereby rendering traditional political divisions obsolete. Patrick Mignon synthesized the contrasting viewpoints when he noted that "rock music is the universalization of both market logic and individualism, the standardized product of cultural industries and the true expression of the people" (Mignon, 1991; 4).[1]

In France, rock music has retained part of its early seduction—insofar as it does not belong to mass culture to the same extent as in English-speaking countries. Although obviously it is now part of mass consumption, it somehow remains on the fringes of consumer society. For a long time, it was restricted to an elite (usually students or members of the working class) that had been "initiated." Rock was an exotic idiom, the music from the other side of the Atlantic, an element of the American Dream, of the American Way of Life. As such, rock has preserved an aura of mystery and acquired a more prestigious, mythical status. French rock magazines, for instance, are more glamorous than their American counterparts; and French rock critics see themselves as missionaries or apostles.[2] The only rock program left on French television is entitled "Rock Culture." And although few French artists could be rightly described as rock artists (when they are, their life's goal is to play in America), most popular middle-of-the-road singers integrate rock sounds into their music.

Considering the conflicting relationship between rock music and mass culture, it is appropriate to assess the value of this culture and, more particularly, the concept of "mass." Some consider it synonymous with standardized consumption, bad taste, and fleeting fads; others, less contemptuous and more positive, stress that "popular" does not rule out "quality." However, the very relationship between rock and mass culture is seldom questioned; almost everyone equates rock music with one of the commonest definitions of mass culture: produced for the greatest number, consumed by the greatest number. It must be that the intimate links of rock music with mass consumption blur all tensions and contradictions between the two.

Indeed, rock depends for its growth on the basic principles of consumer society. To launch an artist, produce a record, or mount a tour takes time, people, and machines—which require heavy investment. American capitalism offers rock its potency and its taste for business ventures. Unlike European businessmen, American entrepreneurs are not suspicious of entertainment. Because popular music, musicals, or plays can be profitable, they deserve the interest of investors. As a result, show business is more integrated in the United States than it is in European countries. In France, rock music was able to develop thanks mainly to student societies, which organized concerts, published magazines, and so on. Major record companies, often the subsidiaries of foreign multinationals, imported British or American rock albums irregularly, under simplified sleeves (words, for instance, were not printed). Rock music represented just a fraction of their turnover. The entire French music industry feared both rock audiences and the questioning of deeply ingrained habits of dealing with mainstream performers. Only in the early 1980s did the specialized companies (studios, halls, tour operators), which still function today, take shape.

In the United States, rock music has benefited from the conjunction of various economic factors peculiar to consumer societies. The inner logic of capitalism demands that consumption be freed from the guilt inherent in it, turned even into a civic duty justified by national economic imperatives. The contradiction between capitalism and consumption, which stemmed from the Protestant foundation of American society, died out. The overall process was amplified by the postwar baby boom. A new class of consumers emerged: the teenagers, freed from the work ethic and commanding large sums of money—which they were encouraged to spend rather than save. They were being educated to consume. To meet this demand various new products appeared, which fitted the adolescent life-style and tastes. Rock 'n' roll was one of them, offering for a few cents unpretentious commentaries on everyday topics (cars, school, parents, love, etc.) over a pleasant musical background.

At this point, a word should be said about the consequences of the integration of cultural products by capitalist economies. If cultural production was to become a profit-making niche, it required the implementation of a mass market. Now, cultural artifacts have no intrinsic worth; their use value is purely hypothetical. Their consumption depends on their symbolic value based—in rock music as in the motion pictures industry—on the star system, which rationalized consumer demand. "The consumer must be created alongside the product" (Buxton, 1985). Hence the setting up of various middlemen, or "gate-keepers," such as critics, disc jockeys, or radio announcers whose task it is to launch new fashions and mold public taste. Such practices of course comfort those for whom rock music is the soulless product of capitalist industry.

Today, rock is solidly established as a major component of mass culture. A few figures should make this clear. Since 1969, overall rock records sales have generated higher profits than the other sectors of the entertainment industry. From 1980 onward—and despite fears of slumps and recessions—rock-related sales (records, videos, concerts) have increased by an annual average of 13.2 percent (slightly less for rock shows alone: 8.2 percent), generating in 1993 a $13 billion turnover. Rock albums (including rap) make up 52.1 percent of the market, as compared to 4 percent for classical and 3.3 percent for jazz. In 1993, six rock albums were certified multi-platinum, that is, more than 2 million units sold that year in the United States. Some even reached 10 million units (e.g., the soundtrack from the film *The Bodyguard*). Also in 1993, 33 albums were certified platinum, that is, above 1 million units sold.[3] Cumulative figures for the United States over several years are even more impressive: 14 million units for the Eagles' *Greatest Hits*, 13 million for Pink Floyd's *Dark Side of the Moon*, 43 million for Michael Jackson's *Thriller*, and more than a billion for Elvis Presley's complete recordings. At the same time, the break-even point for a rock album jumped from 20,000 units sold to 100,000. (Significantly, a look at France's Top 20 sales for July 1994 reveals that only 7 foreign records entered the charts: 4 of rock, 3 of dance music. Likewise, France accounts for only 6.7 percent of the world market for rock music, ranking fifth after the United States, Japan, Germany, and the United Kingdom. The profits generated by rock shows is also telling. In a single concert at New York's Yankee Stadium on June 10, 1994, for instance, Pink Floyd grossed an astonishing $3,765,090.[4]

Also significant is the growing interdependence between rock and movies. Among the all-time top-30 American films, 8 relied for their appeal on a rock soundtrack: *Batman, Ghostbusters, Grease, The Exorcist, Pretty Woman, Rocky, Saturday Night Fever,* and *Ghost.* It is obviously difficult to determine in such cases whether the film or its music drew the crowds; their interaction, most certainly. But choosing a well-known artist or song increases the prospect of success.

More interesting still is the way rock artists have subverted the Grammy Awards, an establishment of popular culture. Until 1966, the most coveted award (Best Album) went to artists such as Henry Mancini, Frank Sinatra, Judy Garland, Stan Getz, or Herb Alpert. In 1967, rock music entered for the first time with the Beatles's *Sergeant Pepper's Lonely Hearts Club Band.* Since then, only rock artists have received the prestigious award, other musical genres having to make shift with minor ones; typical recipients have been Blood Sweat and Tears, the Eagles, Fleetwood Mac, Stevie Wonder, Billy Joel, the Doobie Brothers, John Lennon, Toto, Tina Turner, Lionel Ritchie, Phil Collins, Steve Winwood, Paul Simon, U2, and Bonnie Raitt. Whether or not all these artists can still be labeled "rock" is another issue. With the opening of a rock 'n' roll Hall of Fame or the systematic use by television of rock music in the soundtrack of various commercials, sports programs, or serials, rock has become even more ensconced in mass culture.

The situation is particularly interesting because rock music has always defined itself as a reaction to mass culture. The grounds on which rock has confronted mass culture have obviously varied over time, as this culture itself was altered by the impact of previous rock genres. But rock dynamics stem from the tension between the centrifugal movement required by the entertainment industry and the centripetal dimension of each new musical wave. It may sound paradoxical to credit rock music with a centripetal force, because most artists seem to crave the largest possible success and recognition. However, their work is often sustained by a desire to prevent rock music from growing flat and dull, from losing its roots, its soul. Music has to be brought back to a center, a core, an origin all the more mythical as it combines at the same time with a quest for newness. Each new style consequently entails a redefining of existing links with mass culture as a whole and with previous rock genres. Rock music feeds on this tension between mass-culture expansionism and the artist's will to remain "outside," "on the fringes." Rock progresses through a series of breaks and assimilations. Its final aim is to be popular without selling out.

Year after year, rock artists have modified their demands. The glorification of consumption offered by Chuck Berry and other early rock 'n' rollers can be taken as a disapproval of the ideals still prevalent at the time: work, moderation, disregard for racial minorities and young people. But such a stand was in turn criticized during the 1960s, particularly in the United States, by the hippie movement. Material possessions ceased to be attractive and were secondary to more ethical values that were looked down upon by the society of the time: love, pacifism, recognition of racial and sexual minorities, exploration of the self, concern for nature, and so forth. By integrating the positions of the counterculture, rock became its mouthpiece; it rejected the tenets of mass society, the apology of consumption and of the American Dream, the stranglehold exerted by industry and technocracy over the country's cultural and intellectual life. Different rallying cries appeared ("Small is beautiful," "I'm black and I'm proud") that crystallized the refusal of the dominant cultural and economic ideology.

Obviously, continental Europe was somewhat left aside by these sweeping movements. True, 1968 was for France a time of deep change in which American popular music played a part. To keep in line with the spirit of the time, magazines were launched that devoted considerable space to rock music. But French youth were mere witnesses of what was going on in English-speaking countries. French youth gladly and readily acknowledged the new musical forms, going as far in some cases as translating the songs into French (as the lyrics had become meaningful); but they seldom actually took part in the musical evolution.

In America, the changes in popular music were carried out in the name of authenticity. The new principles were a quest for simplicity and the pureness of the origins, the questioning of large-scale marketing operations and standardization. Throughout the 1960s a number of artists, by putting back in fashion white and black American traditional music and incorporating the rock idiom (folk rock, blues rock), managed to topple classic rock 'n' roll—which had become solidly entrenched in mass culture. Thus, the discrepancy between two deceptively similar notions—mass culture and popular culture—was exposed. The tension between the mass and the fringe (to which we initially referred) overlaps this opposition; after all, within industrialized societies a return to traditional values (here, traditional music) can be seen as a break with the current values of these societies.[5]

The first wave of contestation culminated in the second half of the 1960s with acid rock and the black music associated with the counterculture (soul and funk). The same countercultural dimension can be found at other times and for other musical styles that do not bear any direct connection with 1960s counterculture (whether it be punk, reggae, pub-rock, thrash, hard-core, rap, grunge, etc.); what matters is the break with established traditions, with the musical code.

All these styles operate on the same small-scale basis, the exact opposite of what mass culture advocates. This is true not only of the size of the bands, of the management companies, of the concert halls, of the budgets involved—but also of the musicians' technical know-how. Too high a degree of musicianship and technical command, as befits the demands of the record industry, is considered suspect. Rather, the emphasis is on amateurism and improvization, on careless and ephemeral attitudes. Ideally one should remain a "cult" band, whose success depends more on the grapevine than on the marketing strategies peculiar to mass culture.

The very organization of the record industry reflects the tension between the mass and the fringe. In English-speaking countries, business is shared between separate but complementary bodies: independent companies (the "indies") and large corporations (the "majors"). Multinational corporations are a key element of mass economies, but they are too slow in decision making to match the spirit of rock music; it takes swiftness and flexibility to grasp the volatile quality of new bands and styles. Smaller companies are better equipped in this respect. They are responsible for the discovery and the initial "harnessing" of a great number of artists (in 1956, 33 of the top 50 recordings were released by independent companies). Large corporations—which have the manufacturing, distributing, and marketing clout and the capital necessary for worldwide developments—come in later.[6]

This organization of the record industry brings to light the essential ambiguity of rock music. If most new musical trends result from the criticism of mass consumption (including music), they seldom resist for very long the relentless attacks of the industry and its assimilating powers.[7] The most unorthodox practices are rapidly popularized and made palatable, losing their radical character in the process.[8] A recent example is the Seattle-based band Nirvana, which jumped in a few weeks from the status of garage band to the number one position in the charts. Each musical trend, after a few months of existence, thus faces two alternatives: either to slowly fade away, or to integrate into mass culture. The evolution of the record industry lies along this well-documented process (see, for example, Richard Peterson and David Berger or John Fiske in *Introduction to Communication Studies*), the fierce and unrelenting competition between majors and independents, which is often closer to plunder than collaboration.[9]

Rock music is never countercultural for very long. As a rule, after a short period on the fringes, each new style becomes a mass countercultural movement before eventually joining the mass culture merry-go-round. Mass industry cares little about the subtle differences between culture and the counterculture. In fact, its essential feature is its ability to digest any form of deviancy or marginality. Herbert J. Gans noted in 1974:

the youth culture of the 1960s has now declined, at least in public visibility, and no longer looks as threatening to the advocates of high culture as it did only a few years ago. Indeed, much of that youth culture is now being incorporated into commercial popular culture. (Gans, 1974: 6)

In the end, one may wonder how relevant is the questioning of rock music as it is carried out by the various schools of criticism mentioned earlier. The central question is not one of origin. To ask whether rock is a commodity manufactured and imposed by cultural industries or the authentic offspring of popular culture is pointless. In any case, it takes both to make rock commercially viable as well as artistically exciting; indeed, a commodity that doesn't rely on a popular taste is bound to flop. Consider Todd Gitlin's comment regarding television programs:

capitalism implies a certain sensitivity to audience taste, taste which is never wholly man-ufactured. Shows are made by guessing at audience desires and tolerances. . . .
    Similarly, rock music cannot be content with keeping a low profile. It needs the limelight to thrive. (Gitlin, 1979: 263)

What makes rock so special is its volatile and radical nature. It is actuated by a tension, the necessary resistance to an unavoidable commercialization, that cre-ates new forces, prompts new talents. By regularly breaking free from cultural industries, by opposing the individual to the community, by questioning its in-volvement with mass culture, rock manages to stay alive. It may then resume its position within this culture with a renewed potency, until the next break. Rock music is not a state. It belongs neither to an individualistic counterculture nor to mass culture. Rock could be described best as a passage, an interval, the space between. Rock is dynamic, the dynamic of change.

NOTES

1. For further discussions on the same topic, see for instance Daniel Kingman, *American Music: A Panorama* (New York: Schirmer Books, 1979) 220: "If [rock] is a folk art . . . it is one that was born and is living out its entire existence in the very maw of commercialism. This is what has imparted rock its essentially equivocal nature. In a subject rife with paradoxes, the most basic one is that what began (and in essence still remains) as "under-ground" music—a vernacular, anti-commercial, "protest" kind of art—has become an al-most unimaginably big business"; Devo, interview in *SoHo Weekly News*, n.d.: "what do you think rock 'n' roll is in America . . . besides Propaganda for Corporate Capitalist life?"; "[Rock music] is both fully woven into the fabric of the American corporate structure and endlessly the subject of efforts to censor its rebellious, anarchic impulses. It is safe as milk and a clear and present danger" (DeCurtis, 1992: xii); Dan Graham, edited by Brian Wallis, *Rock My Religion: Writings and Arts Projects 65–90*, (Cambridge, MA: MIT Press, 1993) 89: "Rock is the first musical form to be totally commercial and consumer-exploitive. It is largely produced by adults specifically to exploit a vast new adolescent market whose consciousness it tries to manipulate through radio, print and television . . . . But, ambi-guously built into rock 'n' roll is a self-consciousness that it is a commercialized form and

thus is not to be taken totally seriously by the teenagers who listen to it"; *ibid.* 146: "Rock is the first commercial form of music that contains this self-conscious knowledge of contradiction within its structure."

2. *Les Inrockuptibles*, the most fashionable magazine of the day, is a pun on *Les Incorruptibles*, the French title of the famous 60s television series *The Untouchables*.

3. As of July 1994, for example, 10 albums have already been certified multi-platinum, with Mariah Carey's *Music Box* topping 7 million units. Sources: courtesy of the Recording Industry Association of America.

4. Sources: *Billboard*, July 9, 1994.

5. Cf. Dwight MacDonald, "A Theory of Mass Culture," and Leo Lowenthal, "Historical Perspectives of Popular Culture," in *Mass Culture: The Popular Arts in America*, eds. Bernard Rosenberg and David Manning White (Glencoe, IL: Free Press, 1957).

6. The archetype of this principle can be found in Elvis Presley, who recorded his first songs for Sam Phillips's Sun Studios before being "sold" in 1955 to RCA.

7. The issue has in fact a broader scope; it includes the appropriation of African-American music by white musicians, which can be seen as the exploitation of an authentic folk culture by the industry; but once again, one must bear in mind that even African-American music results from a process of industrialization.

8. As Glenn Gass puts it, rock 'n' roll has become "respectable," "crammed into tuxedos at awards ceremonies, embraced by middle-aged babyboomers, exploited by Madison Avenue as an effective marketing tool and fast achieving the ultimate stamp of legitimacy as a subject for college classes." "Why Don't We Do It in the Classroom?" in DeCurtis, 1992: 97.

9. Recent developments, though, such as the 1993 deal between Atlantic Records and the independent Matador Records, seem to point the way to more collaboration between major companies and independent ones.

REFERENCES

Buxton, David (1985). *Le rock. Star-système et société de consommation*. Grenoble: La Pensée Sauvage.

Chambers, Iain (1985). *Urban Rhythms, Pop Music and Popular Culture*. Basingstoke: Macmillan.

DeCurtis, Anthony (ed.) (1992). *Present Tense, Rock & Roll and Culture*. Durham, NC: Duke University Press.

Frith, Simon, and Andrew Goodwin (eds.) (1990). *On Record, Rock, Pop and the Written Word*. London: Routledge.

Gans, Herbert J. (1974). *Popular Culture and High Culture: An Analysis and Evaluation of Taste*. New York: Basic Books.

Gass, Glen (1995). *A History of Rock Music*. New York: McGraw-Hill.

Gitlin, Todd (1979). "Prime Time Ideology: The Hegemonic Process in Television Entertainment." *Social Problems*, February.

Graham, Dan, and Brian Wallis (eds.) (1993). *Rock My Religion: Writings and Art Projects 1965–1990*. Cambridge, MA: MIT Press.

Harris, James F. (1993). *Philosophy at 33 1/3 rpm: Themes of Classic Rock Music*. Chicago: Open Court.

Heylin, Clinton (ed.) (1992). *The Penguin Book of Rock & Roll Writing*. London: Viking.

Mayer, Margaret M. (1994). *The American Dream: American Popular Music*. Santa Barbara, CA: Front Desk.

Mignon, Patrick (1991). *Rock, de l'histoire au mythe*. Paris: Anthropos/Vibrations.

Turner, Steve (1988). *Hungry for Heaven: Rock & Roll and the Search for Redemption*. London: Virgin.

7 Negotiations and Love Songs: Toward a Verifiable Interpretation of Popular Music

Karl Adams, Henri Drost, and Eugène van Erven

In both Europe and the United States, scholarship and popular music have never been good bedfellows.[1] Musicians seldom read academic journals, and scholars rarely consider pop music a fit subject for academic research. In 1970, American sociologist Richard A. Peterson argued that popular music should not be considered "academic high art culture." Rather than aesthetic analysis, he suggested it would be more useful to study the workings of the music industry, professional careers, audience psychology, and larger social events (Peterson, 1970: 595). His words have been heeded well. If we take the Netherlands as an example, only in the past five years sociologists Rob Kroes and Mel van Elteren have started publishing the results of their research on pop music. In addition, mass communication scholar Paul Rutten of the University of Nijmegen published a dissertation on the subject in 1991. Some of our own research has yielded interesting albeit inconclusive data regarding different marketing strategies for the distribution of American pop music in Europe, ranging from album titles and playing order of songs to completely altered musical arrangements that allegedly appeal better to European tastes.[2] These rare Dutch attempts at legitimizing pop music as a serious subject for scholarly investigation remain incidental and, we feel, unsatisfactory—because they tend to focus either on pop music as a mass media phenomenon or on its sociological periphery while largely ignoring the lyrics and the music of the songs themselves. Without dismissing the undoubtedly relevant findings regarding pop music by sociologists, mass communications analysts, and popular culture scholars, we propose an alternative approach that focuses more on the pop song itself and in which we can integrate our own artistic and commercial experience in the European popular music industry as well as our background as literary and performance studies scholars.[3] After reviewing the three approaches that are most common in European and American scholarship on popular music, we will present our own alternative model of analysis, which we will subsequently demonstrate by means of two Paul Simon compositions.

Scholarly approaches to popular music can be divided into three main categories: cultural pessimism, Popular Culture Studies, and sociology of music.[4] During the 1950s, American cultural pessimists dominated the debate, for which they used data yielded by mass communications research and mass culture studies of the previous three decades (de Fleur and Ball-Rokeach, 1989). They saw their worst nightmares come true when in the 1950s rock 'n' roll gained a spectacular popularity. Intellectuals, educators, clergy, and parents fiercely reacted against its noise, triviality, and obscenity. Thus, popular music came soon to be regarded as having an overwhelmingly negative impact on society. Especially when in the 1960s pop music started covering nearly every devious topic imaginable, exaggerated reactions became rampant.[5] Some even argued that pop was the devil's music and stimulated immoral behavior, revolution, and drug abuse among American youngsters (Huck, 1970). In a similar vein, an American psychologist claimed that all Beatles songs recorded after 1967 had actually been written by a communist think tank, with the purpose of overthrowing the American government (Denisoff and Peterson, 1972: 164–166). Even today, the power of mass media is still the subject of widespread concern. Yet there is convincing evidence that the alleged negative social impact of the mass media should not be exaggerated.[6] In the 1980s, this mostly unsubstantiated fear even led Tipper Gore and a few other senatorial spouses to establish a well-structured lobbying organization they called Parents' Music Resource Center (PMRC). Their main objective was to establish a rating system for sound carriers similar to film; and despite widespread protest, PMRC succeeded in introducing "Parental Advisory, Explicit Lyrics" warning stickers on numerous records and compact discs.

The PMRC phenomenon may seem innocent enough; but in reality it implies contempt for the consumer, whom it regards as a gullible creature that absorbs everything unquestioningly and, therefore, should be protected against itself. This attitude is characteristic of the cultural pessimism approach, which suspected popular music of forcing a prefabricated effect upon its audience, injecting it with clichés and trivialities (Hayakawa, 1957).

In reaction to cultural pessimism, in the 1960s a new discipline evolved from American Studies that referred to itself as Popular Culture Studies. In 1967 Ray B. Browne, one of the pioneers, launched the *Journal of Popular Culture*. In the same period, the Bowling Green University Popular Press started publishing academic books generated by the new discipline. Just like cultural pessimists, the advocates of Popular Culture Studies were predominantly American scholars convinced of the tremendous influence of popular culture and pop music. However, they regarded mass culture much more positively as a victory of the common people over the cultural elite and, indeed, as a means of liberating the oppressed masses (Denisoff, 1971; Pielke, 1986). Although Popular Culture Studies appealed to many young scholars, much of its research remained ad hoc and lacked a common theoretical framework. Representatives of cultural pessimism consequently dismissed Popular Culture Studies for yielding unverifiable data (Lohof, 1973; Geist, 1980).

The third major approach to popular music is sociological. Its primary focus is on the social functions of music and popular culture in general. Europeans such as Simon Frith have made significant contributions to the sociology of pop music. This kind of research is valuable in that it reveals how the music industry operates, how music affects youth culture, how cultural trends develop, how popular taste can be manipulated by the media, and how, in general, American popular culture influences European popular culture (Frith, 1981; Cooper and Cooper, 1993). In an article on American rap music, for example, Dutch sociologist Rob Kroes describes ghetto blasters, scratching, sampling, clips, and the fashion consciousness of African-American street kids (Kroes, 1992: 185–193).

Both European and U.S. approaches to pop music, then, acknowledge its significance as a cultural phenomenon. They recognize what we would like to call the "bardic function" of popular music, which offers its audience a means of cultural identification and communication with its peers.[7] Pop music thus provides pleasurable reassurance and a sense of belonging to a particular cultural generation. However, the above approaches also tend to ignore the musical composition by emphasizing its effects within a mass media realm. And on those rare occasions when the song itself is discussed in European and American publications, its musical and lyrical components are seldom analyzed in a verifiable manner.[8]

THE SONG ITSELF

Using the music and words of the pop song as a starting point for interpretation, linguistic and musicological tools of analysis seem indispensable. Lyrics analysis yields primary and secondary layers of meaning that could be called "literal reference," "thematic reference," and "symbolic reference." Textual analysis alone, however, is not sufficient because it ignores the equally important musical elements. Musical elements can be described by means of universally accepted informal labels such as "tempo," "arrangement," "vocal modulations," "basic chord," and "distinctive sound features." Similar to the primary and secondary textual layers, these labels provide a vocabulary for indicating the verifiable meaning contained in the musical elements of a song. For instance, musical arrangements can highlight textual particulars; choice of instrumentation, sound effects, tempo, and chord patterns can affect moods and emotions; and the performer can choose to emphasize certain textual or melodic aspects of the song through voice variations. Also, the reaction of a live audience may affect the interpretation of a song. Consequently, many contextual variables need to be considered when approaching the pop song itself. We shall discuss these contexts employing the following framework derived from literary theory (Eagleton, 1983; Mileur, 1987):

performance/audience
|
history—SONG—conventions
|
songwriter

Our usage of the term "context" refers to the "meaning environment" of a song as far as it affects the coherence of its form and interpretation. We regard the individual song as the smallest analyzable entity. When appearing in the public domain, it is usually artistically rearranged (or edited), then recorded, and subsequently mass produced and distributed on sound carriers such as cassette tapes, vinyl records, or the popular compact disc. Two questions immediately come to mind: (1) How does the song relate to the other songs on the album? (2) How does the song relate to the entire body of work of the artist under consideration?

It would, of course, be nonsensical to investigate the album context of the songs contained on, say, a *Greatest Hits of 1993* compilation. They will not have more in common than their popularity at a certain point in history and only tell us something about the taste of a mass audience, which may be of interest to sociologists. More can be said about Bruce Springsteen's body of work, which—as Eric Branscomb has demonstrated—can be read as one story with recurring characters that evolve from album to album (Branscomb, 1993).

Performance Context

Popular music is a performing art. Consequently, the creative product of a singer-songwriter cannot be described as precisely as those of literary authors or painters, which can be placed on library shelves or displayed in galleries and therefore can be studied at leisure. Theatrical or musical performances rarely leave tangible traces; often they only exist as residue in the memories of artists and spectators. Even if they are recorded on audio or video, they always lack a dimension of the original event. The context of a performance may severely affect the song itself as well as its interpretation. For instance, various commentators have pointed out that black blues singers have two separate repertoires: one for a partisan black audience, another for white venues (Denisoff and Peterson, 1972: 8).

Context of Conventions

"Convention" in the narrow sense refers to generally accepted patterns or aesthetic structures within a genre. For our purposes, we prefer the broader definition of "all background information that an artist and audience is likely to be familiar with." This not only includes knowledge of what is common practice within a specific popular music genre, but also familiarity with themes, motifs, and historical facts. The relation between the song and its conventions becomes particularly interesting when they are not faithfully applied—as, for instance, in the

Velvet Underground song "Sunday Morning."[9] The sweet lullaby music sharply contrasts with Lou Reed's nihilistic and paranoid lyrics.

Quotations (or "intertextuality") constitute a particular application of conventions. Evidently, the intertext of popular music can be both musical and textual. A well-known example is "American Tune," in which Paul Simon quotes the melody of a chorale in Bach's "Matthäus Passion."[10] And in "End of the Innocence," Don Henley quotes the words "O beautiful, for spacious skies" from Irving Berlin's "God Bless America."[11]

Biographical Context

The relation between songwriter and song is probably the most speculative. Yet many books on pop music have a biographical slant and establish tendentious connections between songs and their author's life. Familiarity with biographical information may enhance the bardic function of a particular songwriter, for knowing that he or she confesses private experiences in a song increases the listener's intimacy and, by extension, the intensity of cultural identification. However, although biographical facts themselves can be verified, proving the connection between biographical context and song is much more difficult, if not altogether impossible.

Historical Context

Evidently, every song or album has its historical context. However, the relation between the song and history is most apparent when it explicitly refers to historical events. This is most obviously the case with protest songs. The older the song, the more relevant it becomes to investigate its historical context. Additional difficulties occur when the historical context cannot be immediately distilled from the lyrics themselves. For instance, anyone who does not know that the National Guard killed four students at Kent State University in 1970 is likely to interpret the Crosby, Stills, Nash, and Young classic "Ohio" differently than someone who does.

APPLICATION: "AMERICA" BY SIMON & GARFUNKEL, *THE CONCERT IN CENTRAL PARK* ALBUM (GEFFEN RECORDS, 1982)

Central Park, New York City, September 19, 1981. An estimated 500,000 people are ready for the third song in the first Simon & Garfunkel concert in 10 years. Art Garfunkel's music and movie career have reached an all-time low. Paul Simon has just encountered his first minor flop with his 1980 *One Trick Pony* movie and album project [**biography**]. The set-list of the reunion concert contains the major hits of the duo and further includes duet versions of Simon's main solo hits. Most songs have been rearranged for a large band of seasoned session musicians [**performance**].

"America" is a folk song [**conventions**] that despite its major chord scheme, has a melancholic mood. It features a conversation between the persona and a girl named Kathy on the "Greyhound from Pittsburg" [**literal reference**]. The girl's name may refer to Kathy, Simon's girlfriend during the better part of the 1960s [**biography**]. The song depicts a game of playful fantasy between traveling lovers, "playing games with the faces" and imagining that "the man in the gabardine suit was a spy" and warning each other that "his bow tie is really a camera."

The traveling image is an instance of the 1960s obsession with journeys back to authenticity [**thematic reference**]. Countercultural youth rejected social codes of bourgeois respectability that governed all civilized interaction [**historical context**]. Thus the persona of Simon's song ridicules the materialist status of marriage: "Let us be lovers, we'll marry our fortunes together; I've got some real estate here in my bag." The persona subsequently expresses his yearning for emotional reorientation as he admits to Kathy that he does not understand why he is "empty and aching." But as if to underscore his reluctance to show emotion, he makes this confession knowing that "she was sleeping" [**literal reference**]. His emptiness is allegedly caused by observing an America that has forsaken the original promise of the American Dream. He believes that all the people in the "cars on the New Jersey Turnpike" somehow share this emptiness and have "all come to look for America" [**symbolic reference**].

"America" originally appeared on the *Bookends* album in 1968, when Paul Simon and Art Garfunkel were 22 years old. In the previous year they had scored their first major hit with "Sounds of Silence" and were on the verge of megastardom [**biography**]. As he had done with Bob Dylan, "Sounds of Silence" producer Tom Wilson combined acoustic guitars with electrically amplified instruments to obtain a new sociocritical folk-rock sound for Simon & Garfunkel that would constitute a significant source of identification for alienated American youth [**conventions**]. Simon's lyrics overtly dealt with countercultural issues such as racism ("A Church Is Burning") and unquestioned tradition ("Mrs. Robinson") on preceding albums [**body of work**]. On *Bookends*, "America" appeared in the context of other songs dealing with the individual's search for self-identity, such as "Fakin' It" and "Save the Life of My Child" [**album context**].

In 1981, many of Simon & Garfunkel's peers feared the return to complacent patriotism of the Reagan era. They felt that America was doomed and possibly looked to their reunited bardic touchstones for nostalgic comfort. With updated arrangements and orchestration [**performance**], Simon & Garfunkel showed the audience that they had grown along with their fans. The 1981 version of "America," however, was performed virtually in the same manner as on the *Bookends* album, with the notable addition of a screaming electric guitar solo that prepares the audience for the song's emotional finale. It made the baby-boom generation feel it still had a voice after losing John Lennon the year before in the same city [**historical context**]. As if pledging renewed allegiance to the American Dream, the Central Park crowd roared along with the lines, "Counting the cars on the New Jersey Turnpike/They all come to look for America"—and Simon's voice audibly quivered as he repeated that same line one last time [**performance**].

APPLICATION: "SONG ABOUT THE MOON" BY PAUL SIMON, *HEARTS AND BONES* ALBUM (WARNER BROTHERS, 1983)

"Song about the Moon" is an optimistic, major-chord, soft-rock song [**conventions**] filled with suggestions on how to break through a writer's block [**literal reference**]. It may also have biographical overtones, as in the early 1980s Simon himself received therapeutic treatment for his inability to create new material [**biography**].

First, the persona explores poetic associations as a possible strategy for song-writing: "if you want to write a song about the moon/walk along the craters of the afternoon/when the shadows are deep and the light is alien/and gravity leaps like a knife off the pavement" [**thematic reference**]. Soon we realize that the persona is actually going back over the basics of songwriting in a kind of self-referential songwriting master class. Thus, he explains how an analogy works: "If you want to make a song about the heart," then "think about the moon before you start/the heart will howl like a dog in the moonlight/the heart can explode like a pistol on a June night." Subsequently, the persona explores possible historical causes for his current artistic impotence: "cut off your hair or whatever is frightening" [**biography**]. After a cryptic bridge about a boy who "laughed so hard he fell right from his place" and a girl who "laughed so hard the tears rolled down her face," the persona reaches a possible solution for his predicament. He implies that no songwriter can ever know beforehand whether a song is going to be good or bad. Thus, in the final phrase the persona plunges into the creative void and, as if to emphasize his newly found liberation, he screams: "If you want to write a song about the moon/if you want to write a spiritual tune/then na-na-na, yeah, yeah, *then do it*, write a song about the moon" [**performance**].

The other songs on the *Hearts and Bones* album, which also contains "Song about the Moon," mainly deal with very private references to mental confusion and failing relationships [**album context**]. They offer very little room for bardic identification. Whereas Simon's songs of the 1960s contained many references to sociocultural alienation and his work from the 1970s hinted at spiritual alienation (e.g., "Silent Eyes" and "Jonah"), *Hearts and Bones* seems to be more about being alienated from oneself [**body of work**]. Apparently, this was not what Simon's peers were looking for after Ronald Reagan announced that he would be running for re-election [**historical context**]. The bad revenues of Simon's *One-Trick Pony*

(1980) had already indicated that Simon was losing clout with his peers. *Hearts and Bones* further confirmed his reduced bardic appeal. Undoubtedly, his new break-up with Art Garfunkel also helped accelerate the decreasing loyalty of his fans [**biography**]. Finally, the album's overt compromise to slick pop arrangements (excessive reverb, drum computers, synthesizers, and Nile Rodgers's funky guitar sound) may have created the impression that Simon had lost his artistic integrity and had sold out to commercial interests [**conventions**]. His peers may have thought he had forsaken his concern with living according to a humanistic moral code, which had been the leitmotif of his work until then [**body of work**].

CONCLUSION

In this chapter we have attempted to point out that most research about popular music evades interpretation of the songs themselves and concentrates mostly on effects and peripheral sociological phenomena. We have tried to redress this by basing our interpretation on the music and lyrics of the individual song and placing it in a verifiable context model. Particularly in combination with any of the other approaches, we believe our method may contribute to a more complete understanding of popular music that encompasses everything from musical and lyrical components to the broadest sociocultural context.

NOTES

1. We use a broad definition of popular music that captures a huge variety of styles including folk, rock, soul, hip hop, blues, and metal. It is difficult to distinguish between these styles, as many artists (e.g., Rage against the Machine, Living Colour, R.E.M., Arrested Development) use combinations. On the difficulty of defining popular music, see J. Shepherd, "Definition as Mystification: A Considering of Labels as Hindrance to Understanding Significance in Music," in Denisoff, *Solid Gold* (1975); and Ennis, *The Seventh Stream: The Emergence of Rock 'n' Roll in American Popular Music* (1992).

2. For instance, Bob Dylan's album *Bringing It All Back Home* was retitled *Subterranean Homesick Blues* for the European market, based on the European commercial success of the single with the same title.

3. Karl Adams is a professional singer-songwriter, Henri Drost is a record salesman, and Eugène van Erven has published two books on performance studies. All three share a literary studies background.

4. Winfried Fluck makes a similar observation in his article "Popular Culture as a Mode of Socialization: A Theory about the Social Functions of Popular Cultural Forms" (1988).

5. In *The Sounds of Social Change*, Denisoff and Peterson (1972: 308) published Vice-President Spiro Agnew's speech on how rock music would bring eternal damnation to America's youth in a disguise of "good, clean, noisy fun."

6. See de Fleur and Ball-Rokeach, 1989, on H. M. Enzensberger's, J. T. Klapper's, and H. D. Lasswell's views on this subject.

7. The term "bardic function" was coined by John Fiske and John Hartley with reference to television in the book *Reading Television* (1978).

8. In *Hitmuziek in Nederland, 1960–1985* [Hit Music in the Netherlands, 1960–1985], Paul Rutten (1991) argues that pop music should be seen as a communication process and that its dominant message is romantic love. Although he reaches his conclusions on the basis of lyrics analysis, his research is unverifiable. He does not acknowledge that lyrics may have secondary meanings that may also be affected by musical elements.

9. *The Velvet Underground and Nico*, Verve, 1967.

10. *There Goes Rhymin' Simon*, Warner Brothers, 1973.

11. *The End of the Innocence*, Geffen Records, 1989.

REFERENCES

Barzun, Jacques (1965). *Music in American Life*. Bloomington: Indiana University Press.

Branscomb, Eric (1993). "Literacy and a Popular Medium: The Lyrics of Bruce Springsteen." *Journal of Popular Culture* 27.1 (Summer): 29–43.

Cooper, L. E. and B. L. Cooper (1993). "The Pendulum of Cultural Imperialism: Popular Music Interchanges between the United States and Britain, 1943–1967." *Journal of Popular Culture* 27.3 (Winter): 61–79.

de Fleur, M. L., and S. Ball-Rokeach (1989). *Theories of Mass Communication*. New York: Longman.

Denisoff, R. Serge (1971). *Great Day Coming: Folk Music and the American Left*. Urbana: University of Illinois Press.

———— (1975). *Solid Gold*. New Brunswick, NJ: Transaction Books.

Denisoff, R. Serge, and Richard A. Peterson (eds.) (1972). *The Sounds of Social Change: Studies in Popular Culture*. Chicago: Rand McNally.

Eagleton, Terry (1983). *Literary Theory*. Oxford: Blackwell.

Ennis, P. H. (1992). *The Seventh Stream: The Emergence of Rock 'n' Roll in American Popular Music*. Hanover and London: Wesleyan University Press.

Fiske, John, and John Hartley (1978). *Reading Television*. New York: Routledge.

Fluck, Winfried (1988). "Popular Culture as a Mode of Socialization: A Theory about the Social Functions of Popular Cultural Forms." *Journal of Popular Culture* 22.3 (Winter): 31–47.

Frith, Simon (1981). *Sound Effects: Youth, Leisure and the Politics of Rock 'n' Roll*. New York: Pantheon.

Geist, Christopher D. (1980). "Popular Culture: The *Journal* and the State of the Study: A Sequel." *Journal of Popular Culture* 14.4 (Spring): 389–404.

Goldberg, Herbert (1970). "Contemporary Popular Music." *Journal of Popular Culture* 4.3 (Winter): 580–585.

Hayakawa, S. I. (1957). "Popular Songs vs. the Facts of Life." *Mass Culture: The Popular Arts in America*, eds. B. Rosenberg and D. M. White. Glencoe, IL: Free Press, 393–403.

Huck, Susan (1970). "Why Is Rock Music So Awful" *Review of the News* 6 (February 11): 17–24.

Kroes, Rob (1992). *De leegte van Amerika: Een massacultuur in de wereld*. Amsterdam: Prometheus.

Lohof, Bruce A. (1973). "Popular Culture: The *Journal* and the State of the Study." *Journal of Popular Culture* 7.4 (Spring): 453–462.

Mileur, Jean-Pierre (1987). "Literary Criticism since 1965." *American Literature Since 1900*, ed. Marcus Cunliffe. New York: Peter Bedrick Books.

Peterson, Richard A. (1970). "Taking Popular Music Too Seriously." *Journal of Popular Culture* 4.3 (Winter): 590–595.

Pielke, Robert G. (1986). *You Say You Want a Revolution: Rock Music in American Culture.* Chicago: Nelson Hall.

Rutten, Paul (1991). *Hitmuziek in Nederland, 1960–1985.* Amsterdam: Otto Cramwinckel Uitgeverij.

Shepherd, J. (1985). "Definition as Mystification. A Considering of Labels as Hindrance to Understanding Significance in Music." *Popular Music Perspectives II*, eds. P. Tagg and D. Horn. Gothenburg: International Association for the Study of Popular Music.

Part III

The Written Word

8 Harlequin Romances in Western Europe: The Cultural Interactions of Romantic Literature

Annick Capelle

The romantic literature series available on the French and Dutch literary markets are almost entirely translations of American novels. Does this mean that "the norms for romance are universal"?[1] Not quite, because a foreign culture supplies a native need. Western European originals of romantic literature are not enough. Why? Romantic literature in popular fiction "is a story about a love relationship . . . courtship . . . marriage," and as the "tensions and issues inherent in love stories are women's concerns, romantic fiction is almost entirely a female form of reading" (Mussell, 1980: 317). A highly social form of the written word is concerned. What does the woman reader from France or the Netherlands get from the sentiments and dreams of American stories that she does not get at home?

To answer this question one has to look closely at how the various models in series romances produced in America, France, and Holland interact, and how the local models correlate and cope with the American original. The translated romances that dominate the market are mainly produced by French and Dutch subsidiaries of the U.S. publisher Harlequin Enterprises Ltd. Harlequin is a worldwide enterprise with the largest international distribution of all romance publishers. As of 1981, Harlequin romances were published in 15 languages in 27 countries; in 1992, these were available in 110 countries in approximately 20 languages.[2]

Under consideration here is the passage of fiction from one system with its own models to another wherein different models prevail. Translators and translations are deeply embedded in the nuances of languages and national values. The translator guides, constructs, and reconstructs more than mere words. The translator selects various norms and constructs a new product. At the same time, one of the most important characteristics of a Harlequin translation is its membership in a series. The serial aspect is nearly the sole distinguishing feature of these texts, whose authors are often unknown. This appears, for example, in the Harlequin advertising campaigns in which the series name—not the writers—is foremost.[3] To some extent, both translator and original author are effaced.

Other literary influences in a series, aside from translator and author, are very important. The publisher selects and presents the texts but inevitably intervenes in the production process as well. The editor also plays a major part: selecting texts, reading manuscripts, proposing titles, suggesting deletions, and representing the series elsewhere (as with promotional material). The result of their activity is especially reflected in the paratexts of the novels, that is, the nonfictional part of the book. Consequently, in what follows I will first examine the publisher itself, the paratexts, the texts themselves, what distinguishes British and American versions of romance fiction from one another, and finally the French and Dutch translations.

THE PUBLISHER: AT HOME AND ABROAD

Throughout the 1970s and 1980s the world's leader in the market of mass-produced romances was Harlequin Enterprises Ltd. Although competition and variable quality have somewhat eroded readers' brand name loyalty, Harlequin still has the advantage of being the "original" contemporary romance series. If the home market is nearly saturated, foreign outlets enable Harlequin's sales abroad to increase steadily.

Harlequin Enterprises Ltd. started in 1949 as a privately owned company in Winnipeg, Canada, called simply Harlequin Books. It published a mixture of romances, mysteries, westerns, and nonfiction. In the 1950s it moved to Toronto and switched to publishing exclusively romances and began regularly importing romances for distribution from the English publisher Mills and Boon. In 1971 it purchased the British company. Most Harlequins continued to come from England. In 1975 Harlequin Enterprises launched Harlequin Holland. In 1976 Harlequin Enterprises began operations in a separate distribution center in the United States, in New York. In the 1980s it started publishing purely American novels, in what until then had been an exclusively British series. In 1978 Harlequin Enterprises established Harlequin France, its second-largest operation outside North America.

Created in 1975, Harlequin Holland functioned as a test-market for the international expansion of Harlequin. Apparently it fully satisfied the expectations. Harlequin Holland started with a big advertising campaign with one single series, the Bouquet series. Originally, only four novels came out every month. Encouraged by the widespread and rapid success of these novels, the Dutch publisher increased the number of series and titles published every month, so that by 1984 the market was saturated. At the end of that year, Harlequin Holland published approximately 35 titles every month, that is, nearly one title every day. In 1985 the firm carried out a large-scale purge and reduced the number of series to four (which still exist). Nowadays, Harlequin accounts for roughly 90 percent of the Dutch turnover and is undeniably the market leader. However, the rapid development and increasing success of romantic literature have clearly come to an end.[4]

The history of the French subsidiary of Harlequin Enterprises is similar to that of Harlequin Holland. When it was created in Paris in the late 1970s, French publishers did not seem interested in romantic literature. Harlequin was a totally new enterprise there, and the French formula of the genre had to be invented. Original French romances did exist but had a limited readership.[5] Harlequin was different. The long introductory parts were deleted, the plot got off to a quick start, the style was invigorating, the number of pages was reduced. Yet Harlequin's streamlined machinery was especially new: its use of marketing reports, questionnaires, and new commercial practices (such as returning the covers of unsold books). Harlequin was immediately successful, so that it was described by some as a "real social phenomenon" (Favier, 1989: 34).

Like Harlequin Holland, the French publisher peaked in 1983 and then sales started to decrease. Possible causes have been cited for this development in both France and in Holland: overproduction, as the increase in the number of series disorganized the market; the general success of other new publications for women; the increasing number of television soaps; the depressing American prosaism; and the erotic scenes characteristic of Harlequin that many readers thought were rather too hard core.

Although the Dutch and French subsidiaries of Harlequin Enterprises have a similar history, their products are not identical. For the sake of this short study, the production of 1989 and 1990 has been examined. In 1989, 506 titles were brought onto the Dutch market. In 1990, 478 were published.[6] Harlequin France published 482 titles in 1989 and 476 in 1990.[7]

Although these figures seem to correspond to each other, the Dutch and the French publishers have different editorial practices. The books are generally translated one year after their original publication, but the various titles are not always translated and published simultaneously in their respective markets. Simultaneous publication is coincidental. Each publisher sets its own policies and seeks a different market—although eventually the same Harlequin authors appear in French and in Dutch.

A systematic comparison of the two publishers' products will help us formulate a few hypotheses. The initial norm determining the nature of a translation relates to the choice between an *adequate* translation (i.e., close to the original) and an *acceptable* translation (i.e., determined by the norms of the target system). We shall see that this choice, different in the Dutch and in the French novels, conditioned the translations so as to create quite different products.

PARATEXT

The paratext is the external aspect of a book that both influences the reader's expectations and exhibits the general attitude of the editor or translator. It helps the critic to determine the strategies that influenced the translated text. Four aspects of the paratext are particularly illuminating for Harlequin Books: series names, titles, covers, and introductory pages.

Harlequin books generously include both American and British writers in the French and Dutch markets.[8] Yet national tastes differ, as demonstrated by the existence of different series. In the Netherlands, British authors are preferred; in France, American authors. National preferences may differ, but the way the outsider is labeled is strikingly similar in the "British" and "American" collections in both France and in Holland. The names of the "American" series are more explicit and evoke a more passionate kind of literature. The "America" group is clearly a more erotic series that stresses the irresistible passion of the two lovers: for example, Red Passion (*Rouge Passion*) or Love at First Sight (*Coup de Foudre*, literally: "struck by lightning"). The "British" series are more conventional, more traditional. They exhibit a strong, old-fashioned focus on adventure, are appetizing and pleasantly pungent, but no more so than the labels Bouquet or Jasmijn would suggest.

Then, if one looks at the titles of all the novels published in 1989 and 1990, one is struck by the large degree of coherence. The French titles very often contain a reference to a geographical place (34%) or/and to a person (42%); in the Dutch titles—especially the "American" ones—a few terms recur at an astonishing frequency. Most often reappearing are *liefde* ("love," 10%), *hartstocht* ("passion," 5%), *geluk* ("happiness," 4%), and *verlangen* ("desire," 4%). Although these references are not as numerous as the French, they altogether represent 23% of the total titles. The translation of titles thus forms part of an image of what a romantic novel is or should be. In the French case, stress is put on an action taking place in a foreign, exotic place and on identification with the main character(s). In the Dutch versions, the passionate, erotic character of the novels is of crucial importance and is reflected in the more general, abstract titles (*titres passe-partout*) never containing any proper nouns.[9]

As a consequence, the titles are not necessarily—indeed rarely—translated literally. Complete adaptation of the title is the norm: often no single semantic element from the original title is kept. Only 5.5 percent of the Dutch titles and 3 percent of the French are literal translations. Although 14 percent of the Dutch titles contain one element from the original (e.g., **Dark** Mosaic: **Donker** *Labyrinth*), 10 percent of the French novels are, likewise, partial translations. Generally speaking, one is under the impression that Dutch translators remain closer to the originals than do their French counterparts.

Can you tell a book by its cover? Well, it depends which side one is talking about. In neither the French nor Dutch versions can the illustrations on the front cover of a Harlequin book be related to a scene from the story. The covers present the two main characters and the setting, thereby expressing a general mood. Sometimes they resemble the American original, sometimes they do not; there seems to be no system here. As for the back covers, the Dutch text is much more explicit than the American text. It reveals a lot of information. It tells about the motives underlying a character's actions and thoughts, whereas the American text remains vague and keeps the tension and suspense higher. Apart from this, the texts are quite similar. The Dutch text seems based on the American one (evident in structure, sentences). The French back cover blurb is less closely linked to the American original. Usually a fragment of the text, which expresses a crucial moment of the story and synthesizes the plot's starting conflict, has been selected and reproduced on the back cover. Here, as in the American text, the reader knows much less when starting his or her reading.

Finally, introductory pages and concluding advertisements differ. The Dutch version is more like the American original. A short biography of the author appears on the first or second page of the Dutch novels. This mostly tells about the writer's hobbies and family situation, and sometimes contains information about her origin or place of living: "Kara Galloway lives in Colorado with her husband . . ."[10] (from K. Galloway, *Hartstochtelijke dromen*). Such information is never found in the French romances.

The last pages of the novels often contain advertisements for other series. One advertisement, presenting the Bouquet series, mentions the foreign character of the romances:

The Bouquet Series is a novel series of *English* origin, which is read by millions of readers all over the world. Next to the original *English* versions, these books are published in 15 languages . . . in Dutch too! Each book from this series offers you a passionate story in an exotic world full of adventure and romance. (from C. Lamb, *Een lang vergeten liefde*)

In the same way, a page containing a presentation of the Super Roman series says:

Written by the best authors from *America, Canada and England*. (from Mary Lyons, *Een onweerstaanbare kus*)

Here is another extract from an advertisement for the Temptation imprint:

STORIES WHICH SEDUCE YOU CONTINUOUSLY! You will find them in Temptation, written by America's best writers! (from J. A. Krentz, *De opstandige bruid*)

The French versions rarely mention the author's nationality. But the foreign origin of the books, especially their international character, is very present, as in:

Dear reader, As every month, we hope to meet you in the Azur and Horizon collections with the Harlequin *authors most appreciated in the world*. (from R. Winters, *La princesse amoureuse*)

The Euromance series, created in 1992, also emphasizes the international character of romances:

A European series launched simultaneously in all the European countries, a reading pleasure *to share with millions of readers* who will discover the same title every month. (from R. Winters, *La princesse amoureuse*)

Similarly it is announced in the Dutch romances:

HARLEQUIN's INTERNATIONAL LOVE LANGUAGE IN: EUROMANCE. Harlequin presents Euromance: romance in all the European countries, without any borders . . . . *Euromance appears in all the languages and countries of the European Community.* (from S. Cook, *Tussen geurige bloemen*)

Although the Dutch editors mention the English and American character of the novels, both the French and Dutch emphasize the generally foreign origin of their products. Particularly important is the readers' membership in an international community of millions of fellow readers.

TEXT

The Dutch texts are generally very faithful to the originals.[11] The French translations are less so. Both the translations and the originals are quantitatively homogeneous. This is a general strategy determining the translations of the series: all the books belonging to the same imprint have approximately the same number of pages—with a maximum difference of five pages. Most originals contain between 185 and 190 pages, and most translations are 145 to 150 pages long. As such, both Dutch and French texts are shorter than their originals, although the tendency seems to be stronger on the French side.

One of the most fundamental translational practices is "nontranslation" (i.e., deletion), which seems to be applied in a coherent manner according to determined norms. The tendency is to simplify the plot: some details in the development of the action are deleted. Scenes that might slow down the pacing of the plot and that are not essential are generally left out. There are fewer descriptive passages, or at least they are made shorter. This is quite evident in the French text: whenever possible, sentences from the descriptive parts are integrated into the dialogues. Many verbal exchanges described or summarized in the descriptive parts occur in the dialogues. Some dialogues are made shorter. Introspections are made shorter; sentences are left out, fused together, or summarized when they might slow down the pace of the plot. Yet introspections describing the heroine's feelings toward the man or the attractive power the hero exerts over the heroine are retained in the French, whereas they are often deleted or considerably reduced in the Dutch. The French text even adds new parts not found in the original.

The Dutch text is a syntactic mapping: a sentence-by sentence-translation, even word-by-word. The French adaptions are "free (if not freer) than the original" (Alphant, 1988: ii). What is important for the French is to recreate the right atmosphere, not to have accurate translation. One French translator confirmed:

The text was to read Harlequin-ish; but translation was entirely free by comparison with the original. This work of adaptation called for experience—competent writing, vocabulary and imagination—as well as compliance with instructions. We would edit out the female protagonist's introspection pages. We'd invent places, clothes, dialogues; we'd change characters. (Alphant, 1988: iii)

As for vocabulary, place names are kept when there is no French equivalent; and when a foreign word is taken over in the French translation, it is written in italics to stress its foreign character (e.g., *ouzo*). This is not the case in the Dutch translations. The French texts try to avoid superfluous contamination by strange, disturbing elements—such as unknown proper names. By contrast, Dutch texts accept—and to a certain extent encourage—invasion by foreign-looking features (e.g., by enriching language with new, exotic elements).

An earnest attempt to raise the level of the narration can be observed in the French texts. There seems to be great variation in the incidental clauses. Repetitions are avoided. Anything vulgar, common, or incoherent is left out. Simple expressions are made more literary. This tendency is summarized by a French translator:

We have strict instructions. . . . Suppress vulgar, commonplace, and incoherent phrases. Translate the English "you" as a distant *vous*, except in intimate scenes. Prefer a grammatical "Fait-il beau?" [Is the weather nice?] to a colloquial "Est-ce qu'il fait beau?" . . . or "Waves broke on the sand in a soft murmur" to "You could hear the sea." (Alphant, 1988: iii)

CONCLUSION

Whereas the Dutch publisher is open to American models and produces *adequate* translations, the French is not ready to import American models unconditionally and produces *acceptable* translations that correspond to local models in the French system. The impact of the American system of popular literature on the production of French romantic novels is less strong than the impact of French literary systems from the indigenous canonized literature.

However, the basic scheme of American, French, and Dutch romances seems not to have changed throughout the years: exoticism, dream, a love story with a happy ending remain the basic elements of all novels produced. The wish to produce exotic texts is not contradictory with the fact that the translated American texts are "Frenchified." Harlequin France wants extreme exoticism, that is, not simply a shift from a French environment to an American one, but to a complete fantasy place.

All the attempts to create French originals have failed because the writers tried to be exotic at all costs and thereby produced unreadable, artificial exotic crea-tions.[12] So, while making use of the exotic elements "naturally" present in the American novels, the French publishers blur the specifically American character-istics.

Apparently, all attempts to create Dutch originals have failed too. Although many were sent to the publishers, they were considered unpublishable; and those published were not successful. Unlike the French manuscripts, the Dutch wrote stories situated in Holland. It seems precisely because these novels took place in Holland that they failed. Indeed, even though Dutch readers are very open-minded and are ready to accept many things, they do not want to be confronted with everyday life.[13] Exoticism seems to be key in all cases. In the Dutch situation, importing of exotic elements via translated novels takes place through the me-diation of the American cultural system. The French translations describe an ex-otic dream world—not *too* American, and clearly French.

NOTES

1. "The norms for romance are universal. . . . A bestseller in Amsterdam is also a be-stseller in Tokyo." Statement by Josiane Mouissie, editorial director of Harlequin Holland, in *NRC-Handelsblad. Cultureel Supplement*, 29 September 1989. [My translation]

2. In 1988, Harlequin sold worldwide nearly six books per second. Cf. *NRC-Handelsblad. Cultureel Supplement*, 29 September 1989.

3. One of the slogans of the 1992 French campaign read: "Les Harlequins, c'est comme les hommes; il serait dommage de n'en essayer qu'un" (Harlequins are like men; it would be a shame to try only one).

4. Ed van Eeden, "Het fabuleuze succes van goedkope romantiek," *Boekblad*, 21 July 1989: 6–7; Peter Nijssen, "Populaire boeken (1): Van 'Pride and Prejudice' tot Bouquet en Favoriet," *Boekblad*, 14 August 1992: 8–9; Peter Nijssen, "Populaire boeken (3): Distributie, verkoop en consumptie. Omzetvergroter of drempelverlager?" *Boekblad*, 28 August 1992: 12–13; Bas Roodnat, "Na ruzie komt zonneschijn" *NRC-Handelsblad*, 14 August 1981: 8–9.

5. The romantic novels were nearly exclusively sold by the publisher Tallandier, which reprinted old romances by Delly, a very popular author of the 1920s.

6. These figures include the output of De Vrijbuiter, another publisher of romantic literature, with which Harlequin Holland shares the market; it represents about one-fourth of the total title production. Although in France, Harlequin France is the undeniable market leader, it also has to account for the existence of the "Collection Passion," published by Presses de la Cité (approximately 13% market share), which will not be addressed here.

7. French sources: *Bibliographie de la France, Notices établies par la Bibliothèque Nation-ale*, 177e année, n° 1–52; 178e année, n° 1–52; 179e année, n° 1–26 (Paris: Cercle de la Librairie, 1988–1990). Dutch sources: *Brinkmann's Cumulatieve Catalogus van Boeken*, 1989–144e jaargang; 1990–145e jaargang (Amphen aan den Rijn: Samson Stafleu, 1990–1991).

8. The British writers were mostly first published in England by Mills & Boon. British authors are mainly present in the Dutch series Bouquet, Harlequin, and Jasmijn; and in the French series Or, Azur, Horizon, Teenager, Blanche, Royale, Prestige, Romance. Amer-

ican authors are published in the French series Rouge Passion, Harmonie, Coup de Foudre, and Désir; and in the Dutch series Intiem, Temptation, Love Affair, Loveswept, Candlelight, and Extase.

9. These tendencies roughly correspond to certain imprints. The word *hartstocht* is especially present in Love Affair and Loveswept titles. Conversely, the French imprint Horizon makes excessive use of geographical references.

10. All the following extracts from Dutch and French titles are my translations. Italics are also mine.

11. The sample on which this textual analysis is based is limited to 17 novels published between 1988 and 1992. The hypotheses put forward are thus of a limited scope and should be mapped further on the basis of a more extended analysis.

12. One such example was the *Collection Turquoise* imprint. Cf. Favier, 1989: 37.

13. Peter Nijssen, "Populaire boeken (2): De producenten. Strakke produktie en uitlevering," *Boekblad*, 21 August 1992: 12.

LIST OF TRANSLATED ROMANCES STUDIED

Abbreviations

BR: Bouquet Series

CA: Collection Azur

CH: Collection Horizon

CRP: Collection Rouge Passion

DD: Duo Désir

DH: Duo Harmonie

HA: Harlequin Holland: Amsterdam

HE: Harlequin Enterprises Ltd.

HP: Harlequin S.A.: Paris

I: Intiem

IE: Intiem Extra

J: Jasmijn

LA: Love Affair

MB: Mills & Boon: London

SB: Silhouette Books: New York

T: Temptation

U.S. Romances

Algermissen, Jo Ann: *Bedside Manner*, SB 1989; *Strijd om de macht*, I 388, HA 1990; *Les chemins du bonheur*, CRP 328, HP 1990.

Bradford, Sally: *When Fortune Smiles*, HE 1989; *Verleidelijk bezoek*, LA 317, HA 1990; *Lou-la-tendresse*, DD 301, HP 1990.

Carlisle, Donna: *Interlude*, SB 1989; *Hartstochtelijke intermezzo*, I 389, HA 1990; *Lady Pamela*, CRP 325, HP 1990.

Dale, Ruth Jean: *Together Again*, HE 1990; *Verrassend weerzien*, LA 354, HA 1990; *Tendres complices*, DD 310, HP 1990.

Greene, Jennifer: *Secrets*, SB 1988; *Parel van de nacht*, T 26, HA 1989; *La perle noire du Tennessee*, DH 225, HP 1989.

Krentz, Jayne Ann: *Full Bloom*, HE 1987; *Vierentwintig rozen*, LA 226, HA 1989; *Les fleurs de l'orage*, CRP 229, HP 1989.

Krentz, Jayne Ann: *The Main Attraction*, HE 1987; *Wild en ontembaar*, LA 167, HA 1988; *La déesse des bords du lac*, DD 314, HP 1991.

London, Cait: *The Loving Season*, SB 1989; *Eerlijke hartstocht*, I 369, HA 1990; *Une seconde nuit à Bénévolence*, CRP 301, HP 1990.
Roberts, Nora: *The Name of the Game*, SB 1988; *Hartstocht in beeld*, T 35, HA 1989; *Une seconde de la vie de Sam*, DH 289, HP 1991.
Ross, Jo Ann: *Eve's Choice*, SB 1988; *Een engel op aarde*, LA 250, HA 1989; *Ombre et mystère en Louisiane*, CRP 255, HP 1989.
Schuler, Candace: *Almost Paradise*, HE 1989; *Exotische extase*, LA 295, HA 1990; *Les songes de Belle de Lune*, DD 294, HP 1989.

British Romances

Arden, Jenny: *A Taming Hand*, MB 1988; *Verlate verzoening*, J 822, HA 1990; *Lune de miel à Sorrente*, CA 1113, HP 1990.
Cook, Sally: *Spring Sunshine*, MB 1991; *Tussen geurige bloemen*, BR 1242, HA 1992; *Un printemps en Crète*, CA 1301, HP 1992.
Donnely, Jane: *When We're Alone*, MB 1989; *Bevrijdende liefde*, J 836, HP 1990; *Le voyageur de l'île de Wright*, CA 1124, HP 1990.
Leclair, Day: *Jinxed*, MB 1990; *Redeloos verliefd*, J 827, HA 1990; *Un peu de sérieux, Miss Malory*, CH 914, HP 1990.
Lyons, Mary: *Dark and Dangerous*, MB 1991; *Een onweerstaanbare kus*, BR 1251, HA 1992; *La diabolique Miss Kate*, CA 1288, HP 1992.
Winters, Rebecca: *The Story Princess*, MB 1990; *Een sprookje van liefde*, J 901, HA 1991; *La princesse amoureuse*, CA 1274, HP 1992.

REFERENCES

Alphant, Marianne (1988). "OPA sur le roman rose" [Corporate takeover of romance]. *Libération*, 7 July.
Cohn, Joan (1988). *Romance and the Erotics of Property: Mass-Market Fiction for Women.* Durham, NC: Duke University Press.
Favier, Annie (1989). "L'amour en grande diffusion" [Mass-produced romance]. *Livres Hebdo* 27 (July 3): 34–37.
Jensen, Margaret Ann (1984). *Love Sweet Return: The Harlequin Story.* Bowling Green, OH: Popular Press.
Mussell, Kay J. (1980). "Romantic Fiction." *Handbook of American Popular Culture*, ed. M. Thomas Inge. Westport, CT: Greenwood Press.
Radway, Janice (1984). *Reading the Romance: Women, Patriarchy, and Popular Literature.* Chapel Hill: University of North Carolina Press.

9 *Reader's Digest:* A Rosy World for Both Sides of the Atlantic

Daniel Baylon

In spite of many demonstrations and explanations to the contrary, nobody really knows what makes a magazine successful. As a case in point, the tremendous development of *Reader's Digest* both in the United States and in the rest of the world, and particularly in France—has often been ascribed to the special gift or "touch" of its founder DeWitt Wallace. As to what this "touch" consisted of, people and so-called specialists seem unable to give a precise definition. Nowadays the magazine, which has not changed much since it was created in 1922, still gathers millions of readers every month.

Just like any other American magazine *Reader's Digest* claims it helps its readers understand the world better; but more often than not, what happens in the world frightens people so that the press has taken to hiding the most unpleasant aspects of reality in order not to scare away the reading public. Various means and devices can be used: skip altogether the most disquieting sides of an event, or forget about the truth and rely on a bland optimism that gives rosy colors to the bleakest occurrences. However, such a departure from facts undermines efficiency and contributes to what has been called the credibility gap. This is why *Reader's Digest*, in both its American and French editions, resorts to more subtle techniques, the goal of which is to control external reality and, so to speak, "digest" it in order to make it acceptable. The brutishness of existence is softened and euphemized so that the buyers of the magazine, even as they are reading about wars, crimes and death, can relax in their armchairs and appreciate the quality of what they are reading.

When it first appeared in 1922, *Reader's Digest* called itself the "Little Magazine" and was in every way quite unobtrusive. Its pocket size seemed unable to compete with the much larger popular magazines; only 1,500 "happy few" subscribed at the very reasonable price of $3 for 12 issues. All the articles had been published in other magazines and appeared in a shorter, "condensed" form, which allowed the editors to cut whatever material they deemed unfit for their readers. Life certainly appeared simple throughout the pages of such a euphemistic anodyne.

When it landed in France in 1947, the magazine still preserved those characteristics. Nothing in its contents or appearance suggested that such an ordinary little magazine would become one of the leading French publications. However, the immediate postwar period was favorable for an American magazine that appeared in French with the more or less avowed goal of transmitting an idealized image of the United States and the American way of life. Since 1944, America had been present in France through its army and its soldiers. They had been acclaimed as liberators; but a small and unassuming magazine such as *Reader's Digest* could even better—and in a quieter way—conjure a reassuring and pleasant image of the faraway country that had won the war. Every month, 31 articles told about the lives of simple people—farmers, workers, schoolteachers—and gave the impression that the same kind of people lived across the ocean and that it was quite easy to understand them. At the same time, French readers discovered an extraordinary and modern country from which they had heard nothing for five years because the German authorities had forbidden any contact with America.

In fact, it was only the alluring side of a global offensive by the American media that was taking place in the wake of the American army. True, French people wanted to know everything about the country of jazz and chewing gum; but behind it all, some businessmen had already understood that huge markets were at stake. The attempt to sell the American way of life went hand-in-hand with a form of international cooperation. Just like *Reader's Digest*, *Time* and *Life* considered they also had a twofold mission: to show America as it really was and thus prove German propaganda false, and to promote American firms and their know-how. In America, idealism and business can become hopelessly entangled. Thus, by its very arrival in a country like France, *Reader's Digest* was euphemizing reality exactly as it had done in the United States in the 1920s and 1930s. It essentially gave a vision of life centered on individuals in a community where any reader could feel at home. The end product suggested that hope had come back and that, after the war, life could start all over again.

Throughout the years, both in America and France (and in the rest of the world), *Reader's Digest* has remained faithful to its unassuming formula that works like a magic charm. The general unobtrusiveness of its articles plays an important part in the commercial function of euphemization. The press cannot disturb or disquiet its readers, as it needs them to live and thrive just like any capitalistic enterprise. So journalists must find a balance between the problems and difficulties of the hour and the way to present them, which must please the readers without shocking them too much. Thus, the titles of articles on the cover page of

Reader's Digest are carefully engineered to tease and attract the readers. Both the French and American editions play on suspense, first creating anxiety and then bringing relief. Some of the titles are slightly disquieting: "When Your Doctor Doesn't Know" or *"Un enfant perdu dans le désert"* ("A Child Lost in the Desert"); but very quickly other titles comfort the reader: "Making the Most of Your Money" will help us get rich, and "There's Joy in Giving Yourself Away" will make us feel good and cater to our soul.

In both countries, euphemization can be partly ascribed to the pressure of advertisers who are reluctant to place ads in a magazine that devotes too much space to pessimistic news or unpleasant stories. But in fact euphemization pervades the very core of the *Digest*, and the editors claim that it gives their public a sounder view on life (as if they derived wisdom from what is sometimes called a social function fulfilled by the magazine). For instance, one of the main difficulties of the individual in society lies in a direct conflict with another individual, an unpleasant situation that may lead to failure, defeat, and frustration. For the *Digest*, this must be avoided at all costs. So it works hard at eliminating aggressiveness in its readers, mentioning only easy targets such as "they" or "the administration" or "the government." Thus, we know where and who the enemy is; however, he must not look too much like ourselves or we will be unable to bear the stress. Then the conflict will be made anonymous or eliminated through compromise. And the reader will be led to feel the need for a common search for a solution that will satisfy everyone. Before World War II, the magazine tried to create a type of behavior for the members of the huge American middle class; after the war—thanks to the same devices—it has tried to homogenize and, of course, euphemize the various European middle classes following the American pattern.

The press is supposed to inform, educate, and entertain us, and it has often been accused of failing to do so in a proper and decent way. Journalists usually respond that they merely report what is going on in the world, which is generally *not* decent or proper. Front pages are thus full of murders, wars, and other horrible events—the usual fare of the average newspaper reader. And readers seem to like it simply because, unknown to them, euphemization is already at work. Whatever the horror of a crime, whatever the callousness of a murderer, the press—and the *Digest*—try to explain everything, to give it a place within the frame of our moral, human, or psychological conceptions in order not to have it floating somewhere in our minds, between reality and nightmare, creating a feeling of uneasiness verging on anguish. There must be a norm that becomes the measure of everything. To euphemize is to create the sort of norm that codifies the psychological distance between the event and what is accepted as normal by society. Everything cannot be integrated, but such a norm supplies the reader with a representation of the phenomenon and helps him compare it with something he already knows. Thus, the June 1993 issue of the French edition published an article entitled *"Cancer: le courage d'en rire"* ("Cancer: The Courage to Laugh about It"); and when we read about riots in Los Angeles, we mostly hear about acts of heroism that warm our heart, not about the violence among minorities or in communities that have been humiliated and frustrated for too long. In both cases, the real problem disappears behind a "feel-good" smokescreen.

The disquieting aspects of a situation are made innocuous as if they were sterilized by a norm that eventually puts everything on the same level, creating a coherent and stable world protected from changing and chaotic impressions.

Such a strategy rests on various techniques at all stages of the magazine's production. The very size of *Reader's Digest*, the same in its American and French editions, constitutes an element of euphemization. Wallace did not like large magazines, which are difficult to handle and cannot be read anywhere for want of room. With its small size, the *Digest* is a familiar object that one can put in one's pocket and carry everywhere to be read at any opportunity. This aspect hasn't changed since 1922, and it gives the magazine a permanent and reassuring look. In spite of its mass circulation, it looks like the work of a craftsman made for people with good taste and an average standard of living. The feel of its sleek pages adds to our pleasure without aping the luxury paper on which posh art reviews are printed.

Our first visual contact confirms this impression. Now, reading is not the simple activity one might imagine. Editors try very hard to facilitate it, and the layout of *Reader's Digest* articles nearly always consists of two narrow columns with short lines of seven or eight words. Thus, the reader grasps the meaning easily and his interest and attention are maintained as his eyes constantly look for the beginning of a new line.

Moreover, through the choice of articles, editors try to blur the most unpleasant aspects of our society and to stress what they consider positive. Religion, holidays, travels, everyday problems, and what the magazine calls "philosophy of life" are the main subjects, together with education and how to be a good citizen. These articles must be cheerful and optimistic even as they acknowledge that life is not always pleasant, as everyone knows. But thanks to euphemization the magazine allows for it and can forget about it afterwards. To mention these unpleasant sides is in fact a way to dominate them. In particular, it is convenient to begin an article with something terrible happening to the main character. The story can develop from this terrible past event toward something that will be better and bring the solution. Thus, the beginning of "I Had to Learn the Truth" in November 1992 reveals euphemization at work: "The young soldier was covered in mud, with one leg hanging by a thin strip of skin and the other almost as badly mangled. His arms were broken, a finger missing, and he was bleeding from his left eye." Obviously things cannot be worse, and the reader feels that eventually the situation will improve. Sure enough, three pages later we learn that now the man is able to play the piano, that he goes scuba diving and has just completed a year at the university. The more formidable the obstacles, the more striking the euphemization; the more adverse destiny is, the greater the hero—and the less the reader—will be aware of the difficulties at stake.

Among other techniques, oversimplification and manichean duality play a significant role. But special mention must be given to repetition. Theoretically, to use repetition is to stress, to amplify the subject. But an overdose of the same element weakens it because of the lack of interest born of too frequent use. *Reader's Digest* publishes many medical articles, often telling the story of a child who develops a rare or unknown disease and whose parents fight a losing battle over months or even years. Who could remain indifferent when reading about this kind of suffering? It is too pure and too genuine a feeling. It does not correspond to what the editors want to communicate to their readers; thus, repetition helps readers get used to this kind of situation so that their response becomes mechanical and empty.

Finally, euphemization rests on two simple elements, the conjunction of which allows *Reader's Digest* to build another world that looks like ours but that possesses only certain of its characteristics. Hopes and secrets are the keys to knowledge, as they are meant to fill the reader's need for information without disquieting him. Hope comforts us and makes us forget our worries through the expectation of better days. Thus, the magazine kindles hope with a clever device. It puts forward the idea that our ignorance or inability to act do not come from our stupidity or from sheer impossibility, two very frustrating possibilities, but simply from the fact that we do not know the secret of the operation. Once we have been told the secret, our life becomes different: "The secret, says this therapist, is to focus on what you can, not on what you can't, do for your partners" ("Marriage Bed Burn Out," August 1992). In July 1992, the French edition tells us *"Les secrets de l'amour qui dure"* ("The Secrets of a Lasting Love"). Of course, every subject has its secrets. The whole complexity of the world boils down to a simple formula that will open the doors of success once it has been revealed.

Such a constant use of euphemization corresponds to a worldview meant to make us accept the world as through the building of a compromise between idealism and realism. To begin with, the reader must be convinced that the economic system has nothing to do with his own difficulties. For centuries people have been debating whether it is better to change the person or to change the institutions; but for *Reader's Digest*, the stress obviously lies on individual responsibility. Only an individual can bring about meaningful changes, so economic grievances are systematically played down. This leads to a double euphemization: on the one hand, an institutional problem becomes an individual problem; on the other hand, the individual is told that whatever the circumstances, there is always something to be done. The enormous amount of advice on how to behave in difficult circumstances finds its justification in the eternal pursuit of happiness: so the reader knows what he or she should do, thereby avoiding stress and frustration. Besides, euphemization helps us cope with everyday life—for instance, by bridging the gap between the peaceful life most people would like to lead and the statistically documented violence of modern societies. Such a system, which amounts to a model or a norm, helps people find their bearings in life but at the same time envelops them within the norm and prevents them from imagining anything else.

A calm acceptance of life as it is seems commendable. Greek and Latin philosophers advocated it. However, stoicism is not what *Reader's Digest* teaches. On the whole, it would probably accept the idea that happiness can be founded on duty and virtue; but the American way of life and its stress on a consumer society have little to do with the wisdom that stoic philosophers study throughout their lives. Nevertheless, the magazine approves of the idea that we must be aware of the strength of destiny, behind which looms an all-powerful God who created the world according to His own plan. Thus, to rebel against the order of the world (the social order, for instance) is futile and useless. Quite conscious of the austerity of such a conception, *Reader's Digest* tries to comfort us and give us hope through euphemization. The cathartic effect of other people's misfortunes is well known. To show what happened to an average American is to exorcise it, and the purging of old fears seems to guarantee that it will not happen to the reader.

Like Emerson, the magazine does not like the idea of a reward in the next world—it seems to imply that sinners get theirs in this one. Unable to suppress evil, the magazine endeavors to use it by suggesting that even the most horrible situations can yield some good. An accident or a disease must not be a negative event in an individual's life; it carries meaning because it signals an intention, a will in the universe. So, in an extraordinary reversal, we must refuse to despair, fight to survive, and eventually restore hope in other people. A famous football player, paralyzed after an accident, got the idea of looking after other people in the same situation; Magic Johnson's HIV infection led him to fight AIDS. In this way a sick person never remains alone, isolated from other human beings; on the contrary, his new mission allows him to feel useful and be an active member of society.

To complete this acceptance of the world, the magazine establishes a subtle compromise between idealism and realism. On the one hand, *Reader's Digest* wants its readers to become responsible and informed citizens who will not be surprised by strange, extraordinary, or cruel events. However, wars and atrocities are apt to frighten readers, and as a consequence they might want to forget about it all—which is not appropriate for citizens of a democratic country; besides, such an attitude can lead to the protection of a selfish, comfortable, but narrow middle-class life. Euphemization will reassure people and prove that life is indeed worth living. The magazine knows quite well that one does not live on bread alone, so it looks after the souls of its readers. If the way of life advocated by the *Digest* belongs to everyday reality, one can also find a form of idealism. But there again, dangers lie in store for the readers. With an ideal vision of the world we forget about reality, are carried away by exaltation, and cease to be pragmatic. Of course, the magazine never forgets to remind its readers of great moral principles: all men are brothers, and goodwill brings the solution to all problems. Most of the time intuition, feeling, and impression are preferred over thought, analysis, or proof. Nevertheless, this idealism is deeply rooted in everyday, matter-of-fact reality; and euphemization keeps it on a human scale. On the one hand, the hard, static, material world needs to be softened so as to bring about if not enthusiasm, at least some sort of adherence; on the other hand, a far-fetched and inaccessible idealism causing frustration must be transmuted into a peaceful spiritual life. Somewhere in the middle lies a golden mean that links readers with the real world while leaving them something to dream about. Euphemization allows us to think that on the whole we live in an acceptable world in which the material and the ideal can be had together. Where Gatsby eternally pursues the green light without ever reaching it, the *Digest* is wise enough or prudent enough to split up its quest so as to multiply the goals and increase the odds in favor of success. Eventually a double pleasure is achieved inasmuch as we keep the impression of "reaching toward" without the frustration of never getting anywhere.

Popular magazines claim to help people lead a better life in a society where things are not always easy. Traditionally they are presented as crusaders for the public good, trying to adapt institutions to society. Some of them, however, seem to try to adapt society to its environment—as can be observed with *Reader's Digest*. After praising the American system for more than 20 years, the same devices have been used since World War II to convince foreigners that what is good for America is good for the rest of the world as the values and euphemized worldview of the American middle class have spread and multiplied all over the world.

Should the process be condemned? After all, one could conceive of a softening of reality for those who do not like strong emotions. But euphemization for all corrupts the very nature of the job the press is supposed to do. The result is superficial, the journalist avoids difficulties, and the reader is left defenseless when confronted with a complex situation because the way toward real knowledge and genuine thought has been blocked.

BIBLIOGRAPHY

Bainbridge, John (1946). *Little Wonder: Or the* Reader's Digest *and How It Grew*. New York: Reynal & Hitchcock.

Baylon, Daniel (1989). *L'Amérique mythifiée: le* Reader's Digest *de 1945 à 1970*. Toulouse: CNRS/Presses du Mirail.

Heidenry, John (1993). *Theirs Was the Kingdom: Lila and DeWitt Wallace and the Story of the* Reader's Digest. New York: Norton.

Roeder, Otto (1954). *Der Konzern der guten Herzen; Geschichte einer journalistischen Welteroberung*. Oldenburg: G. Stalling.

Schreiner, Samuel, Jr. (1977). *The Condensed World of the* Reader's Digest. New York: Stein & Day.

Wood, James P. (1967). *Of Lasting Interest: The Story of the* Reader's Digest, rev. ed. Garden City, NY: Doubleday.

10 "Seriously Lurid": The Pitfalls of Publishing American Crime Fiction in Britain

Andrew Pepper

It is said that great artists are never truly appreciated in their home towns, or, in the case of American popular culture, their own nation. Conventional thinking tends to suggest that although the general mass of the American population gape enviously at the historical longevity and highbrow status of European culture, they do so at the expense of properly appreciating the artistic virtues of home-grown popular culture. Hence, this line of thinking goes, it has only been due to the efforts of the European intellectual that film noir was born as a recognized genre, that hardboiled icons such as Jim Thompson were excavated from publishers' archives, that jazz was elevated to its current status as major art form, and more recently that contemporary American crime fiction—a body of writing represented among others by Elmore Leonard, James Ellroy, and James Lee Burke—was dragged up the cultural escalator and bestowed an artistic and literary credibility previously denied to it at home. Certainly, American crime writers such as Chester Himes, Jerome Charyn, and James Ellroy, whose own fictions have radically challenged the conventions of the genre, have felt better appreciated in Europe than in America—Charyn and Himes both moved from New York to Paris; and Ellroy, tongue firmly in cheek, suggested that he seemed to be most popular in France because, in his words, "they love this kind of perverted American shit."[1]

Yet feedback from the London publishing world paints a different picture, at least in commercial terms. Struggling to convince a skeptical reading public about the merits of American crime fiction, British editors have resembled European soccer coaches trying but failing to elicit the best from their multimillion-pound imported stars—excellent results on the players' home turfs fail to translate into success abroad. The appeal of hardboiled crime fiction is, of course, inherently limited by its hard edge, showing as it does an often unpleasant side of society. Yet while writers like Ellroy and Burke enjoy quasi-bestseller status on their home territory, a new novel achieving hardback sales of 60,000, they might only sell one-twentieth of that amount in Britain, even in relative terms a disappointingly low figure. As Bill Massey of Orion Books philosophically states, "To be frank, if you want to know how publishers view American crime fiction, it's as a rather problematic area where sales, in general, lag significantly behind critical reputations."[2]

To claim that American crime fiction is only commercially successful in the United States and only critically successful in Europe is too broad a generalization. Yet difficulties associated with marketing and packaging American crime fiction in Britain reflect a more general European situation whereby American popular culture is either dismissed as mere escapism or deified as highbrow art. U.S. publishers have pursued an unashamedly populist approach, packaging even the most radical, left-field crime novels (e.g., by Charyn and Ellroy) in brash, lurid covers—and judging by sales levels and by the quantity of new crime fiction being published, their approach seems to have been successful. In Britain, though, where American crime fiction has a necessarily low-key presence in the market (necessarily because the American cultural background is more accepting of the issues and locales described in the novels), publishers have faced a much tougher decision: whether to follow the American model and treat it as mass market entertainment, or to take it up the "cultural escalator" and view it as highbrow art.

As part of what can loosely be termed "popular literature," American crime writing is attractive to those who read to be entertained, but at the same time its often bleak, unpleasant view of American society gives it appeal beyond those readers only seeking escapist thrills. The danger, then, lies in straying too far from the middle ground—in pushing it too far upmarket into the domains of "literature," a move that threatens to alienate the form from its populist roots; or too far downmarket, into fiction's bargain basement, a move that denies specific American crime writers (notably Ellroy, Burke, and Leonard) the serious platform their writing deserves.

It is, of course, dangerous to speak about American crime fiction as one homogeneous entity, especially in relation to this high culture/low culture debate. Certain crime writers, such as Jonathan Kellerman and Patricia D. Cornwall, produce accessible, mainstream fiction and have genuine mass market appeal; others, such as Gar Anthony Haywood, who writes private investigator novels set in the south central ghettos of Los Angeles, simply don't sell beyond a limited "cult" audience. In terms of Kellerman, whose thrillers detail the exploits of a Beverly Hills psychologist, Bill Massey of Orion Books ascribes his success to the comforting worldview his novels support—"they have a veneer of sophistication, the main character's a psychologist, he's into stocks and shares, its all quite nice"— whereas Hillary Hale of Little Brown credits some of Cornwall's considerable appeal to her creation of a female investigator who is neither a private investigator nor a police detective "but has a very legitimate reason to be involved."[3]

Beyond the fiction itself, Little Brown's success (especially with Cornwall) owes much to insightful packaging that suggests the writing is both adult and sophisticated, and populist and entertaining. The matte laminate, spot varnish covers signify a sophistication that sets them apart from standard genre fictions—this is the move upmarket. The embossed images of, for example, a knife (Kellerman's *Over the Edge*) or a gagged woman (Cornwall's *Postmortem*), and the small pocket-book size, signify a thriller element and indicate mass market appeal.

The question of book size is not merely cosmetic, but one dictated by the structure of the book trade in Britain. *A format* is the small, pocket-book paper-back size. *B format* is the larger, more expensive size. WH Smith (which accounts for 20 percent of the total U.K. market) and wholesale distributors (who supply motorway service stations, supermarkets, and airports) are not keen to stock paperbacks in B format because of the higher price. Hence a decision to publish in either A or B formats can seriously affect potential sales, as well as signify either mass market or literary credentials. Indeed, the impact of Smith's or the whole-salers' stocking a title can be stunning, at least in commercial terms. Hillary Hale suggests that one reason why Cornwall outsells Kellerman by a factor of 20 relates to exactly this issue. "With Kellerman, it's about 60% in shops like Waterstone's and 40% in Smith's. With Cornwall it's 20% in Waterstone's, 40% in Smith's and 40% through the wholesalers—and that's why she's so much bigger."

For Gar Anthony Haywood, though, the ride has not been as smooth. Indeed, the treatment of his novels is one example of the potential dangers of taking American crime fiction too far downmarket. Maxim Jakubowski, owner of London's Murder One Bookshop, and John Williams, author of much crime fiction reportage and editor of the Serpent's Tail hardboiled fiction imprint Mask Noir, both agree that Haywood's novels are essentially conventional private investigator narratives. But Williams in particular points out the extraordinary tenets of Haywood's writing: his dissection of L.A.'s south central culture that neither panders to racism nor depicts its inhabitants as victims.[4] However, Pan Macmillan published Haywood's first two novels as part of its no-frills Crime Case list, thereby diluting the impact of his work's exceptional qualities among a swathe of standard detective yarns. Each novel sold just 600 copies, mostly to public libraries, and never made it into paperback; and Macmillan consequently decided to drop Haywood from its list. One could argue that his type of crime fiction might fare better if directed toward a smaller, cult audience specifically interested in hardboiled urban crime fiction, rather than those who read simply for entertainment. Indeed, the fact that his most recent novel *You Can Die Trying*, which uses the aftermath of the 1992 Los Angeles riots as subtext, has been picked up by Serpents Tail, (which produces high-quality, high-price paperbacks in limited numbers) seems to bear out this point.

The recent collapse of Arrow's crime fiction imprint Mysterious Press also adds fuel to this particular fire. The imprint, whose name was borrowed from the

flagship American Mysterious Bookshop, produced swathes of crime fiction—
some British, some American, some hardboiled, some what editors call "cosy"
crime—all in the same format and on the same list. Oliver Johnson of Arrow
Books argues that the list failed because they saturated a market that simply
couldn't absorb all the material. But John Williams makes a more telling observation: "They put out hardboiled writers like James Ellroy and James Lee Burke.
But on the same list they also put out a lot of cosy, British procedural writing
which utterly diluted the impact of the list. You couldn't walk into a bookshop,
pick up anything with Mysterious Press on it knowing what it would be." In other
words, the project of treating all crime fiction in the same way, taking all crime
fiction down to the level of lowest common denominator, automatically assumes
a homogeneity that not only doesn't exist but also distracts from the individual
merits of certain crime novelists.

The real danger of such a move downmarket is the perception that writers
whose work is published alongside other standard genre entertainments are
merely pulp novelists rather than authors worthy of serious critical attention. This
danger is especially pronounced in the case of James Ellroy, who perhaps more
than any other American crime novelist has sought to redefine and push back the
conventions of the genre. In fact, his work has mutated so much in the past ten
years—from relatively inauspicious procedural beginnings to the epic scope of
his four recent novels, the L.A. Quartet, which rewrite the entire history of the
city in the 1950s—that his U.K. publishers, Arrow, repackaged and reissued all
four books, swapping the pocket-book design with covers supporting B-movie
images of men in fedoras and trenchcoats for upmarket, higher-price B format
designs. This move was deemed necessary by his British editor, Oliver Johnson,
in order to properly reflect the change in his own work: "We agreed that his
writing was tending towards literature more than popular entertainment; therefore
the move to the B format, classy monochrome covers, and a higher price represented a push for a more literate audience."[5]

The project of treating certain crime novelists seriously is a necessary one;
taking writers like Ellroy up the cultural escalator (to borrow Stuart Hall's phrase)
introduces their work to a younger, more literate audience that might have otherwise written it off as pulpish entertainment and hence unworthy of close critical
attention. Yet there are problems with this approach as well. The more that hardboiled fiction is dressed up to look like serious literature, the more it will be
alienated from its popular roots. According to John Williams, crime fiction is
different from what he calls literary fiction precisely because of these roots: "they
have a necessarily close relationship, born, if nothing else, out of the demands of
writing for a mass, not a literary audience" (Williams, 1991: 8). Crime fiction, he
maintains, is different from literary fiction because it is read primarily by what he
calls an unsophisticated audience—people who read books that appeal but have
no fashionable status. For him, literary fiction is strongly fashion-driven, with
writers moving in and out of favor on practically a weekly basis. At least in terms
of American crime fiction, his point is well taken. Hauling it too far upmarket

threatens to sever the genre from its traditional readership and allow literary fads to dictate who and what gets published.

Whether this fate will befall James Ellroy is not clear, and early indications from his publishers suggest that their search for a new audience has been successful. Yet other American crime writers, notably James Lee Burke, have been caught out by this British publishing push to "intellectualize" the genre. Whereas U.S. publishers have achieved significant sales by marketing and packaging his novels— part thrillers, part exploration of the issues and history affecting southern Louisiana—as brash, populist entertainments, his British publishers have adopted the opposite approach, dressing up his work in dull monochrome jackets and treating it as pseudo-literature. That Burke was discarded by Random Century after a number of failed attempts to find an audience shows the dangers of such an approach. Not that all blame can be directed against the packaging, though. Other factors, such as the author's relative anonymity in Europe and the unfamiliarity of his novels' setting, have hindered attempts to break him into the mainstream. Yet his current editor, Bill Massey, accepts that colorless packaging has worked to overemphasize the seriousness of his writing and underemphasize the fact that his novels also work as plot-driven thrillers. "The Burke titles in Vintage, paperbacks that looked serious, signified that this was highbrow stuff, not to be picked up for a bit of light entertainment. Maybe we've overdone that route."

Much American crime fiction does fall between two stalls. *Clockers*, a novel by Richard Price, is both a police procedural narrative in which a homicide detective investigates the murder of a black youth, and a serious exploration of issues affecting life in a grim, inner-city housing project. Bill Massey speaks about the need to treat it as serious entertainment—or, to borrow a phrase from the rap band BDP, *edutainment*. A novel whose main character is an unreformed crack dealer cannot be sold or read as mere escapism, but to dress it up as serious art deters those who might enjoy the whodunit element of the plot. The resultant paperback is an effective compromise: pocket-book size, lurid cover design on a sophisticated matte surface. As John Williams points out, there is too often an assumption in publishing circles that an intellectually serious thriller must be made to *look* serious, rather than made to look seriously lurid. "There is probably a lot more design skill in producing a good A format cover than a ghastly, pseudo-literary B format cover."

John Sutherland suggests that one crucial role of popular fiction is to express and then fulfill certain needs that readers bring to the novels—among them, providing comfort and reassurance (Sutherland, 1981: 34). However, Stephen Knight argues that crime fiction functions to assuage the anxieties of its middle-class readers (Knight, 1980: 5). A recent questionnaire, specially commissioned for this study and conducted at London's Murder One Bookshop among a sample group of 60 readers,[6] revealed that almost 60 percent of those questioned confessed to reading American crime fiction primarily for escapist reasons. Furthermore, although more than half were personally familiar with Jonathan Kellerman's work, less than 40 percent admitted to reading Ellroy and just 10 percent to reading anything by Gar Haywood. That Kellerman's thrillers offer the most comforting portrait of Los Angeles—and Haywood's, the most uncompromising—is no coincidence. Indeed, although there is literally no room for neat resolutions in Haywood's fierce South Central milieu, Kellerman actually acknowledges the artificiality of his plot resolutions. "I think in this age there's so much a sense of loss of control, particularly about crime. I look out of my window and I see race riots, literally; but in my books I can make it come out the way I want."[7]

All this suggests that whatever serious credence academics, publishers, and writers themselves place in the contemporary American crime novel, it is still read primarily as entertainment. Yet there are also strong signs that these motivations are changing, as a new climate prevails and a new generation of readers is introduced to the genre. Of those questioned over the age of 40, less than one-quarter claimed to read American crime fiction to engage with some kind of grimly realistic portrait of contemporary America; yet when the same question was put to those under age 40, this percentile figure rose to almost half. In addition, although Kellerman was fantastically popular with readers over age 40 (some 82% claimed to have read one of his Alex Delaware thrillers), among readers under age 40 this figure fell dramatically to just 33 percent. In contrast, at least one of Ellroy's ferocious, multilayered L. A. Quartet novels, read by just 35 percent of the older group, was familiar to almost 60 percent of the younger group.

Of the younger group, half admitted to reading American crime fiction for escapist reasons; but half also claimed they read crime novels to engage with a range of pressing social issues: drugs, guns, poverty, crime, inner-city life. Ion Mills, founder of the small crime fiction press No Exit, also feels the two categories are not mutually exclusive. He accepts that his own interest in hardboiled fiction comes partly from a desire to escape into another world—"I read this kind of book for escapism, hoping to God that what happens, never happens to me"— but he is also keen to stress that he is not interested in safe, contrived, easily resolvable stories. "Crime fiction is not like historical romances, which are pure escapism and very safe; it's real, it's on the cutting edge."[8]

The challenge for publishers, critics, and even writers must be to treat American crime fiction in this same way: as fiction that has a serious point to make on a wide range of pressing social issues, from institutional corruption to gun control, as well as fiction that sets out to entertain. Like much American popular culture in general (e.g., film noir, jazz, and blues), contemporary crime fiction should not be written off merely as escapism. Equally, it should not be deified by European (and American) enthusiasts to the point at which its popular appeal, its vitality, and its accessibility all count for nothing. After all, hardboiled fiction, like jazz and film noir, was created to be enjoyed, not to be seriously studied.

NOTES

1. James Ellroy, in a phone conversation with A. Pepper (January 23, 1994).
2. Bill Massey, Editorial Director, Orion Books; interview with A. Pepper at Orion

House, Upper St. Martins Lane, London (March 11, 1994). All further references to Massey refer to this note.

3. Hillary Hale, Editorial Director, Little Brown and Co.; interview with A. Pepper at Brettenham House, London (April 12, 1994). All further references to Hale refer to this note.

4. Maxim Jakubowski, Owner, Murder One Bookshop; interview with A. Pepper at Murder One, Charing Cross Road, London (April 15, 1994). John Williams, Editor, Serpents Tail; interview with A. Pepper at Kensal Rise, London (August 4, 1994). All further references to Jakubowski and Williams refer to this note.

5. Oliver Johnson, Editorial Director, Random Century; interview with A. Pepper at Random House, London (March 4, 1994).

6. Conducted by A. Pepper at the Murder One Bookshop, Charing Cross Road, London, between May and June 1994, among a sample group of 60 readers.

7. Jonathan Kellerman, "A Criminal Mind: An Interview with Kellerman," Catherine M. Nelson, *Armchair Detective* 26.1 (Winter 1993): 93.

8. Ion Mills, Editor, No Exit Press; interview with A. Pepper at Harpenden, Herts. (April 29, 1994).

REFERENCES

Collins, Jim (1989). *Uncommon Cultures*. London: Routledge.
Knight, Stephen (1980). *Form and Ideology in Crime Fiction*. London: Macmillan.
Mandel, Ernest (1984). *Delightful Murder*. London: Pluto Press.
Sutherland, John (1981). *Bestsellers*. London: Routledge.
Symons, Julian (1994). *Bloody Murder*, 3rd ed. London: Pan.
Williams, John (1991). *Into the Badlands*. London: Paladin.

Part IV

Food

11 Pride and Prejudice: American Cuisine, the French, and Godliness

Mireille Favier

"American *cuisine!*" my friend exclaimed with a glint of outrage in his eyes, "What the hell are you talking about?" He was a critic in a rather posh gastronomic review. The I-am-not-amused look on his face reminded me too late that to some cooking fundamentalists, not only was my unfortunate choice of words (American *cuisine*, for God's sake!) utterly tactless, but it actually verged on sin.

The two of us being French, we shared a natural, inborn pride in the indisputable prominence of our cuisine over all other existing or tentative ones. To us French people, cooking is indeed a serious, if enjoyable matter—and when it comes to the even more serious subject of our excellence in the field, no degree of doubt or irony is to be tolerated. There is no joking with the most sacred component of our national identity. Any breach in the consensus passes for a threat. At the least teasing attempt to compare us, even to the Italians, we see red and scream blue murder. At the merest suggestion that Americans can cook, war looms.

The critic's withering look was the sober, mature equivalent of the youthful guffaws that met the question "What do you think of American cuisine?" when I made a quick, impromptu survey among my own students (age 18 to 24) at the Parisian School of Applied Arts. Let me put it this way: if I were American, I would crawl away, hide my shame in some corner, and cry.

The result of this survey (however limited, imperfect, and nonscientific) was overwhelming. To these young people, who have chosen art as a future career and agreed, when asked, that cooking is an art, American food means *fast food*—some even say *junk food*. As they were trying to describe it more accurately, they came up with sorry adjectives: fat, stodgy, too sweet and soft (or indeed "mushy"!), savorless, shapeless, undefined, unrefined, artificial, chemical! No less. One soothing remark in the biting flow, however: American food is fairly better than English food! Were I English, I would consider suicide.

One youth said: "Americans have no history, so to speak. They started from scratch. Unlike Europeans, they have no gastronomic traditions. In the early days of the American pioneers, there was a sense of danger and urgency that excluded the time it takes to cook refined dishes. The time, plus the knowledge, plus the know-how."

In a word, Americans have an excuse (their short history) for producing such poor, disappointing food—does it still deserve to be called so, given the scathing epithets? But how come the very same youths who railed against hamburgers admittedly consumed their fair share of Big Macs? Is sheer masochism their sole excuse? Urged to explain the contradiction, one young man conceded: "When you're hungry, broke, and in a hurry, you can't afford to be very demanding. Everybody goes to fast-food restaurants these days anyway, but it doesn't mean I don't know the difference between a hamburger and real food!"

Now *that* is interesting; fast food is not *real*.

After imposing it worldwide through marketing methods that have the grace of a bulldozer, Americans may have fallen victims to their own imperialist success. Panzer-burger may be king, but its kingdom is a sham. The hamburger is a humbug. You often spend more time standing in line at a McDonald's counter, waiting your turn, than actually eating. This is not the best way to make food taste real. The hamburger culture is the reign of the lowest common food denominator, with a frustrating lack of variety in taste and texture that discourages curiosity, erodes extremes, and eliminates surprises, whether good or bad.

Andy Warhol, the pop-art pope who fantasized himself as a machine-artist producing totally impersonal, standard images, lavishly commented on U.S. popular culture. He said: "All the Cokes are the same and all the Cokes are good. Liz Taylor knows it, the president knows it, the bum knows it, and you know it."[1] The same could be said of the hamburger. In our country, it would not be a compliment.

Unreally sweet and soft, unchangingly bland, fast food is a perfect food for kids, too. No wonder they love it; they lick the oozing ketchup (more cosmetic than tasty, another *unreal* condiment), make a happy mess of it, and thumb their noses at good manners.

Reduced to a few always-identical staple items (better identified from their name than from their taste, I'm afraid), it is also a perfect food for bulimics. Freezing the imagination, abolishing variety and relish, inanely repeating itself across the globe, fast food is a sort of nonfood for millions of anonymous nobodies who blindly down their warm, soft, pre-chewed (but rightfully authenticated) mash the way a bulimic gobbles almost anything up indiscriminately. Even the unheated content of a can or last night's leftovers—just to fill a void.

What void is America trying to fill (and many of us in its wake) with this fast-made, fast-eaten, fast-forgotten food? Could it have anything to do with the anguish of the uprooted, the inextinguishable hunger for an ever-elusive identity? For all its *fastness*, U.S. food offers more complexity than is apparent. In spite of a decidedly unpalatable reputation in our country (backed by advertising clichés, stale, imported U.S. television serials, and the multiplication of fast-food chains) Americans often know better—but mostly at home.

Their gastronomic tree may well have few, feeble roots. However poor it may be in history and traditions, the United States has a much richer story to tell, geographically speaking. There is no such thing as a real, national, "federal" gastronomy; instead the U.S. cooking heritage proceeds from a succession of additions and adoptions, rather than from the harmonious blending of long-simmered ingredients. Its inventiveness is essentially ethnic.

A patchwork from the start, American popular culture very much remains so, and the food culture is no exception. Instead of emerging, wholly recognizable, from the original melting pot (this great unattainable dream), U.S. food claims a multiple identity best expressed through a variegated jumble of ethnic habits and influences: Italian, Jewish, Asian, Mexican, among many others. As for more specifically "American" dishes or products, from clam chowder and chicken pot pie to T-bone steak, pecan pie, and maple syrup, only the most traveled French people know and speak about them, acknowledging the existence of "another" American cuisine, generally discovered in situ; for it is otherwise little exported, rarely advertised (if at all), and largely ignored.

This American cuisine deserves a better, fairer treatment, but its champions are few and isolated—a cockleshell in a rough sea of prejudices—unable to counter the landslide of rejection in France of American popular food. Such massive disparagement certainly raises many questions. Among others: Are French people, for all their deep-rooted faith in their superior food civilization, up to their own reputation? They will occasionally admit: "All right, we don't cook yummy elaborate dishes every day. So what?" Understood: "We could if we would." (Subunderstood: "Should they want to, Americans couldn't for they just don't know how.")

Why this almost naive arrogance?

Our absolute confidence in our own cooking perfection can't be accounted for without a common reference to a common, unspoken norm of excellence—if not shared by, at least implicit for, every one of us. Thus, even the least imaginative French person (as far as food goes), the least gourmet one can literally spend hours talking about mythical *petits plats* exhumed from the past—not necessarily their own, mind you, but a fraction of some collective food memory mysteriously transfused to him/her long ago through their mother's womb as part of a genetic heritage.

Could it be that today our claimed excellence in food matters relies mostly on an illusion, a fantasy? Could French gastronomes be floating through air, boasting of a colorful, prestigious, but vanishing past that is getting flimsier over the years? Unknowingly they may well become gradually disconnected from what they still value as the most authentic part of their identity.

A U.S. mass-circulation magazine recently pointed out: "Nurtured on images of past glory, the French are finding it hard to adjust to a world in which the encroachments of modernization . . . threaten the traditional way of life" (*Time*, October 4, 1994). Indeed, in just a few decades, working lunch constraints, women's work, deep changes in the family structure, along with the accelerated development of the food industry, have eroded oldtime habits and perceptions. We are, at times, confronting the new, confusing problem of having to identify the content of our plate: vegetarian, fish, or cheese steaks, false crab, imitation shrimp, and the like offer unexpected, unwelcome, and not very stimulating riddles to our abused senses, as modern food has more and more to do with engineering. "What are we eating today?" never before had this unsettling double meaning.

To some pathological malcontents, a half-full glass is grudgingly seen as half-empty. I resolutely—some would say unrealistically—side with optimists; even supposing that our gastronomical paradise is already half-lost, I prefer to think it has been blessedly half-preserved. I contend it is not unrealistic to believe in a few perennial features of our food civilization, for what is at stake here is not only the *nature* of our food in all its modern and sometimes regrettable avatars, but our ingrained *attitude* toward it—a whole gourmet philosophy. Unlike American food habits, still largely characterized by a childlike simplicity, ours have had centuries to shed the rawness of early experimentation and achieve their present maturity. Although the clearcut memory of our turbulent beginnings eludes us by now, our most unconscious tastes and uses have been irrevocably shaped by the density of our past.

In the American so-called melting pot, not much actual melting occurred, mostly for lack of time; and it is no coincidence if the only homogeneous food culture the United States has hitherto produced is fast-food culture, its most controversial achievement. The main ingredient in the melting operation is time; and we, on the contrary, had plenty of that.

Throughout our history, we have developed a sort of natural complicity with time and integrated it as a positive value. Originally a rural society, France had to build up patience as a direct consequence of its year-long sedentary confrontation with nature. For our peasant forebears, duration was taken for granted as part of the cycle of seasons. It takes time for seeds to germinate, trees to bloom, and crops to grow. More time for wines and spirits to mature in the cool shade of our cellars; for the pervading, strong-smelling smoke of a wood fire to flavor the hams and salamis left to dry hanging from the farm ceilings; for milk to slowly mellow or harden into cheese on rows of racks in gloomy, odorous rooms; for meats, herbs, and spices to simmer. Time again to make preserves. There is a time for everything, impatience is youthful, and ours is an old country. How could we not be irritated by Americans' impatience and haste? How could we understand their drive to annihilate time?

Much space and little time are America's double-edged assets. Distances are huge, and part of the taming of such an extensive land has consisted of building crisscrossing networks of motorways. Straight, time-saving despite drastic speed limits and police controls, they have induced a new, functional way of traveling. While driving almost hypnotically along what, to me, suggests giant conveyor belts, I was often amazed at the elliptic road signs that say GAS and FOOD at a short distance from exits. It would be difficult to acknowledge a few basic needs in a more unsophisticated, utilitarian way! It is a fact: at regular intervals, cars and humans need energy refills. But nowhere have I seen it expressed in a drier, sadder fashion. Filling though unfulfilling, food is fuel for the human machine. Instant food or instant urges, it only calms an itch.

In France, one never quite forgets—or is quickly reminded—that food is not only a need but a source of pleasure, even on the road. If we get bored by the minimal food available in *restauroutes* or gas-station stores, we seldom have no other solutions. France is a surprisingly small country when it comes to finding something good to eat—be it only a crunchy sandwich. Driving a few miles further down the road to stop at a gastronomical landmark (whether renowned according to national, local, or individual, purely subjective, standards) is no big deal. Every region in the country, every precious *terroir* is literally strewn with them. Wherever we are, we are never far from them. Ask truck drivers, or ask traveling agents, an inexhaustible mine of information and source of *bonnes adresses*.

All the foreigners I know who have lived here long enough to develop some sort of day-to-day relationship with French people have, at one time, experienced a very particular bout of vertigo, a sense of being practically assaulted by our number one obsession. "Honestly, so much food, and so damn too much *talk* about food is exhibitionist," said an American friend of mine. "It's downright pornographic!" I guess he was only half-joking.

Conversely, I have often teased Americans about their down-to-earth, practical, and again efficient approach. Whereas they seemed mostly interested in absorbing the right amount of vitamins and proteins with their food, I was possessed by the daunting task of balancing flavors.

Chemistry versus alchemy. Food cripples versus food perverts . . . . Can there ever be an end to this dialogue of the deaf? Probably not. French and American eaters observe—when they don't simply ignore—one another with mingled curiosity and irritation, across an unfathomable ocean of misunderstandings.

In a small country like ours, producing a little of almost everything, quality and balance prevail. All is a matter of sometimes fussy measuring out, of finding the exact proportions. In America everything is out of proportion—vast natural landscapes, huge natural disasters, giant highrises, bumper crops, ultraproductivity. It is the land of bounty, with the cornucopia as a symbol and the hypermarkets and malls as the oversized temples of a consumer society gone berserk. And Big Mac is the modern ogres' greed-killer, a food made (ready-made) for individual, selfish, solitary eaters—again, food for bulimics.

Nobody can live on air, and hunger betrays us as mortals. If fast food is the raw, standard response to the rawest of all biological needs, the French cuisine may be an attempt to deny this crude reality. We don't cook and eat the way we do *because* we are hungry, but to forget about our hunger through elaborate ceremonies that involve all our senses, engage our imagination, and imply both the closeness of sharing and the distance of talk. Cuisine is a magical act; and the most celebrated of all capital sins—*la gourmandise*, which no English word translates accurately—encompasses our doom *and* our salvation.

Modern civilization is largely obsessed by the *look* of things; the packaging can be more important than the product itself, superficiality has become an ethic (who has time for depth anyway?), and overblown visual effects often replace aesthetic emotion. In France too, where food always refers to something more than food, we acknowledge the importance of appearances. But it seems to me that even our appearances are backed by an organic relation to our past; images and signs, to some degree, still have structure and content.

A recent ad posted everywhere in the *métro* said: "A table, la France!" In a sort of autumnal, intimist light, a bottle of the promoted, cheap plonk (with an elegant label, however) stood beside a smoked ham and a loaf of crusty country bread, conjuring up both a rich, common rural tradition and images of gourmet togetherness. This rural memory goes hand in hand with a strong bourgeois tradition, which in turn bespeaks old court models. We may not be aware of all the ins and outs of our gastronomical past, but we *are* aware of, and bonded by, its existence. We take it for granted. Internalized from childhood, recognized by other countries, it is also part of class pretenses and stereotyped social rituals. It belongs to us and we are afraid to lose it. When we deemed its natural transmission threatened by modern life, did we not open an *École du goût* to educate or re-educate our children's taste? It is evidence enough that although this gourmet tradition may be a burden at times (the French who can't cook often feel they have to apologize!), it is still as vital to us as the air we breathe.

To me, the Danish film *Babette's Feast*[2] best exemplifies what I find most difficult to convey about the French attitude toward food. See it, savor it. The movie is about a *cordon blue* cook, Babette, who makes her first "real French dinner" after 14 years of enforced abstinence from cuisine while living amid the bleak, puritanical society of the Jutland peninsula. As one of her dinner guests remarks, Babette turns "a simple meal into an affair of love, abolishing all distinctions between physical appetite and spiritual appetite."

Architect and gastronome Jean-Claude Ribaud wrote: "Cooking is a choir in which everyone plays their own part and which expresses the singularity of a people."[3] For the French, cuisine is very much a religion with dogmas and priests, missionaries and fanatics, dissenters and heretics. Babette stands out as a great priestess of this very ancient cult. Her feast is a pledge of love and gratitude to her companions, a hymn to life that has the fervor of Gregorian chant. Her gift for cooking is unique, of course, and few means reach such selfless, exhilarating perfection. Yet all meals pertain to some sacred domain, however remote, however invisible.

God has long been hovering about France's kitchens. Paul Bocuse knows it, the president knows it, the man in the street knows it, and I know it too. God has obviously deserted fast-food restaurants with a shudder; but one hopes He may now be roaming Berkeley's self-styled gourmet ghetto, or silently encouraging the Clintons' newly appointed American chef. Who knows? After all, God is everywhere. God is even in the *pot-au-feu*—Saint Theresa of Avila knew it and said so. Why not in the chicken pot pie? For the ways of God are unfathomable.

NOTES

1. Andy Warhol, *From A to B and Back Again: The Philosophy of Andy Warhol* (London: Pan/Picador, 1975) 96.

2. *Babettes Gaestebud*, Denmark, 1987, 105 mins., dir. Gabriel Axel.

3. *Autrement* 138 "Menus, mots et maux" (June 1993):

12 "Wash Your Hands with Coca-Cola": Coca-Cola's European Tribulations

Laurent Ditmann

> In Germany, it is a German business; in France, it is a French business; in Italy, it is an Italian business.
>
> Coca-Cola executive, 1950s

While on a research trip to France in the spring of 1993, a Frenchman working in American academe—henceforth referred to as Professor D.—decided to pay a visit to an old high school friend—henceforth referred to as Professor W.—now a history and geography teacher in a rural middle school near the small town of Fère-en-Tardenois. As classes were still in session, Professor W. invited Professor D. to observe a group of sixth graders during a history period. Professor W. introduced his friend to a group of rambunctious 12-year-olds as a French expatriate living and teaching in Atlanta, Georgia. Trying hard to impress the children, Professor D. asked them whether they knew anything about the great southeastern metropolis. Hoping somewhat to hear about Martin Luther King, Jr., CNN, or *Gone with the Wind*, Professor D. was taken aback by the unanimity and enthusiasm of the response: "Atlanta, c'est la ville où il y a Coca-Cola." This writer will assume that no translation is needed here.

It remains to be determined what, if anything, this story reveals in terms of the real level of Americanization of European adolescents. A way of answering this question would be to observe that one could hardly imagine as energetic a response coming from an ordinary group of American youths at the simple mention of, for instance, Gevrey-Chambertin or Château-Lafitte. As anecdotal as it may seem, this encounter between the French and American worlds illustrates a well-established point: Coca-Cola is currently one of the best, if not the best, recognized name-brand in the world. As luck would have it, it is a U.S. brand closely associated with the American way of life, or with some hypothetical and supposedly stable American identity. It is an integral part of a number of activities, social practices, and icons that can readily be identified as pertaining to American popular culture: music (recording stars Paula Abdul and M. C. Hammer have promoted the brand), sports (Coca-Cola has exclusive rights to most ballparks in the United States), and fast-food restaurants, to name just a few.

What qualities are almost magically imparted on the product by this seal of "Americanness"—should such a word make sense—is a highly debatable point. According to cultural critic Roland Barthes, it seems that because the carbonated beverage is little more than water laced with sugar, the latter ingredient plays a paramount role on a semiotic and psychological level: the consumption of Coca-Cola would then denote the cultural and dietary primacy of sugar, which one could equate with the "sweetness" of life.[1] It is very likely that for the sixth graders, the American way of life, as exemplified by countless feature films and series they may see on television, epitomizes the concepts of leisure and pleasure, additional proof that Europeans have a superficial understanding of contemporary America.

The most troubling and paradoxical aspect of the anecdote is probably that the grandparents, and perhaps even the parents of this generation of French teenagers, may have entertained radically different notions about Coca-Cola, both as a firm and a product. It is not improbable that at one point in the past, say between 1945 and 1975, some of these adults wholeheartedly rejected the carbonated beverage as a token of American imperialism. Yet if France's reaction to the opening of Euro Disney and the General Agreement on Tariffs and Trade (GATT) negotiations is any index, one can justifiably contend that although anti-Americanism has certainly not subsided in Europe, Coca-Cola is now more widely accepted and consumed by Europeans than ever before.

How can one account for the complex relationship that has developed over the past century between Europeans and Coca-Cola? First, it should be noted that there has never been a unified and homogeneous European attitude vis-à-vis the beverage: Europe's love of or hatred for the drink has depended and still depends largely on where one is in Europe. It should be pointed out that the current consumption of Coca-Cola products in two southern European countries (e.g., Spain and Italy) may differ by a wide margin, the same being true of two northern European countries (e.g., Norway and Great Britain).[2] Nevertheless, for the sake of clarity and brevity, a certain degree of generalization will have to be tolerated here, and two basic methodological assertions accepted. First, because Coca-Cola, although present in Europe since the 1920s, has developed its market mostly since World War II and west of what used to be the Iron Curtain, this discussion will mostly focus on Western Europe. Second, because this author is French, a lot will be said about France, although it is by no means this author's contention that France perfectly exemplifies all European characteristics. Simply, this discussion will attempt to outline the major phases of Coca-Cola's involvement in

Europe and, with a hint of semiotics, explicate some of the reasons—pertinent to Coca-Cola's advertising policies of universalization and corporate culture of inclusion—for the growing success of the firm on the Old Continent. Readers interested in more specific accounts of the brand's successes and mishaps in Europe should be satisfied with Mark Pendergrast's (1993) and Frederick Allen's (1994) thorough discussions of the brand's history.

Both Pendergrast and Allen would be likely to side with those—either critics or proponents of the drink—who view the "Ideal Nerve Tonic and Stimulant" brewed and patented in 1886 by Atlanta chemist John Stith Pemberton as an unmistakable sign of the American civilization's irresistible rise, a praise—or accusation—rarely if ever leveled at Coca-Cola's arch-rival Pepsi-Cola. A telltale sign of this ideological distinction between the two brands can be found in the fact that Pepsi was given access to the Soviet and Eastern European markets as early as 1975, a period when the Coca-Cola company was still being treated by Soviet authorities as some supremely sneaky extension of the CIA. In any case, both authors are careful to remind their readers that Coca-Cola did not appear in a vacuum, either ideological or geographical. Although they can hardly dispel the secrecy around the famous Formula X7, they do not entirely yield to its mythology of absolute originality. In fact, our French sixth graders might be greatly perplexed by the reading of these studies; Coca-Cola replicated a beverage popularized in the late nineteenth century, and a French beverage at that. Vin Mariani was a concoction of coca leaf invented in the 1860s by a Corsican turned Parisian, Angelo Mariani (Pendergrast, 1993: 24–25). The product, successfully commercialized in the United States, inspired a number of imitations, including one of Pemberton's early experiments known as French Wine Coca. Although significantly different from alcohol-rich Vin Mariani, Coca-Cola was initially to suffer from this distant parentage: Vin Mariani also contained a much larger quantity of coca leaf derivative than Coca-Cola, which for many years was plagued by accusations that its consumption could lead to chemical dependency.[3] It took years of struggle to convince consumers and potential clients that, to borrow from the first Coca-Cola corporate wizard Asa Candler, "It is not dope! There is no dope in it" (Pendergrast, 1993: 104).

Although the domestic triumph of the brand was almost immediate, the international success of Coca-Cola was long in coming. It is remarkable that roughly two decades after it was introduced in the United States, the product was being commercialized only in a very limited number of neighboring countries such as Canada and Cuba. As far as Europe was concerned, Coca-Cola became a household name mostly after World War I, when corporate giant Robert W. Woodruff, within a climate of economic and political isolationism, boldly created Coca-Cola International in 1923 in an effort to revive a faltering corporation threatened by its perennial competitor Pepsi-Cola (Pendergrast, 1993: 161). Allen submits that Woodruff's corporate acumen in relation to foreign markets is a matter of well-cultivated mythology rather than fact. Some of his initial experiments went terribly awry: in France, for instance, bottling partners R. A. Linton and George Delcroix provided cafés with flawed and unsterilized preparations. As a result, they were on occasion physically confronted by bistro owners (Allen, 1994: 171). In the Netherlands, an unfortunate translation of the promotional slogan "Refresh Yourself with Coca-Cola" actually read "Wash Your Hands with Coca-Cola."[4] Yet Woodruff—who knew that one of the cardinal rules of good management is to know when and to whom to delegate—learned from such mistakes and quickly built a team of efficient and committed European representatives. Those men, fitting their market hand in glove, were to lay the foundations of Coca-Cola's post–World War II expansion.

One such individual was the German Max Keith (pronounced Kite). Keith, a cunning businessman rather than an ideologue, did not hesitate to associate with Nazi dignitaries in order to promote a beverage that was prominently featured at the 1936 Berlin Olympics.[5] In spite of the war, Keith remained successful in his endeavors, managing to keep his factories going by producing an alternative drink, Fanta, today one of the brand's most widely sold products.[6] In the postwar years. Keith successfully sold Coke to the West German populations by utilizing the super-Aryan image of prizefighter Max Schmelling, a former Nazi idol. Such practices, although heavy on the nationalistic component, constituted the blueprint of Coca-Cola's later policies of assimilation of local identities. In like fashion, other Coca-Cola men, little embarrassed by ideological manipulations, spared no effort to sell the drink to devastated European countries as well as in other parts of the world. Their labor came to fruition in the aftermath of World War II as the company further expanded its operations to an additional 76 countries (Allen, 1994: 3).

Regardless of ideologies and propaganda later at work during the Cold War, the fact that the drink literally arrived to many European areas in the wake of U.S. landing barges played no small part in the likening of Coca-Cola's expansion to an American colonization, be it virtual or real. In truth, it would be difficult to separate the silhouette of the World War II GI from his bottle of Coke, a linkage made explicit by Woodruff just a few days after the Japanese attack on Pearl Harbor: "We will see," he is quoted as saying, "that every man in uniform gets a bottle of Coca-Cola for five cents wherever he is and whatever it costs."[7] It was no rare sight to see Coca-Cola "Technical Observers," as their official title went, setting up bottling installations in the immediate aftermath of a military offensive. Unfortunately for the brand, in the same way as the GIs were first warmly welcomed all over Western Europe and then later rejected by the populations they had fought to liberate, Coca-Cola paid a steep price in the 1950s for its more or less voluntary association with American imperialism (Wall, 1991; Kuisel, 1993: 52–69).

During the climactic years of the Cold War, Coca-Cola's image suffered in most European countries a degradation experienced possibly by no other U.S. company: bottling installations were picketed and occasionally sabotaged, delivery trucks vandalized, and employees verbally and sometimes physically victimized. It goes without saying that Eastern European countries were almost completely deprived of their ration of soft drink. Hard to believe now as it may be, Coca-Cola was in the late 1940s and early 1950s considered by many as a kind of concentrated poison responsible for a variety of physical ills, a belief greatly facilitated by the drink's secret formula and unclear origins. Italians, for instance, feared bouts of "Coca-Colitis," and the French were warned of the spawning of a generation of *cocacoliques* (Allen, 1994: 6). In Germany and Austria, scathing pamphlets inspired by Communist propagandists claimed that Coca-Cola was indeed the true "opiate of the masses" (Pendergrast, 1993: 244–245). French Communists, in a rather unnatural alliance with wine growers and water bottlers, tried in 1949–1950 to have the drink banned from the country, suing to have Coca-Cola treated as illegal medication due to the presence of infinitesimal amounts of phosphoric acid among its ingredients.

In all fairness—and it should be noted that this writer never drinks carbonated beverages—it seems obvious that the Europeans' fears had little factual basis either in terms of ideology or chemistry: contrary to popular belief, there is no documented side effect to a normal consumption of the drink; and Coca-Cola's political involvement in the affairs of sovereign states, although it should not be dismissed as entirely insignificant, has always been limited.[8] Allen discusses the lobbying campaign led by Stephen P. Ladas, sent to Makinski as reinforcement from the United States, to stem the tide of anti-Coke resentment in the French political world. A subtle combination of financial and commercial incentives, coupled with veiled threats of retaliation against French products sold in the United States (especially Champagne wines), were used to coerce France's Ministry of Health to pass a special ordinance making Coke acceptable to the French food authorities (Allen, 1994: 8–15). One feels, however, that such practices hardly constituted the hostile takeover of the French economy and government that some feared. As did other Europeans, the French, having other things to worry about, learned to live with the widespread availability of Coca-Cola, a great advantage in times of shortage and rationing. Furthermore, they apparently learned to like it, at least a little.

That Coca-Cola's Western European operations survived such trials speaks highly of its corporate savoir faire and resilience, the same qualities that were again tested in the 1985 "New Coke" affair. Yet Coca-Cola's dealings with Europeans were such that no quick fix could guarantee the brand's success in European countries. Coca-Cola had to instill the love of the product in populations for whom, regardless of ideologies, sweet carbonated beverages meant practically nothing. One could argue that the true reason for France's lack of congruence with the drink was that a fundamentally non-European operation was at work through the beverage, one that took drinking even beyond matters of taste and personal appreciation. It is possible that Europeans first found it difficult to consume Coca-Cola in compliance with the unspoken principle, detailed by Barthes, that in Europe "food has a constant tendency to transform itself into a situation."[9] Barthes argues that in French terms (and the point could be made in respect to a large portion of the Old World), "it is not at the level of its production that the sense of a food item is elaborated, but at the level of the preparation and use" (Barthes, 1979: 169). Coca-Cola shuns the two crucial questions of the preparation and timely consumption of the product: coming from nowhere in particular, it is linked to no specific and identifiable technique of production, and attached to no specific activity. Its consumption was further impaired by its function as a relaxant—one trumpeted by the brand for decades, yet a relatively vague and alien one to European cultures until recently. Generations of Europeans had to grow in the sense of relative comfort and security provided by the 1960s and 1970s before the "Pause that refreshes" could become a relevant concept.

Coca-Cola could not easily be inscribed within the structured and rigid confines of European time and space. In Europe, and especially in France, traditional food products are closely associated to their *terroir*, the unique spatial and human environment that entirely conditions the product's characteristics—specifically the most basic quality of taste. With Coca-Cola, the *terroir* concept appeared as entirely unapplicable.[10] It is a well-known fact that Coca-Cola's origin cannot be allowed to be determined[11] and has to remain not only secret, as the famous Formula 7X, but also vaguely transcendent.[12] Therefore it took more than political pressure and kickbacks to change Europe's opinion about the product. What it took was a systematic and sustained, 20-year campaign to redefine Coca-Cola as a sort of nondenominational product, one whose consumers, instead of toeing the line between nationalism and Americanism, would enter the domain of benevolent and leisurely universalism.

Credit for this should really go to the founding father of Coca-Cola advertisement, William C. D'Arcy. As early as the 1920s, he defined marketing guidelines sufficiently flexible to accommodate local and national idiosyncrasies, a principle later adopted and amplified by Woodruff.[13] The idea that allowed Coca-Cola to gain a significant market share in Europe was the universalization of its image coupled with the company's close association to local capital and production structures. While making Coke everybody's drink instead of a "purely" American drink, the corporation also took advantage of its flexible bottling organization to rely more heavily on national economies. This process did not always occur without glitches: in 1988, for instance, Coca-Cola allied itself with Pernod, France's largest beverage company. In addition to marketing differences, it seems that the alliance with a company closely associated with an alcoholic (and Mediterranean) beverage connoting middle-aged to elderly consumers could not succeed—and the unhappy couple separated.[14]

Although it never concealed its American origin, Coca-Cola had to lose some of its Americanness to become a truly popular product, in the same way that the corporation had domestically downplayed its southern identity. Over the past 20 years Coca-Cola has developed a corporate identity integrating cultural sensitivity and ethnic diversity. This is best illustrated by the attribution of the position of CEO to Cuban-born Roberto Goizueta, a rare occurrence in the American corporate world. In the same manner, the corporation has acknowledged the existence of national tastes, commercializing a number of beverages aimed at satisfying local clienteles: Peach Fanta from Botswana, ginger-flavored Thai Krest, Japanese Mone made with honey, or Paraguayan Simba containing pineapple extracts. In keeping with the famous 1971 "Hilltop Commercial"—a celebration of peace and ethnic harmony—the most recent promotional campaign orchestrated worldwide by the brand with the slogan "Always Coca-Cola, always the real thing" epitomizes this desire to satisfy a universal, totally nondescript consumer who is no more male than female, no more old than young, no more European than North American or Asian. Coca-Cola is sold everywhere to anybody and is therefore endowed with no specific ideological baggage. Rather than "something," it means "everything" or, perhaps, nothing. Such ideas are seminal to the recorded speech delivered by former company president Don Keough to visitors at the Coca-Cola Pavilion, the brand's museum located in downtown Atlanta:

In the final analysis, Coca-Cola doesn't belong to us. It belongs to you, to anyone and to everyone who has ever shared a moment with a Coke . . . . Coca-Cola is so natural to the different cultures and lifestyles in nearly 170 countries round the world. Every day, over a million people worldwide earn their livelihood from Coca-Cola, this simple bit of refreshment . . . . Yes, Coca-Cola is big, very big, but we never lose sight of the fact that Coca-Cola has a very simple purpose, and that it is to offer people of the world a moment out of the day to relax, to enjoy, and to be refreshed.[15]

In Europe, over the years, the implementation of such principles has encountered overall, if variable, success (especially considering that Coca-Cola has always been interested in new "exotic" markets rather than the Old World, where Pepsi's presence has traditionally been strong[16]). In the early 1980s, the opening of a McDonald's restaurant—and therefore a Coke outlet—in Moscow was hailed by many as one of the great successes of Mikhail Gorbachev's *perestroika* and *glasnost*. It was also clearly the triumph of Coke's new identity, one that, after the fall of Communism, warranted a complete opening of Eastern European markets to the brand. In the late 1980s in France, the per person consumption of Coca-Cola, under the guidance of William Hoffman, rose above the 50-drinks-per-year mark. It reached 61 last year, still a lower-end figure as compared with Mexico's 273 drinks a year, and 296 in the United States (Pendergrast, 1993: 411–413). According to the company's 1993 report, Coca-Cola enjoys a comfortable leadership margin in most European countries, especially in France, Great Britain, and Germany.[17] Undoubtedly Coca-Cola has succeeded in finding its own niche not only on the European market but also in the European world and psyche. Yet it could be argued that our French *collégiens* identified Coca-Cola less with an American identity than with a seal of sheer transnational modernity. Coca-Cola does not negate European concerns, ideals, and paradigms; it covers them up and neutralizes them. Whereas Barthes notes that beverages could be ultimately divided into two "Eurocentric" categories according to their metaphysical values, Wine and Milk,[18] the great innovation proposed by Coca-Cola has been to create a supplemental, autonomous, and unique category. From the sign of super-capitalism, Coca-Cola has become more than a drink, a line of drinks, or a firm: it is now synonymous with innocuous (i.e., nonideological) consumption. Could it be said that Coca-Cola is the element that renders Barthesian ideological critique irrelevant? For a simple mixture of sugar and water, that would be quite an achievement.[19]

NOTES

1. For Roland Barthes, sugar—especially in its "soft drink" form—is as much an institution as wine. He adds: "I remember an American hit song: *Sugar Time*. Sugar is a time, a category of the world" (Barthes, 1979: 167).

2. Coca-Cola's 1993 annual report indicates the following per capita consumption in drinks per year for European countries:

		Growth rate (10 years)
Average	32	6%
Norway	238	—
Germany	180	6%
Spain	155	—
Benelux/Denmark	145	7%
France	61	13%
Great Britain	95	13%
Italy	90	9%
Romania	26	—
Poland	23	27%

3. Both Allen (1994) and Pendergrast (1993) detail the company's fight to rid its name from any negative connotation. Pendergrast, however, suggests that Asa Candler slightly altered the original recipe, which may have called for ten times the amount of coca leaf later used in the formula (1993: 89).

4. Pendergrast, 1993: 173. Apparently, worse mistakes were made—such as the original Chinese translation of "Coca-Cola," which meant "Bite the wax tadpole."

5. Cf. Pendergrast's Chapter 13, "Coca-Cola Über Alles" (1993: 218–231). Allen notes that 100,000 cases of Coca-Cola were sold in Germany in 1993 (1994: 246), a tribute to Keith's predecessor, Ray Powers.

6. The sacrifice of the brand name was a matter of pure expediency for Keith; the war made it simply impossible to receive syrup and ingredients from the United States. Pendergrast clearly shows that Keith's fundamental loyalty was to the brand.

7. Watters, 1978: 162. Also see Pendergrast's Chapter 12, "The $4,000 Bottle: Coca-Cola Goes to War" (1993: 199–217).

8. Cf. Frundt, 1987. Also see the last chapters of Watters (1978), in which he discusses Coca-Cola's influence on Georgian, American, and world affairs.

9.

[T]oday, at least in France, we are witnessing an extraordinary expansion of the areas associated with food: food is becoming incorporated into an ever-lengthening list of situations. This adaptation is usually made in the name of hygiene and better living, but in reality, to stress this fact once more, food is also charged with signifying the situation in which it is used. It has a twofold value, being nutrition as well as protocol, and its value as protocol becomes increasingly more important as soon as the basic needs are satisfied, as they are in France. (Barthes 1979: 172)

10.

[Preparation and cooking] have long roots, reaching back to the depth of the French past. They are, we are told, the repository of a whole experience, of the accumulated wisdom of our ancestors. French food is never supposed to be innovative, except when it rediscovers long forgotten secrets. The historical theme, which was so often sounded in our advertising, mobilizes two different values: on the one hand, it implies an aristocratic tradition . . . on the other hand, food frequently carries notions of representing the flavorful survival of an old, rural society that is itself highly idealized. In this manner, food brings the memory of the soil into our very contemporary life . . . . By way of a thousand detours, food permits [the Frenchman] to insert himself daily into his own past and to believe in a certain culinary being of France. (Barthes, 1979: 171)

11. This point parallels that made and belabored by Jean Baudrillard about U.S. civilization. See, for instance, "Utopia Achieved" in *America* (New York: Verso, 1989): "America ducks the question of origins; it cultivates no origin or mythical authenticity; it has no past and no founding truth . . . . It has no ancestral territory . . . . The U.S. is utopia achieved" (76–77).

12. The religious aspects of Coca-Cola, such as its use as the beverage of communion, is well documented by Pendergrast (1993: 400–401). Also see Laurie M. Grossman's article "The Big Problem Is: If They Tell, That Wouldn't Be Kosher, Either," *Wall Street Journal*, 29 April 1992: B1, in which the issue of Coke's compliance with kosher rules is discussed.

13. This is perfectly exemplified by a D'Arcy memo entitled "The Philosophy of Coca-Cola advertising," quoted by Watters (1978: 30): "Because there is never any telling where and when an impulse will take hold on a customer; and because we know that when this impulse does come it will be monetary; it is essential that we confront our customer with the product, well advertised, in as many widely distributed spots as possible . . . . We are interested in both sides of the railroad tracks."

14. Cf. John Rossant and Scott Ticer, "Why Pernod Didn't Go Better with Coke: Coca-Cola Wants Its French Bottler to Surrender Its Franchise," *Business Week* 3057 (June 20, 1988): 64.

15. See also Roberto C. Goizueta, "Globalization, a Soft-Drink Perspective," *Vital Speeches* 55.13 (April 1, 1989): 360–363.

16. See, for instance, Cynthia Mitchell, "Coca-Cola vs Pepsi: Showdown in South Africa," *Atlanta Journal-Constitution*, 4 October 1994: F8.

17. In countries such as Sweden, Italy, Greece, and Austria, Coca-Cola's edge depends on Fanta, not Coke.

18. See *Mythologies* (New York: Hill and Wang, 1972) 58–61. On page 59 he notes: "Wine gives thus a foundation for a collective morality within which everything is redeemed: true excesses, misfortunes and crimes are possible with wine, but never viciousness, treachery or baseness; the evil it can generate is in the nature of fate and therefore escapes penalization, it evokes the theater rather than a basic temperament."

19. In his introduction to Brillat-Savarin's *Physiologie du goût* (Paris: Herman, 1975), Barthes notes (1979: 8–9) that a critical articulation of classical gastronomy, as extolled by

Brillat-Savarin, hinges on the dichotomy between *besoin* (need) and *désir* (desire). It is clear that the consumption of Coca-Cola dislocates these categories. The "pause that refreshes" is caught inbetween this polarity, too unimportant to be needed and too immaterial to be desired.

REFERENCES

Allen, Frederick (1994). *Secret Formula: How Brilliant Marketing and Relentless Salesmanship Made Coca-Cola the Best-Known Product in the World.* New York: HarperBusiness.

Barthes, Roland (1979). "Toward a Psychology of Contemporary Food Consumption." *Food and Drink in History, Selections from the Annales (Economies, Sociêtês, Civilisations),* vol. 5., eds. Robert Forster and Orest Ranum. Baltimore: Johns Hopkins University Press.

Coca-Cola Company (1994). *1993 Annual Report.* Atlanta: Coca-Cola.

Frundt, Henry J. (1987). *Refreshing Pause: Coca-Cola and Human Rights in Guatemala.* New York: Praeger.

Kuisel, Richard F. (1993). *Seducing the French: The Dilemma of Americanization.* Berkeley: University of California Press.

Pendergrast, Mark (1993). *For God, Country and Coca-Cola: The Unauthorized History of the Great American Drink and the Company That Makes it.* New York: Scribner's.

Wall, Irwin M. (1991). *The United States and the Making of Postwar France, 1945–1954.* Cambridge: Cambridge University Press.

Watters, Pat (1978). *Coca-Cola: An Illustrated History.* New York: Doubleday, 1978.

Part V

Social Customs

13 The Barbie Doll

Marianne Debouzy

The appearance of the Barbie doll in 1959, a few years after *Lolita* (1955), marked a turning point in the socialization of little girls and, more generally, in social practices connected with childhood. Hence my interrogations concerning the significance and implications of this change replacing a child doll by a woman doll.

Was this phenomenon absolutely new? Had there been no fashion dolls in the nineteenth and twentieth centuries? One could mention "Bleuette" in France and many others (Theimer, 1985). Thus the Barbie doll might suggest the life cycle of dolls to be a perpetually recurring one—babies succeeding fashion dolls and vice versa. However, Barbie has a number of singular features: her sexy pinup look, her success of over 30 years, the symbolic nature of her persona and worldwide commercialization.

Playing with dolls is a children's game, in a double sense, for it is a game played by children and its object is traditionally a child. It is also an adult's game because the child projects herself in the future as a mother. But Barbie is of indeterminable age, presumably a teenager yet actually a woman. People make no mistake about her bosomy appearance or about the universe built around her, which gives her a clear adult identity. And so we raise the question of the child's relationship to that doll. The little girl does not play the role of mother but of woman. But what kind of woman?

With the Barbie doll, the function of parent vanishes. The girl who plays is no longer supposed to be a mother. In the large "family" that has surrounded Barbie at different times, parents have been totally absent—unlike other products that manufacture families with parents, such as "Dr. John Littlechap."

To understand the significance of the Barbie phenomenon, I will examine the elements of the historical context in which she was born and that are relevant to her persona. I will look into the doll's origins and her status as commodity (who produces her, where, for whom?) and then study her as a toy (shape, physical and technical evolution). By analyzing this character's significance and message, I will decipher *Barbie thought* as an expression of *Barbie culture*.

HISTORICAL CONTEXT

The 1950s witnessed the Cold War, the baby boom, the "affluent society," the "feminine mystique," and the triumph of consumerism. Those were the years when family values such as motherhood and childhood were exploited to the fullest. The commercialization of these values did lend particular importance to one stage of the youth's life cycle—teenage years. The word "teenagers" then gained wide currency, and teenagers acquired visibility through rock music, transistor radios, bobby socks, and hot rods. Teenage culture was commercially exploited as never before, and teenage girls hit the social scene as majorettes, cheerleaders, or prom queens. The big screen glorified two models of female beauty: the voluptuous woman exemplified by Ava Gardner and Heddy Lamar; and the adolescent beauty, not yet a full woman, embodied by such actresses as Debbie Reynolds and Sandra Dee. One could argue that the two types eventually combined into childlike *and* sexy Marilyn Monroe.[1]

Thus, the seductive power of the teenager asserted itself, as could be seen in cinema stars and in the Barbie doll. Her early "activities" were typically those of teenagers: she would babysit, go to the prom, be a cheerleader. Barbie did change over time. In the 1970s she became a student, in the 1980s a career woman. Always she indulged in sports and adopted the latest fashions. However, until recently Barbie remained faithful to the feminine ideal of the 1950s, that is, cut off from any professional activity.

I can add that the baby boom of the 1950s allowed toy manufacturing to expand dramatically and thereby contribute to mass culture. The Barbie doll thus became one of its emblematic products. Until a few years ago, the official story of the doll's creation (still found in some magazines) was that it was designed by Mattel founders Elliott and Ruth Handler for their 13-year-old daughter Barbie, who loved to dress paper dolls. However, the truth came out over ten years ago and turned out to be slightly different. Barbie was plagiarized from Lilli, a German doll first presented at the Munich fair in the early 1950s. Maybe Ruth Handler then purchased the patent (Zinsser, 1964).[2] What is interesting is not so much the suppression of facts, which was necessary to the creation of illusion, as the two-way relationship between Europe and America. American mass culture often drew its inspiration from Europe, but its products and stories have had to be adopted in the United States before being marketed throughout the world.

THE DOLL AS COMMODITY AND TOY

Mattel is one of the largest toy manufacturers in the world. In 1992 it employed 15,000 staff in 24 branches and 8 plants across the world. Initially the Barbie doll was produced in Japan and the United States, then in Third World countries: Malaysia, the Philippines, Korea, Taiwan, the Republic of China, Hong Kong, and Mexico. The main source of Mattel's profit, Barbie is sold in more than 100 countries. The firm, which is based in El Segundo, California, claims to have sold over 700 million Barbies worldwide since 1959. This doesn't include the millions of accessories—bags, clothes, shoes—that go with the doll. According to Mattel, little girls in the United States own an average of seven Barbie dolls each. French girls age 3 to 11 owned an average of two in the 1980s but reportedly an average of five in the 1990s. All records seem to have been broken in France in 1993, with 4.5 million dolls sold.[3]

Some collectors reportedly possess 5,000 or even 11,000 different Barbies. From these figures one might infer the existence of a multitude of dolls. In fact, there is one basic model, one and the same doll in different attires. The 11.5 inch, anatomically incorrect plastic figurine (Motz, 1983: 128–129), "a perpetually pubescent girl," "with a pert bust line, shapely hips and well-turned calves,"[4] had a facelift in 1967. Her face has grown softer, her limbs have lost their original stiffness, and in recent years she has even learned to speak. As advertised in 1992, the Teen Talk Barbie could utter four sentences selected out of 270 programmable ones. One of the sentences—"Math class is tough"—aroused the ire of feminists and math teachers and was later suppressed. Until 1990, the only doll advertised on television was white, although a black doll had been available since 1967. Asian and Third World dolls have since appeared, but they are usually westernized ethnic dolls.

Mattel has produced a number of dolls that are presented in the fan press and advertised as Barbie's family and friends: Barbie's boyfriend Ken (1961), her best friend Midge (1963), her little sister Skipper, and her "modern" cousin Francie, among others. The circle of friends widened in the 1970s and narrowed afterwards. Simultaneously, a number of dolls based on fashion models, television stars, and Miss America (1972) also appeared.

BARBIE CULTURE

Barbie's birth was accompanied by the creation of a universe not only peopled with other dolls but replete with objects, accessories, and equipment of all kinds—from roller skates to computers, not to mention hula hoops, makeup kits, swimming pools, yachts, and a variety of pets.

Fan clubs and even Barbie Block Clubs were also created. In 1963, Barbie's fan mail amounted to 10,000 letters every week. *Barbie Magazine* posted 100,000 subscribers. In 1982, Mattel-France started a fan club that soon claimed a membership of 300,000. The point was made quite clearly by a Mattel executive: "Our goal is to use this formidable tool—personalized mail—to capture our customers. 300,000 for a start . . . . They constitute a privileged target for our products."[5]

For years now, ads, television shows, films, videos, CDs, the press, and the media have made Barbie a "superstar" and created a Barbie culture that inspires children's play. Mattel has always endeavored to promote the image of Barbie as a real person. The introduction to the postcard booklet *Forever Barbie* describes her as follows: "She is devoted to family and friends . . . . She has never been fickle. Barbie and Ken have been devoted sweethearts since 1961."[6] Barbie's "biography" is a succession of professional activities: "Barbie has always worked for a living. As a baby- and teen-model . . . as an airline stewardess, an entrepreneur. More recently, she has been a commercial airline pilot, a physician and a rock star . . . . Barbie has also signed up for military duty as an Air Force pilot, a Navy chief petty officer and an Army captain." This type of discourse, relatively recent, is a response to detractors who condemned Barbie's life-style as a typically consumer-oriented, leisure-class type. One passage from the introduction particularly deserves to be cited: "In 1967 while the United States struggled with racial integration, Barbie took a bold step. One year before President Johnson and the Civil Rights Act, she became the first doll to have a black friend, Francie. The following year, Mattel introduced Christie, another black friend, with racially correct features." Surprisingly, Mattel never made up scenarios of the Freedom Rides and Selma March in which Barbie had the lead.

Another important element in the doll's "humanization" is her family—not that constituted by other dolls, but her "genuine" family. In the mythical account of their creation, Barbie, Ken, and Skipper were identified with the Mattel founders' children, whose names the dolls received. Still, much more than Mattel, psychologists, doctors, and teachers have contributed to endowing Barbie with the status of a person. They have lent her a power, an influence that one would associate with a real human being rather than with a piece of plastic. This was especially true in the years that followed Barbie's appearance. During a 1964 medical symposium on teenagers, Dr. Alan F. Leveton, chief of family therapy at Mount Zion Hospital, remarked: "Barbie-instigated problems already harass the therapists here." Psychologists and doctors accused Barbie of making little girls anorexic in their desire to look like her. Educators also deemed it disquieting that "this teener in training shoves tots into the world of bras, girdles, dating dresses and teenage marriages."[7] A late 1960s Mattel survey showed that the average age of girls playing with Barbie had fallen from 10 to 6. Today the average age seems even younger. Barbie's popularity with very young children raises questions: What does it mean to be a little girl in U.S. society? Are there still little girls in such a society? Some commentators harbored doubts as early as the 1960s: "Most girls think of Barbie 6 or 7 years older than themselves, which puts her anywhere from 12 to 18. But she dresses 21 and up—a symbol of the American urge to hurry our children into the trappings of adulthood, if possible eliminating their youth altogether" (Zinsser, 1964). For another it was clear: "Barbie, Ken and three doll associates have been designed for little girls who hate to be little" (Bess, 1965: 26).

The question as to whether Barbie invites little girls to become precocious teenagers or even adults actually raises another, more fundamental one: Does Barbie have an influence, and of what sort, over children? A widely accepted idea seems to be that Barbie is a role model. This notion refers to a very "personalized" view of the way in which individuality is constructed. You will become what other people have been before you by imitating them in their social role. But beside the fact that the notion of role is problematic, such a view is all the more simplistic because it fails to take into account the complex web of social, economic, and personal realities that go into the makeup of an individual. It reduces the process of growing up to a sort of model-copying. As to what kind of model Barbie provides, consensus is lacking, even among feminists.

According to Mattel-France, the "strength of the Barbie doll" is "to embody the physical and moral ideal of America and western culture." No less. In a more recent statement, Mattel claims that, "While it is true that Barbie is fashion-conscious, she also has been a very positive role model—and in many ways a leader." The radical critics of the 1960s stressed that the content of the role had been defined by Mattel Corporation: "The children . . . grow up with Mattel-made expectations . . . . The company wants the little girl to grow up to be a big-spending, busy, powerful, frigid woman" (Bess, 1965: 26–27).

It was precisely for her role as consumer and sex object that feminists criticized Barbie in the 1960s and 1970s. Barbie's gospel is "conspicuous consumption," the acquisition of material goods that are socially valued—mostly fashionable clothes liable to make one "popular." In this perspective, Barbie's many "friends" assume a new significance, reminiscent of David Riesman's analysis of sociability in the consumer society: "Making good becomes almost equivalent to making friends." When popularity or acceptance by one's peers becomes one's main goal in life, "people and friendships are viewed as the greatest of all consumables: the peer group is itself a main object of consumption."[8] For Marilyn Ferris Motz, the creation of Barbie and her friends allowed children to buy themselves "a peer group," "to collect friends literally."

The Ken doll shows how far the instrumentalization of human relationships can go. All comments, whether favorable—"Barbie, the ideal teenager, sexy but innocent"[9]—or not—"Barbie presents a smoothed-over version of the female anatomy, clearly designed to titillate rather than to provide sexual satisfaction to herself or Ken" (Motz, 1983: 129)—make it clear that nothing has ever happened between the two. Ken is nothing but one more accessory: "If you go to a party, you need a masculine touch. That's about all that Ken provides," concluded a *Ramparts* journalist (Bess, 1965: 26–27).

Finally, Barbie's message, in Motz's words, is to "be rich, be beautiful, be popular and above all have fun" (Motz, 1983: 129). Yet her message is not deciphered in the same way by everyone. Today, some feminists defend the Barbie doll, claiming with Mattel that she has had a positive role. Should we take it as a sign of the times that Barbie fans who became grown feminists contend that the "Barbie persona was a woman of power who, even at her most generous, never deferred to Ken?" According to some feminists, she was "a truly revolutionary doll, one that inspired, rather than oppressed, young girls' imaginations" (Cordes, 1992).

Such are some of today's comments, but do they tell us anything about the actual influence of the doll? How do we know what use children make of dolls and what impact they have on their adult lives? Do children enact the suggestions of *Barbie Magazine* or follow the scenarios presented by Mattel? It is difficult to answer the question; anyhow, the answer is probably yes *and* no. Investigations conducted by educators and anthropologists suggest that Barbie's packaged stories do guide the games of children, but the children also make up their own stories (Batté, 1987; Brougère, 1992).[10] If any object can be turned into a toy, any toy can be diverted from its expected use.

The problem is that the packaged stories and the world created around Barbie embody values and models glorified by the media and advertising and omnipresent in society. All this most likely shapes children's imaginations and channels doll games in given directions. The anthology *Mondo Barbie* provides comforting testimonies, however; the ways of using, misusing, and diverting Barbie from her expected uses seem innumerable. One can reasonably hope that there remain many a corner of children's imagination that have not yet been Mattel-ized.

CONCLUSION

One can only admire Mattel's marketing skills, its sense of public relations and media power, its clever presentation of Barbie as a person. Not to mention its capacity to co-opt all fads, including the most advanced ones. Barbie is always "in"; thus, Mattel can go from cross-dressing to cross-selling to gender-bending! Yet is this enough to explain *barbiedollism*, the enduring success of Barbie and her emblematic character?

Now a world-famous star, Barbie has acquired social significance through accessories, garments, equipments, and all the showy bric-à-brac that surrounds her. She has become a popular heroine thanks to the scenarios devised by Mattel. In order to turn children into consumers, modern fairy tales must be told. Mattel is a toy manufacturer and a teller of tales on a world scale. Big Brother is also Big Mother. However, Mother Mattel has replaced Mother Goose. And the firm intends to retain exclusive control over these stories, as an anecdote reported in the April 3, 1993, *San Francisco Chronicle* shows:

For some months, a San Anselmo psychic named Barbara Bell has been getting in touch with Barbie's spiritual essence. She ran an ad in a psychic magazine, offering to answer letters on the doll's behalf at $3 per.

Two hundred letters poured in. Barbie replied on pink stationery, sweetly and sagely. Barbie says don't worry, everything will work out, love your neighbor. Sincerely yours, Barbie.

Now, it seems, it must all end.

"Your use of the Barbie name may adversely affect the wholesome, positive, family-oriented image of Barbie," said a two-page letter from Mattel headquarters in Southern California. 'We demand that you immediately discontinue." . . .

There is no room for compromise, said the Mattel people. "Barbie does not dabble with the occult thing," said spokeswoman Donna Gibbs. "Channeling and the occult are not what Barbie is about. She is a toy for children. I don't believe you can speak for a doll."

But you're speaking for a doll, aren't you?

"That's different."[11]

This story is revealing. In recent years, the Barbie doll has occupied a particular position in U.S. society. What makes her such a presence that one can invoke her spirit? Why does she arouse such consuming passions? A man whose collection of Barbie dolls had been stolen exclaimed: "They meant everything to me. I could do without eating. I don't know if I can live without them."[12] Some women are known to have identified with Barbie to the point of undergoing painful surgery to look exactly like her. Why are so many people so fascinated by a doll as to fancy it is a person? Does this tell us something about a world in which human beings are treated increasingly like pieces of plastic? The triumph of Mattel's marketing is the triumph of make-believe. The typical product of the celluloid universe was the star—that of the plastic era is the Barbie doll. Significantly, marketing specialists argue that the Barbie doll is a substitute for "absent partners," the unborn siblings of the mother who has left home. In short, we live more and more in a universe of substitutes.

I started by saying that the appearance of Barbie was a turning point in the socialization of little girls. Indeed, it was a "revolution" in the concept of childhood; it tended to eliminate the latter by rushing children into the world of adults and casting them as future buyers and potential consumers. The Barbie "revolution" was also that of a society less and less capable of distinguishing between make-believe and actuality. Born in the 1950s and still triumphant in the 1990s, the Barbie doll is just another one of those monstrosities produced by the imaginings of a social order that generates fabrications of all sorts.

There have been worse cultural catastrophes than the Barbie doll. But when we look at things through her eyes, we can only conclude that the *barbiedollization* of the world is well on its way.

NOTES

This chapter was first presented in French at the May 1993 FAAS conference "Popular Culture in the United States." All similarities between the ideas expressed by M. Debouzy and those of M. G. Lord's book *Forever Barbie* (1994) are therefore purely coincidental.

1. Lois Banner, *American Beauty* (Chicago: University of Chicago Press, 1983) 283–284.

2. See also Boy, 1987.

3. Elisabeth Chambard, "Barbie chérie" [Darling Barbie], *Le Progrès de Lyon*, 24 December 1993.

4. James Stern and Michael Stern, *The Encyclopedia of Bad Taste* (New York: HarperCollins, 1990) 32.

5. Quoted in Philippe Gavi and Isabelle Lefort, "Barbie, guest star du marketing," *Le Nouvel Observateur*, 19 January 1989: 59.

6. All quotations in the rest of this paragraph are excerpted from this introduction.

7. "The Barbie Doll Set," *Nation*, 24 August 1964: 407.

8. Quotations from Motz, 1983: 129–135. For more information, see Riesman et al. on sociability and the friendship market in the U.S. in David Riesman, Nathan Glazer, Reuel Denney, *The Lonely Crowd* (New York: Doubleday-Anchor, 1950, 1953) 316–319. "The Denial of Sociability."

9. Mattel-France corporate pamphlet, 19–20. For more information, inquire Mattel France (SA). Fabricants de Jouets, 64 av. Victoire BP 23, 94310 Orly.

10. My thanks to Nathalie Batté for communicating to me her interesting thesis.

11. My thanks to Doris and Charles Muscatine for bringing this article to my attention.

12. Carol Masciola, "Stolen 5,000 Barbies, Unplayed With," *International Herald Tribune*, 15 October 1992.

REFERENCES

Batté, Nathalie (1987). "La poupée Barbie et le jeu des enfants" [The Barbie doll and children's play]. Unpublished master's thesis, Department of Anthropology, University of Paris X–Nanterre.

Bess, Donovan (1965). "Barbie and Her Friends." *Ramparts*, April.

Boy, Billy (1987). *Barbie: Her Life and Times*. New York: Crown.

Brougère, Gilles (ed.) (1992). *Le Jouet, Valeurs et paradoxes d'un petit objet secret* [Toys: Values and paradoxes of little secret objects]. Paris: Autrement.

Cordes, Helen (1992). "What a Doll! Barbie: Materialistic Bimbo or Feminist Trailblazer?" *Utne Reader*, March–April: 46–50.

Ebersole, Lucinda, and Richard Peabody (eds.) (1993). *Mondo Barbie*. New York: St. Martin's Press.

Faure, Michel (1985). "Barbie, la blonde et l'Amérique" [Barbie: The blonde and America]. *Libération*, 2 April: 22–23.

Forever Barbie: A Postcard Book (1991). Philadelphia: Running Press.

Hoffmann, Frank W., & William G. Bailey. (1994). "The Barbie Doll." Hoffmann and Bailey, *Fashion & Merchandising Fads*. New York: Harrington Park–Haworth Press, 27–29.

Lord, M. G. (1994). *Forever Barbie: The Unauthorized Biography of a Real Doll*. New York: Morrow.

Motz, Marilyn Ferris (1983). " 'I Want to Be a Barbie Doll When I Grow Up': The Cultural Significance of the Barbie Doll." *Popular Culture Reader*, eds. D. Geist and J. Nachbar. Bowling Green, OH: Popular.

Theimer, François (1985). *Barbie, une poupée de collection* [Barbie, a collectible doll]. Paris: Polichinelle.

Zinsser, William K. (1964). "Barbie Is a Million Dollar Doll." *Saturday Evening Post*, 12 December: 73.

14 Serial Heroes: A Sociocultural Probing into Excessive Consumption

Robert Conrath

Shopping is more American than thinking.
"What are you taking with you, Jeffrey?" "Oh you know, a toothbrush,
underwear, a heart, shoes, a liver, deodorant, a few fingers, mouthwash . . . "
(from *The Law of Remains: The Story of Jeffrey Dahmer*.
A play by Reza Abdoh, first performed in Los Angeles in 1992)

In light of the late twentieth-century American social practices, the most "barbaric" and, I shall argue, most "apocalyptic" form of extreme behavior and its media-consumer iconization, *serial killing* has become a sort of "sewage-farm" for everything that has gone awry in the postmodern American world. In order to justify the culture-specific premises of my argument, however, I shall conclude my explorations by juxtaposing them with the transcultural horizons of acceptance and rejection of violent cultural representations outside the United States. As counterexample to the serial killer–celebrity, I have chosen someone who is very much his antithesis and has found his home *away from home*: the loser antihero of the American *roman noir*/crime fiction.

Because a swath of European examples is likely to muddy the already turbulent waters of late twentieth-century popular culture, I shall concentrate on the case of France. Cross-cultural analysis is that much more enlightening as we move stealthily and surely forward to a fully global market economy, one in which the lines of cultural demarcation, high and low, national and universal, dominant and marginal, are blurred continually.

Culture is at its most tenacious when it remains flexible. American popular culture in Europe has a long and very tumultuous history, and many forms and practices have never taken hold on the Continent because they don't correspond to any emerging—indigenous or artificially imposed—sociocultural space. Some objects of mass consumption on the other hand have not only been adopted (and often to the incomprehension of Americans: the success of Jerry Lewis in France is a prime example), but they have also been transformed in order to accommodate needs inherent in their country of adoption. By looking at these two examples, I hope to be able to show why one of them remains "despairingly American," whereas the other has received its letters of noblesse in France.

SACRIFICE IN AMERICA

Since the beginning of the twentieth century, the phenomenon of serial killing appears to have shifted almost entirely to the United States. Scant documentation, and a press essentially limited to urban centers, make it difficult to calculate its importance prior to the twentieth century.[1] But what will become startlingly clear is that the convergence of an advanced free market capitalist economy, and the escalation of mass media and the culture industry, have made our awareness of (and therefore interest in) serial killing much more acute over the last 20 years. I shall argue that these factors have also to some extent been responsible for the increase in actual cases.

The United States houses just over 5 percent of the world's population and yet 75 percent of its serial killers. Protestant mother England, home to grandaddy Jack the Ripper, follows a very distant second and Germany is third. *Hunting Humans: The Encyclopedia of Serial Killers* (Newton, 1993) the most complete compendium of its kind, lists 295 major cases of serial killing (generally four or more murders) for the United States in the twentieth century. England and Germany together account for only 47. France is a very distant fourth (after Canada), with only seven major killers listed. In order to throw light on the inflated discrepancy between the United States and Western European countries, I think it best to first analyze in some detail the reasons why serial killing has become such a specifically American practice.

We have been aware for some time now of the escalating obsessions that Americans have with their more extreme forms of violent behavior, but we rarely question the underlying structures of the marketing strategies involved. What sociohistorical factors have made this such a lucrative and popular endeavor in the first place, and what corresponding public *mise en scène* has been responsible for its cultural mapping?

The obsessive affliction of course strikes both sides of the Atlantic to some extent. The fascination with America's fascination with the darker corners of its subconscious is hardly a recent affair. The hinterlands of the American psyche reached France in the middle of the nineteenth century via Baudelaire's translations of Poe. And 70 years later, when the first hardboiled crime novels were translated, the French reading public was fully accustomed to the world of American barbarism that the serial killer so apocalyptically manifests today. Yet the latter's near-celebrity status elicits more perplexity than affinity from abroad. Do we here in Europe risk falling into the same media-culture-industry traps, or are we protected by history and cultural difference?

The thresholds for tolerance to violence in America have, to borrow Stuart Hall's expression (Hall, 1978: 225), been pushed unrelentingly forward over the last few decades for reasons that are both real and imaginary. Because both primitive sacrificial drives and today's cybernetic virtual realities, serialized worldviews, and behavior are at play, the story of our serial killer is a narrative of multiple meanings. The omnipresence of television and video as testimony to public confession have conditioned the readability of such extreme phenomena, and the unbridled consumption-ethos and "trash for cash" tabloid deontology of the 1980s has made this communal bloodthirst marketable.

Violent crime is culturally foregrounded, a sociohistorical construct that takes on as many forms as there are social groups to commit it. Statistics bear out vast differences in how one social matrix or another acts on its violent impulses and what forms of control and punishment are implemented to curtail them. Does it murder its children, stone its adulterous wives, kill with submachine guns or with knives, execute its perpetrators, or try to reform them? More important, how does a given society choose to *represent* and to *talk about* these crimes?

As we move into an information-saturated global market economy today, with "televised reality" dictating our lives, crime has increasingly become a struggle for "image ratings." Symbolic domination and its attendant "knowledge" are conferred almost solely through the "visual"; and the epistemological slip that has occurred due to the proliferation of "reality television" and the rapid blurring of traditional distinctions between "real news" and "fictional representations" has brought the *real* seat of power to the image-making industries. Image powerbrokers define and redefine almost daily the media representations and forms of discourse that will contain the criminal act. They also master the simulacra of crime; and s/he who, according to Warhol, can lay claim to his/her fifteen minutes of fame on the screen legitimizes his/her existence, and is temporarily empowered.

The breakneck speed at which we in Europe watch the progressive slide of America toward these omnipotent but fleeting visual realities has raised innumerable questions concerning the role they play in our own production of violent crime. Is there any hope of resisting violent *virtual* domination short of resorting to reactionary backlashing of the type that has surfaced in the United States?[2] I believe so, but hope rides on the possibilities of renewed critical discourse and not on the apparent inevitability of increased censorship.

TABLOID HERO

The production of criminal superstars is a timeless preoccupation for the American public. U.S. history has been punctuated with what Paul Kooistra refers to as "social bandits," violent Robin Hood–style do-gooders who have surfaced during times of social strife and crisis, and who, acting out their constitutional rights as "individuals," have been integrated into the social discourse as popular catalysts for rebellion. Jesse James and Billy the Kid, Butch Cassidy, and more recently Patty Hearst, Charles Manson, or Bernard Goetz the subway vigilante—all have reached stardom by violently representing disenfranchised or frustrated segments of the population.

But the late 1980s saw the iconization and superstar status of a different kind of violent anti-hero individual: often suburban, middle-class, with an above-average IQ (Bourgoin, 1993; Noris, 1989), and largely gratuitous in his motives, the serial killer hit tabloid headlines with an egotistical mandate whose money-grubbing corollary was the megalomaniacal likes of Donald Trump and Michael Milken. Brett Easton Ellis's scandalous *American Psycho* (1991) brought the two together in Patrick Bateman, a Wall Street yuppie–serial killer.[3]

The idea of what constitutes an emancipated individual is of course sociocul-turally dependent. The subject qua individual is constructed from the stuff of a given society and its forms of institutionalized social behavior. With the rise of savage, freewheeling capitalism at the end of the last century, and the implemen-tation of social Darwinism, the "free individual" who was no longer shackled to government or master became one of the most cherished icons of American de-mocracy. The translation from the context of "lone avenger" (an individual who defies centralized, alienating, and unjust powers and is pivotal to that great Amer-ican tradition of puritan autonomy, manifest in doxic *ideologemes* such as "every man for himself," "the right to bear arms," "the defense of private property," "the best government is the one that governs the least"), to a French social and political context wherein class divisions, omnipotent government, and Voltairian ideals of tolerance and individual liberty are juggled with "the common good" in the social unconscious, means that when confronted with a marginal, extreme manifestation of the individual such as the serial killer, we are rarely speaking of *the same individual*. The myth of the individual is the backbone of the great American experiment—what Walt Whitman referred to as "the destiny of me."

Ironically and perhaps tragically, this particular individual today increasingly reflects the principles of mass reproduction, and not the mythical autonomy for which Americans once fought so hard.

RANDOM SERIALS

The serial killer is the perfect structural mimesis of a television serial mentality, a figure who has escaped from the American television subconscious. He offers the same structure with different variables each time he kills. Once this series is over, once Jeffrey Dahmer (the Milwaukee cannibal) or Ted Bundy (the co-ed killer) has been caught, we know that the newspapers, and then the studios, will come up with another series built along the same intrigues, the same storyline, with new characters, new horrors.

Yet the *seriality* of the serial killer is veiled under a much more attractive and deceiving form: random action. The function of a serial is to make one believe in its novelty, its random appearance. The apparent irrationality of actions and arbitrary choice of victims belies a very logical, linear, and fetishistic impulse in the serial killer (he chooses redheads, brunettes, Asian boys). He works in a very defined pattern that usually only becomes clear months, sometimes years, later.

This reflects the art of channel-surfing, nothing more than a tired and perversely cynical attempt to impose difference and randomness on a series of objects, actions, narratives that are all structurally similar. If television is a sort of serialized superego that reflects our hopelessly linear cultural stasis, then the serial killer, who functions in the same mode of repetition, is the most logical, dysfunctional, psychotic extreme of which we, serialized victims, are capable.

Yet each murderer thrives on his *apparent* uniqueness, on his absolutely personalized, fetishistic, ritualistic *mise à mort*. His is a desperate cry for recognition as an authentic individual in a democratic society where mass-produced egos continually bear down on the struggling, fragile subject. And what is a celebrity in the postmodern world but the reconciliation of mass production and uniqueness? Madonna, the artist formerly known as Prince, and Michael Jackson all point the way to this single aberration in the assembly-line production of persona. Individuality and its eventual transgression of the masses can nowhere be better attained than in the suppression of "the other," the one who continually reminds you of your tragic, mediocre role as interchangeable extra. Genet, de Quincey, and de Sade all understood that killing, as an aesthetic and creative act, sets one off from the sloppy, banalized action of the common man.

CONSUMING, COLLECTING, AND METONYMY

The serial killer has a disquietingly banal, self-effacing profile. He looks like everyone else who hangs out at the mall. He is the ur-American whose id has flipped out. Serial killing is not the expression of deeply suppressed underclass rage, complete social alienation, or even acute schizophrenia, but usually a *vital* (both visceral and at times intellectual) drive to kill, an uncontrollable pleasure that—like any uncontrollable pleasure—thrives on repetition. The case of recently executed John Wayne Gacy is exemplary. He had been married, lived in the suburbs, had a bad haircut, and could have been *everyman's* uncle. Over 30 dismembered bodies were discovered in a crawl space underneath his middle-class bungalow.

These criminals give a subjective clarity to what has become an increasingly dysfunctional project: the American dream, freedom of the individual to shop as he or she pleases. Serial killers stalk their victims like they shop for clothing, with a discerning eye for the subtle differences between generic products that make one of them special, unique. They represent "gone shopping" gone awry in a day and age when shopping has become a personal quest for authentication.

The serial killer consumes his victims radically. He is an insatiable collector; and as Baudrillard has pointed out in *L'Echange symbolique et la mort* (1976), the collector perpetually lacks the one object that will complete his collection. He will never find it, of course, because all his meaning is derived from his lack. For the serial killer, the perfect victim is always only perfect as long as pleasure, always ephemeral (the time of an orgasm, say), is able to last.

Collecting is a very particular and highly codified form of twentieth-century consumption, and the serial killer is a postmodern manifestation of popular-consumer-collecting-culture at its most extreme. He consumes his collection in the worst possible way; not metaphorically—for example, eating the corpses as communion—but rather metonymically, taking all of his meaning and expressing his sense and continuity of self through a series of bodies as linear accumulation. *Body-objects* are linked together and just as quickly replaced. The more bodies and the more body parts he can enumerate, the more authentic he becomes and the longer he can stave off his return to nothingness. The parts have no meaning outside of the series. One ritualistic killing becomes meaningful only insofar as it is related to another and another and yet another. This is exactly how the serial mind works and how much of contemporary mass-popular culture is sold. It is the structural raison d'être of the vast majority of television too, and the serial killer taps into it with ease.

American Psycho's Patrick Bateman consumes his victims in the same way he consumes cocaine: in as large quantities as possible and at whatever the cost. His obsessive accumulation of *hardbodies* and Armani suits reference each other in much the same way as his corpses and his coke do. Outside the chain, a vacuum of meaning.[4]

TELEVISION, THE BIG SCREEN, AND THE EPISTEMOLOGICAL SLIP

One of the most glaring tenets of postmodern popular culture is the collapsing together of the traditional epistemological categories of fact and fiction, veracity and verisimilitude. The idea that the two are solidly intertwined increases tenfold the media attention focused on an extreme social phenomenon such as serial murder. The case of Jeffrey Dahmer the Milwaukee cannibal and Hannibal the Cannibal Lecter, protagonist of the box-office hit *The Silence of the Lambs*, one real and one fictional, is worth mentioning. In 1991, while *The Silence of the Lambs* was consuming the box office, Jeffrey Dahmer's little house of horrors was discovered. The two indisputably fed off each other. Articles started appearing in which the relative merits of the two stars were compared, and people began speaking of them in the same breath. They both suddenly inhabited the same discursive space. They were both terrifyingly (*virtually*) real.

The socio-discursive matrix that holds, molds, and subsequently defines how we relate to and process this information—and more important, how we talk about these events—has now been collapsed into one. There has been a total epistemological leveling.

American popular culture has always been visceral, the lingua franca for a country of immigrants. Violence became its grammar, the rules and common denominator that every one could relate to on the most basic level. But it began as a unique, thoughtful, necessary, and "fictional" violence. What has happened over the last 15 years is that television has usurped that grammar, and the critical-fictional distance once so necessary to purge forms of social violence, the *big* screen, the public ritual, has been closed. Television has rendered all violent acts indistinguishable. It invades our private space, the space that we once returned to in order to digest. The serial killer is a product of the pervasive penetration of media technology and televised representations into our daily lives, into the intimacy of our bedrooms, our dreams, our language. At the same time, violence has lost its cathartic value; it no longer exists as a mediating apparatus for filtering out and deciphering the message. It has become, echoing McLuhanites everywhere, the message itself.

Television's virtual reality places the viewer in a simulated world of death and destruction from which he escapes only by having totally incorporated this "second reality" into his/her own "real" world. The serial killer, as he is propelled into this "fictional" reality, represents this simulated gesture, a totally epistemological crossover. He is everyman, the one you watch television with, the one you *virtually* are.

Yet it is interesting to note that two of the most potent critiques of this social mishap came to us from Europe in 1992: the Austrian video-film by Michael Haneke *Benny's Video*,[5] and the cult Belgian independent film *Man Bites Dog* (*C'est arrivé près de chez vous*).

Benny's Video is the story of a young, alienated, bourgeois teenager who spends his days editing home videos and who, very nonchalantly, one day kills a girl while taping the event. His parents discover the video and proceed to "make the body disappear." After all, a body exists solely as evidence of a video, which itself is only *virtually* real. Moral dilemmas are removed when the real has become its own image. Meanwhile, the *other* has been reduced to virtual status—almost real—real enough to simulate orgasm, but completely reified as *human other*. Is it therefore of any great surprise that necrophilia often plays such an important role in serial killer activity?

Man Bites Dog is a black-and-white docu-parody that follows, with a hand-held camera, the amusing and then not-so-amusing trials and tribulations of an amateur serial killer as he progressively implicates his "objective" camera crew in the slaughter. The point at which voyeur becomes participant is hard to pin down, but a total meltdown occurs during the gang-rape and murder of an immigrant woman and her husband. What we experience as viewers is the invisible-nightmare crescendo wherein our appallingly naive presuppositions of objective truth suddenly implicate, through video participation, our subjectivity, the last refuge for distance from the act, for critical thought. It is a poignant commentary not only on the contemporary crisis of reality but also on the long-held suppositions that evil is always *other*. It has now, thanks to the infinite possibilities of *virtualizing* our fantasies and horror, become us. Rimbaud's famous "*Je est un autre*" has now become "*Je sont les médias.*"[6] What better figure to emblematize the banalized seriality of contemporary evil than you, the "guy next door," serial killer. Me.

THE SPECTACLE OF THE CULTURE INDUSTRY AND THE FEAR OF GENESIS

The media events surrounding the tracking and capture of each of these monsters (the serials killers) are viable means of avoiding more pressing political issues in America. It is much more exciting (and strangely comforting) to listen to the gory tales of Jeff "the Chef" Dahmer's necrophagist habits or John Wayne Gacy's crawl space than it is to the daily barrage of drive-by shootings and overdoses in the ghetto, particularly when the latter demand a concern for the history, context, and genesis of the event.

What has turned the serial killer into a Hollywood commodity-spectacle is that his life has been reduced to a densely packed, two-hour feast of necrology, torture, and death; his life has become a brief spectacle whose sense is derived entirely from its interchangeability and its inevitability, its potentially random serialization and *not* the uniqueness of its narrative. In a word, there is no genesis.[7] When everything is now cause for spectacle, spectacle becomes meaningless.

In the film *Henry, Portrait of a Serial Killer*,[8] censored when it first came out and critically vilified by the tabloid press, the most frightening fact is that *there is no spectacle*. Death occurs in the most perfunctory and ugly of fashions without any of the elaborate "heroic" antics we have grown to expect in the serial killer anti-hero à la Hannibal Lecter. Henry is a loser, existentially adrift in a world of anonymous nomads all trying to somehow legitimize or, at the very least, bleakly manifest their existence. At the end of the film, Henry drives off. No morals, no closure in *this* world. What Henry is trying to say is that he kills therefore he is. The film has become a cult classic in France. The radical nihilism that surges through its characters has nothing of interest to the average American viewer, weaned on criticism-free spectacle.[9]

FROM *SERIE NOIRE* TO SERIAL KILLER

It was precisely this emptiness, which the American crime novel of the 1940s and 1950s expressed so well, that fascinated the postwar French intelligentsia. Not only was the genre adopted in France, but it was essentially legitimized. Its literary and social mandates were quite the opposite of those that characterize the serial killer today.

The American *roman noir*/crime novel (whose protagonist was usually a criminal, but sometimes a private eye) was seen by its French reader as a beacon of counter-discourse, as a genre that had somehow slipped through the hegemonic net of the American dream, the Horatio Alger stories and the Norman Rockwell paintings, baseball and barbecues. It was a genre, the consequence of years of depression and prohibition and war, that had produced a profoundly critical vision of the violent American *Weltanschauung*, a real foil to the ethical and political hegemony of the new, powerful, self-assured dreamland of Disney's postwar America. Under the floorboards, they seemed to be saying, was a despairing, dichotomous social reality. The American dream was the American illusion for many.

A good number of these novels were read in France with a political mandate in mind: capitalism and violence make good, perhaps even inescapable, bedmates. In the bleak pulp worlds of Jim Thompson and David Goodis, Left Bank intellectuals were able to extract a dark "existentialist" vision of the world, a world of losers and loners perpetually set upon by "the system." The "series" of the *série noire* was an ironic nod to the culture industry's "mechanical reproduction of art." One would never confuse Jim Thompson and David Goodis with Coca-Cola and Westinghouse. Their "serialization" in the *série noire* was merely an attempt to highlight the alienated world that *mechanical man* was living (or perhaps more to the point, dying) in, while the capitalist consumption ethos ran wild.

"America hates a loser." The best and most critically potent writers of the American *roman noir* were novelists whose books are littered with has-beens making one last stab at social insertion, victims of society, yet these characters have never entered the *collective* imagination as representatives of anything vaguely American. Their works were popular during the 1950s and 1960s in the United States because of their loosely veiled sexuality and graphic violence, in much the same way as the serial killer (with new levels of tolerance) is today. Taken at the first degree with a purely sensationalist and visceral reading, the deeper critical representations of a highly manichean economic and political structure that transformed poverty and social marginalization into components of evil were lost. Once their thrill value had been exhausted, they were worthless. French critics and intellectuals read further and extracted an indictment of American capitalist society from the blood and the alcohol that ran through the pages. These novels were critical catalysts in the war against the rich, and most of them have never been out of print in France.

The serial killer as he is portrayed on the other hand is the manifestation of a reactionary politics of consumption and nomadic independence. His has become a story of power, a story of brains and brawn and autonomous, serialized, antiauthoritarianism. In his story, the victim has no biography and only exists as a brief moment, a narrative climax, a gesture in the autobiography of the killer. Victims, after all, are losers. The real hero of *The Silence of the Lambs* is the genius Hannibal Lecter.

CONCLUSION

I have intentionally avoided the more obvious sociohistorical reasons for the relative absence of serial killing outside the United States: availability of firearms, decentralized government, geographic mobility, a frontier past, and Protestantism.

Instead I have attempted a hermeneutics of serial killing as sociocultural and textual practice (here the text was television). Myth-making and the social practices it intersects with form a whole; they are part of an organic, continuous process. Creator, producer, and consumer function within the same cultural space and continually feed off each other. If one is to understand the continuing presence of serial killers in the United States today, one must also look toward the consumers and producers of this cultural phenomenon and realize that far from being a simple aberration of "the system," their activity is grounded in some of the most prevalent practices of the American free market capitalist economy. This in turn nourishes the hegemonic activity of a culture industry that too often rehabilitates its marginal elements in order to turn them into profitable commodities.

When Jeffrey Dahmer's house of carnage was discovered in Milwaukee in 1991, television rights to his story were being negotiated within the hour. Thierry Paulin and his lover were arrested in 1987 for the murder of nine elderly women in Montmartre, the worst French killing spree since Marcel Petiot was arrested in 1944, and it took seven years for filmmaker Claire Denis to make a *spectacle-free* film about their savage rampage. Yet, even so, the film was destined to play in art-houses for *cinéphiles* who in all likelihood never even watched television.

NOTES

1. Criminology as a science (and therefore "criminal man" as an object of study) is generally thought to have emerged with the publication in 1876 of Cesare Lombroso's *L'Uomo delinquente*. It is therefore difficult to speak of a genus *serial killer*, or of an identifiable criminal *type* before the end of the century.

2. The bizarre coalition that has formed between reactionary critics such as Michael Medved (*Hollywood vs. America*, 1992), the Christian Coalition, and radical feminists is a phenomenon quite incomprehensible to most Europeans.

3. As with every hyped event or person, the serial killer has found himself at the vortex of a complex network of merchandizing: not only biographies, film rights and made-for-TV movies and documentaries, but also the obligatory appendages of the culture industry— T shirts, board games, comic books, trading cards, and Halloween masks.

4. On the impact of serial killing on contemporary art, see Grandjeat, 1994.

5. Although Haneke's film takes place in a well-to-do suburb of Vienna, the problems confronted with virtual realities and video representations are certainly more prevalent in the United States today than anywhere else.

6. Literally, "I is an other" has become "I are the media." [Editors' note]

7. In this respect, the strangely disturbing and equally touching autobiography of Jeffrey Dahmer's father, Lionel, *A Father's Story* (New York: Little Brown, 1994) is uncommon. Trying to make sense of the horrors committed by his son, he traces their life together, hesitating at each detail that might somehow reveal the monster within Jeffrey.

8. John McNaughton's *Henry, Portrait of a Serial Killer* (1989) is one of the only serial killer films to have questioned the dubious role of television in creating these monsters (Nevers, 1992).

9. The Bobbits, the Menendez brothers, Tonya Harding, O. J. Simpson . . .

REFERENCES

Answer Me! 2 (Hollywood: Goad to Hell Enterprises, 1992). Special issue on serial killers.

Baudrillard, Jean (1976). *L'Echange symbolique et la mort.* Paris: Gallimard.

Bourgoin, Stéphane (1993). *Serial Killers: Enquête sur les tueurs en série.* Paris: Grasset.

Conrath, Robert (1994). "The Guys Who Shoot to Thrill: Serial Killers and the American Popular Unconscious." *Revue Française d'Etudes Américaines* 60 (May): 143–152.

——— (1995). "Pulp Fixation: The Hardboiled American Crime Novel and Its French Public." *Para•doxa* 1.2 (May).

Ellis, Brett Easton (1991). *American Psycho.* New York: Vintage.

Grandjeat, Yves-Charles (1994). "Ce désir d'objet obscur: art et consommation chez Mike Kelley." *Revue Française d'Etudes Américaines* 60 (May): 153–160.

Hall, Stuart, et al. (eds.) (1978). *Policing the Crisis.* London: Routledge.

Jenkins, Philip (1988). "Myth and Murder: The Serial Killer Panic of 1983–85." *Criminal Justice Research Bulletin* 3.11: 22–29.

——— (1989). "Serial Murder in the United States, 1900–1940: A Historical Perspective." *Journal of Criminal Justice* 17: 22–39.

Kooistra, Paul (1989). *Criminals as Heroes: Structure, Power and Identity.* Bowling Green, OH: Popular.

Leps, Marie-Christine (1992). *Apprehending the Criminal: The Production of Deviance in Nineteenth-Century Discourse.* Durham, NC: Duke University Press.

Nevers, Camille (1992). "A l'ombre des serial killers." *Cahiers du cinéma* 461 (November).

Newton, Michael (1993). *Hunting Humans.* 2 vols. New York: Avon.

Noris, Joel (1989). *Serial Killers.* New York: Doubleday.

15 The *Mayflower* Need Not Sail Back: The US of A Is Going European

Claude-Jean Bertrand

Loud has been the whining and gnashing of teeth on the Old Continent about the invasion of US pop culture. Yet I believe that far too much has been made of the Americanization of Europe (Bertrand, 1987a)—and far too little has been said about the Europeanization of the United States.

Certainly, modern technology, which is a joint product of Europe and the United States, has played an immense part in homogenizing life-styles on either side of the Atlantic (and elsewhere). But the reciprocal influence goes deeper. What makes it possible, of course, is the commonality of culture.

The basic Europeanness of the United States is indisputable, although it is often eclipsed by the great myth of the New World. The United States could in fact be considered the largest European nation. One could even argue it was the first, the only one in which all Europeans have merged into one people. Despite the angry buzzing of multiculturalists, the rock-hard historical fact is that the language(s) and original culture of the North American colonies came from Europe. And that Africans, then later Asians, were made to conform to it. Only fanatics can ignore the fact that over 75 percent of the present U.S. population is white non-Hispanic, hence of European descent[1]—and that a majority of them sailed over only 80 to 140 years ago. Personally, I would add Hispanics, whose culture is certainly far more Spanish than Amerindian: that would increase the proportion to over 80 percent.

But what I wish to highlight here is the *increase* in Europeanness on the western side of the Atlantic since the 1960s. It has gone largely unnoticed. One reason it has been ignored is the traditional insularity of the United States, born of nineteenth-century political and economic isolationism and reinforced in the twentieth by the drastic protectionism of its cultural industries.

Another reason is the post–World War II hegemony of the United States. After 1945, it did stop turning its back on the rest of the globe—but its dominance on the world stage, military first, then economic and cultural, endowed it with the arrogance of the cultural imperialist impervious to foreign influence. Americans became convinced that they were *the* model for the world and had nothing to learn from the rest of society. Admittedly, the non-U.S. world had shown a regrettable inclination to fascism, communism, wars local or global, genocides, and gulags.

AN IDEOLOGICAL ISLAND

Americans have always been reluctant to admit that their nation was essentially European: this derives from the immigrants' original determination to reject the Old World in which they had experienced little but poverty, despotism, persecution, pogroms, and war. They wanted a new life in a virgin world, as the Elect People in the Promised Land, where some dreamed of building the Kingdom of God and others of achieving utopia. Unlike Canada and Mexico, which reproduced the Old World, the United States developed as an island nation away from the evil continent. Americans do not realize how insular they have always been (Bertrand, 1995).

The European visitor to the United States feels the difference by a thousand little jolts, which together can drive him into a state of cultural shock—although in recent years the Old Continent has adopted quite a few U.S. ways, from jeans to sitcoms, from urban graffiti to hamburgers.

Food, a not unimportant matter for the French, provides in the United States the first twinges of exoticism: salad to begin meals; then a little veal, lamb, or fish; no rabbit or duck, no stewed meats or innards; cottage cheese, peanut butter, and no decent chocolate; pale coffee, tasteless beer, wine coolers—but no liquor made from fruit or grapes. Not to speak of people's strange table manners—and the amazing number of very overweight people. "There's no business like obeseness," they say; maybe Uncle Sam should yield to Uncle Michelin as a symbol of the United States.

The United States is insular in far more serious ways. It stands now as the only nation not to have adopted the metric system—apart from Myanmar and Liberia, not two of the most advanced countries in the world. And it is impossible stateside to use a non-U.S. electrical appliance: the plug, voltage, and frequency are different. Moreover, U.S. television has opted for the NTSC (National Television Systems Committee) color system, together with only a handful of other nations, which are (Canada) or have been (Japan) under direct U.S. influence. Few Americans know they have, for several decades, been getting a far worse picture than users of the PAL (Phase Alternation by Line) or SECAM (*sequential couleur à mémoire*) system.

Speaking of television, it shows striking differences from the European scene. The three major networks air only U.S. programs. In prime time, a mere 2 percent of foreign material is broadcast, three-quarters of which is of British origin. And the networks have not shown a French movie for at least 20 years, although France is the second-largest exporter of films in the world.[2]

After living for some time in the United States, the European visitor discovers the excellence of certain institutions, such as four-year colleges, foundations that support museums and symphony orchestras, or supermarkets that stay open 24 hours a day. One also discovers the mediocrity of public services, such as urban transportation, intercity passenger railroads, garbage collection, police, postal service, and secondary education.

In 1994, the United States remained the only developed nation not to have a national health insurance system, and the only one to have allowed the medical and legal professions to go filthy commercial. Doctors have become merchants of health, who deem house calls far too unprofitable—and have to weather a storm of malpractice suits. The number of lawyers in the United States is staggering: one for every 400 inhabitants, approximately six times more than in France. They seem to indicate an obsession with righting wrongs by suing.

Striking signs of insularity exist in two other fields of activity: sports and religion. The United States is the only country whose two major sports, baseball and (American) football, are not commonly practised anywhere else except in nations next door (Canada) or in those that at some point were occupied militarily by the United States (Cuba, Japan).

Whereas religion has withered in Europe, it is as lively in the United States as it is in the Third World. Some data are startling: two-thirds of Americans belong to one of over a thousand churches, sects, and cults; every week, 42 percent of them attend religious services; approximately a thousand radio stations specialize in religion or gospel music; televangelists beg on some television channel at almost any time of day. Further, few in the Old World can believe that some U.S. textbooks hardly mention the Darwinian theory of evolution, for fear of offending "creationists."

To old-time conversionist religion and its stress on "new birth," Americans probably owe their constant expectation of happiness—and their ceaseless quest for quick fixes through drugs, mantras, gurus, and various White Knights. Another effect of religiosity is the mind-boggling puritanism of the United States. It is, for instance, difficult in Europe to believe that in 1990 in Virginia, a man was sentenced to ten years in prison for indulging in consensual oral sex. Or that one never sees an unclad female thorax on the beaches or on network television, not even in commercials.

But reactions to the taboos seem worse: cheap pornographic weeklies; fascination with the sexual capers of politicians; plagues of obscene phone calls; dramatic numbers of unmarried teenage mothers (three times higher than in Europe); and, mainly, the replacement of sex by violence on the big and small screens, where people never stop beating and killing each other. Strangely, the mayhem goes on in real life as well, with 24,000 persons being murdered every year (almost half the number of Americans killed in Vietnam over a period of more than eight years).[3] Very few people in Europe fear to go out after dark, or lock the doors of their cars when driving, or own guns or organize vigilante patrols.

Social violence also appears in the guise of intolerance. A century-old history of racism and nativism, of McCarthyism in the postwar period and "political correctness" in the post–Cold War period: probably they also spring from the frontier tradition of simplistic manichean religion.

Finally, puritanism generated the "work ethic," which Europeans would rather leave to the United States—"work for work's sake"—and the worship of the almighty buck; these both prevent full enjoyment of life. Workaholism and greed are partly responsible for the destruction not just of the extended family but even of the nuclear family. Europeans cannot understand how so many American "families" can be headed by a single adult, with the result that latchkey kids are left to fend for themselves.

THE OYSTER OPENS UP

In the twentieth century, U.S. insularism started to erode, imperceptibly at first, then from the 1960s onward more and more obviously. Americans have realized that isolationism weakened them on the global market and reinforced their rivals. R.-J. Ravault calls traditional U.S. policy "boomerang imperialism" (Bertrand and Bordat, 1989): the country exports its cultural products everywhere, with the effect that foreigners know the United States well and can discern its strong and weak points. But the United States imports very few cultural goods, and that generates an immense lack of interest in the outside world and a terrible ignorance of it—in spite of the self-righteous rhetoric about respecting different cultures.[4]

Actually, the opening up has been due to a coincidence of forces. One major factor, I believe, has been the social ascent of descendants of second-wave, non-WASP immigrant groups. The integration of a huge number of Catholics, and of less numerous Eastern European Jews, was long and difficult, partly because they did not appreciate the established model—and they gradually altered it. As is now well documented, whereas second-generation immigrants tend to reject their country or region of origin, the well-integrated third or fourth generation takes pride in being non-WASP. Just compare the names on the lists of credits scrolled at the end of movies or television programs now and 40 years ago. Another factor of change has been the homogenization of the very mobile population under media influence. The norms that spread to the central plains and to small towns nationwide were those of New York and Los Angeles: largely European, Catholic, or Jewish. Meanwhile, African and Asian influence has remained extremely weak.

More recently, however, the struggle of blacks and Hispanics to obtain respect for their own cultures has introduced in the United States a multiculturalism that Europe has always had to accept—because the Continent consisted of such different nations and the nations often consisted of such different provinces. For instance, two of the popular series on U.S. television in the early 1970s, which introduced blacks (*Sanford and Son*) and white ethnics (*All In the Family*) as heroes, were adapted from British programs, *Steptoe and Son* and *Till Death Us Do Part*. (Although *I Spy* [1965–1968] was the first regular U.S. dramatic television series starring a black in a major, respectable role: Bill Cosby.) Pluralism, which history forced on the Old Continent long ago, has now replaced WASP-ish conformism in the United States and has spread to one sector after another: fashion, sex, religion, or food. Admittedly, mass society has helped the transformation by giving people both the opportunity and need to be different.

Yet another cause of the opening up relates to the knowledge of the Old World imposed on Americans by unfortunate events: the two world wars,[5] and then the 1948–1989 Cold War, which prevented a return to isolationism as in 1918, forced thousands of GIs to reside in Europe, and focused popular attention on what was taking place on either side of the Iron Curtain.

Also after World War II, the huge increase in Americans' standard of living, the development of a leisure society, and inexpensive air travel made tourism common even among the less wealthy classes. Between 1950 and 1975 the number of passports issued in the United States doubled, and it doubled again during the next ten years. The number of American travelers to foreign countries doubled between 1980 and 1990 (AA 259).

The average American's curiosity about and knowledge of the outside world were further stimulated by a rise in the educational level (AA 152), especially in college education (from 6.2% of the population in 1950 to 21.4% in 1992) and the remarkable institution called the junior year abroad. These factors increased the emerging realization that the United States is not utopia and that U.S. solutions are not always the best.

Tastes too have become more sophisticated: what was once elite is now becoming common. The aristocracy always kept very close, and fruitful, links with the Old World as a whole (not only Britain) in literature, art, architecture, cinema, and music.[6] Since World War II, the U.S. elite has increased in size. The exploding media have encouraged the hoi polloi to follow suit, which triggered an interest in high culture. Television news showed abundant pictures of that part of the globe where journalists and cameramen prefer to be stationed, that is, Europe. Mainly, the media mixed European ingredients into pop culture. Some were visible, such as the Beatles and the Rolling Stones, who revitalized rock 'n' roll. Others were occult, such as the crowds of artists and craftspeople working in every corner of Hollywood. In fact, the cosmopolitanism of the dream factory probably accounts for much of its current international success.[7]

EUROPEANIZATION

To perceive the degree of change, which has been slow, one must contrast the mental image one has of the United States of 50, 40, or 30 years ago (from personal experience, or from books and movies) with the state of the Union now.

Much insularity remains, especially in the Midwest and South; but everywhere, for better or for worse, originality is crumbling away from the American cookie.

"Europeanization" refers to mental attitudes that are common in most of Western Europe and have been unknown, or rare, in the United States among integrated citizens until recent times. The term also refers to the more visible introduction of products or behaviors that used to be uncommon in the United States. The watershed period was the 1960s, when youth and minorities dramatically questioned U.S. conformism. Since then, interest in things foreign has grown in even larger circles of the population, so that it has gradually reached even sections of the populace that do not realize what is and is not European.

Products

An emblematic craze of the 1960s made the Volkswagen "bug" ubiquitous: the small, economical, safe, handsome, reliable car was the exact opposite of the classic American automobile. Now the chic cars are no longer the Lincoln and Cadillac, but the Mercedes and BMW. Incidentally, a less obvious but more useful import during the mid-1970s was a 30-year old French invention, the steel-belted radial tire.

On U.S. highways now, and in public places such as airports and museums, the signs of an international (i.e., European) pictorial code are used. Since the early 1970s, drivers no longer need to decipher instructions written in English, such as No Entry / Wrong Way / Turn Back: a glance at the red circle with the horizontal white bar is enough.

Speaking of codes, it tickles me that the U.S. elite has adopted not just Perrier and bidets but also jargon-spewing philosophical gurus such as Barthes, Baudrillard, Deleuze, Derrida, Foucault, Lacan, Lyotard—or Habermas. Quite a few of their writings I am tempted to consider as intellectual products exported because they are too stale for native European consumption.[8]

However, Europeanization is interesting in that it now reaches the masses. Change is particularly evident in a sector that has become crucial nowadays (Bertrand, 1987b; Bertrand, 1989): media products are no longer the same. There was a time when all newspapers were local and primetime television consisted of three almost identical programs made up of sitcoms, action series, and movies. Not so anymore.

On the airwaves, noncommercial radio and the Public Broadcasting Service (PBS), serving different audiences successively, first introduced good programs with no commercials in the tradition of European public broadcasting. Moreover, in contrast to the Big Three networks, cable and satellites, with their plethora of channels, are now able to provide world news; political debates; children's shows; educational, religious, and cultural programs; uncut movies; and documentaries. They have made television as diverse at almost any time of day in the United States as it always has been in Europe over a week or a month.

USA Today, the first national daily born in 1982, has become the second-largest newspaper in the country. Although much derided, it has had a significant influence on the press. Although most Americans do not realize it, *USA Today* is very much a European daily: no local news, short stories, comparatively little advertising, clear packaging, attractive layout.

Keeping in mind that muckraking in the early 1900s was the work of radicals, the renaissance of investigative journalism since the 1970s is interesting: it indicates a move away from "impersonal, descriptive reports" toward Old World, activist journalism. More generally, as one eminent U.S. media expert puts it, "U.S. newspapers and television have begun to leave behind their search for impartiality . . . . The trend suggests a return to European-style journalism" (Dennis, 1994: 2).

Life-style

The decline of small-town nostalgia was signaled on the small screen in the 1960s by the decline of western series and suburban sitcoms and by the increasing popularity of police series and urban sitcoms. It was reflected, even in the suburbs, by apartment living, European-style. It seems to be one among many signs that more Americans wish to enjoy life in the modern world—as opposed to living an ersatz rural existence, raising large families and laboring even in their spare time at mowing lawns.

Over the last 30 years, on the occasion of regular visits to the United States, I have witnessed a trend toward more open enjoyment of sensual pleasures. Food first. For some years now in the big cities (and even in some small towns), people have patronized ethnic restaurants, collected cookbooks, watched gourmet cooking programs on television[9], and practised the art themselves. Foreign foods have filled stores: pizzas, quiches, croissants, baguettes, brie, yogurt (Yoplait, Dannon—French brands). Farmers markets have multiplied, where people can find tasty fresh vegetables and herbs.

In terms of drinks, scotch and vodka have been popular for some time. But now wine is being served with meals everywhere.[10] Even in the Midwest, dry white wine has become a popular drink at cocktail time—and even there you can find sidewalk cafés (at least within shopping malls). Tasteful local beers have made a comeback. Even the European habit of drinking spring or mineral water rather than chlorinated tap water has caught on.

The love for European ways has extended from pampering the body to exercising it. In sports, skiing caught on in the 1960s (promoted by the French champion Jean-Claude Killy), then cycling (an American, Greg Lemond, even won the Tour de France). In 1994, the startling U.S. success of the World Cup called attention to the fact that 16 million Americans play soccer, more than play baseball or football.

At the same time, although the use of tobacco (a drug indigenous to America) is declining, an open appreciation of sex is replacing puritanical hypocrisy. A greater tolerance first developed for sexy clothes: the bikini swimsuit came from

France, and later the miniskirt from Britain. An early sign of liberalization was the success of *Playboy* magazine in the 1950s, the first among the large-circulation girlie magazines. These became even bolder, and then were replaced by hard-core movies in the early 1970s. Even the networks became a little more adult in their televised movies and sitcoms (e.g., *Mary Hartman, Mary Hartman* or *Soap*). In the 1980s, video pornography became popular as the VCR became a household fixture. Thus, according to surveys of sexual behavior, such diabolical behaviors as fellatio, cunnilingus, and sodomy were popularized—although they are still considered felonies in a number of states.

A consequence of the "sexual revolution" was the coming out of homosexuality. Interestingly, having now obtained a tolerance that had been commonplace in continental Europe for many years, gays in the United States have launched protest movements demanding more and more rights, which their European counterparts have never felt like doing.

Greater tolerance of any kind of sex exists in continental Europe than in the United States. It has existed at least since the Renaissance, in common practice if not in laws and rites. Is it because of ancient compromises made by the Catholic Church? Because of a tradition of Mediterranean sensuality? It goes further than that. In my highly objective opinion, Europeans have a wiser, more sophisticated, complex, tolerant concept of mankind.

Ideology

Modifications in tastes, when numerous, reflect a shift in mentality. When people alter their attitude toward food and drink, cars and sex, sports and tourism, it seems likely that their view of the world is changing. To understand this evolution in the United States—what I call its greater Europeanization—we must dip into the American psyche and analyze American *Weltanschauung*, or ideology.

As I see it, the core of American ideology consists of three basic values: an attachment to individual freedom, combined with a belief in individual progress[11]—plus, of course, as for all living creatures, an obsession for security. The ideological triangle is of European origin. On the Old Continent, individual freedom and progress were essentially Jewish-Greek values. But in the early Christian era, epidemics, famines, invasions, and wars led Europeans to grant top priority to security, at the expense of freedom and progress. They sought spiritual security in a single, all-encompassing Church that stood as an intermediary between the puny creatures and the Almighty Judge. Physical security they sought in the protection of feudal lords or absolute kings. Thus, in Europe the "security" angle of the ideological triangle pointed upward.

When Europeans crossed the ocean to the New World, they found an immense territory with vast resources. Potentially everyone could find land there and make a fortune. If prevented from doing so in one spot, one was free to move elsewhere. So the protective but oppressive institutions of the Old World disintegrated. For the colonists, security remained important but secondary: the "freedom" and "progress" angles of the triangle became uppermost. Thus, their ideology changed while remaining essentially the same.

Admittedly, "freedom" and "progress" are vague terms that can be interpreted differently. Americans seem to have developed three—or rather four—versions of their gospel.

The first can be labeled "pietist." It is that of people who, in this vale of tears, concentrate on preparing for the afterlife. Freedom for them is freedom to choose salvation.[12] Progress for them is to move from sinfulness to saintliness, which is possible on this earth, with no outside help. What one must do is labor in one's calling, build a family, serve one's community and country. Those who do not respect the rules can be left to the police and the courts. The pietist believes that society cannot be improved until all its members have been converted. American society anyway is the "least worst." The rest of the world does not deserve attention except to fend off its assaults.

The second interpretation, which I call "Darwinist," is the best known. For many years it was the only one the media presented. Many Europeans believe it sums up the entire U.S. ideology. "Darwinists" look on society as a jungle wherein each of us must fight in order to survive and try and dominate others. In that struggle we must be free, not fettered by tradition or institutions. The strongest, hence the best, must prevail. Natural selection means progress. The world's resources will be exploited. Those who work will earn enough to live on. There is no need to bother about the others. Similarly, on the world stage, the United States, being the most powerful nation, must rule. Whoever rejects that notion is an enemy—not just of the United States but of humankind as a whole, for it means rejecting progress.

The third interpretation does not sit well with left-wing Europeans, even though they have developed a more accurate perception of U.S. diversity since the 1960s. I call it "progressive."[13] It is clearly different from the first two. Progressives believe that all men and women should be free (i.e., able to enjoy equality of rights and opportunity) to progress toward whatever they call happiness—through cooperation, not through competition. Progress must be in the quality of the life you lead, not in the quantity of the products you own. The progressive's ideal is participatory democracy. It would be best to do without governmental intervention, but the State is needed to protect each individual's rights and to preserve the common wealth. The progressive is very critical of the United States, but in an optimistic way. As it is, the country best combines individual rights and economic development. One day the American dream will be achieved, and it will be a model for the world.

Another version of the ideology has become more common in the twentieth century—that of the bureaucrat. It originated among the antebellum agrarians, small East Coast farmers satisfied with their fate. It took off in the second half of the nineteenth century when huge private firms created battalions of wage-earners, often recent immigrants of Catholic origin. In the twentieth century, enormous public institutions also gathered more and more salaried employees.

In the twentieth century, because of two world wars, the Great Depression, and the emergence of the communist bloc, security has taken unprecedented prominence in the United States: the two largest items in the federal budget became Defense and Welfare.

Since the New Deal, "government" has meant Washington, D.C. Localism has declined: Americans are Americans, not immigrants, not citizens of a particular state. Small towns have faded away, and so has grassroots democracy. The media were supposed to serve their community: for economic reasons, they now depend on wholesalers in New York and Los Angeles (networks, wire services, and syndicates). Centralization affects all private industries: companies are becoming not just national, but multinational. And it affects municipal and state managers: everybody now depends on the federal government and on federal income tax money. Citizens count on Washington to protect the nation through diplomacy and the armed forces, to keep the economy prosperous within a world context, to regulate big business so as to protect the consumer.

The bureaucrat certainly loves the laws and ideals of the nation—but with no passion, within the limits of his selfish interests. If he is an executive, he wishes to succeed—but without too much effort or too much risk. If he is a white-collar or blue-collar worker, he feels he is a prisoner of a social stratum and of a dull job. Progress for him is an increase in salary or leisure. To be free means to enjoy life, that is, mainly to consume. The bureaucrat is far more interested in rights than in duties; he is inclined to accuse others whenever anything goes wrong for him.

More positively, the bureaucrat also seeks a more spiritual kind of security. Not only does he practice genealogy more and travel to the lands of his ancestors, but he shows growing interest in the nation's past. This is evident in the restoration of old buildings (e.g., the Washington, D.C., railroad station) or historic neighborhoods (e.g., in Philadelphia and Minneapolis). It also is evident in the greater care taken to conserve the environment.

In other words, the triangle of U.S. ideology has for some years begun moving in the European direction with the "security" angle moving up.[14] Its orientation now is not too different from the position of the European triangle. The whole of Western Europe has for at least 20 years been democratic and economically liberal. As the region became richer and more stable politically after 1945, its inhabitants developed a stronger attachment to individual freedom and a deeper faith in progress; hence a lessening passion for the past and a growing interest in the future, that of a united Europe. Their ideological triangle has been tilting in the American direction.

CONCLUSION

Much has been written about the democratization, modernization, privatization, and Americanization of Europe. What demands more attention is the parallel evolution of the United States in symmetrical complement to Europe. The North Atlantic civilization is certainly growing more and more homogeneous, but we must keep in mind that this is a two-way process.

Americans, I believe, must pursue their re-Europeanization for one major reason: to ensure that the American experience has a happy ending.

Even though Western Europe developed modern civilization and spread it all over the world, it also spent centuries fighting internal wars. Now the feuds and the horrors have peaked and ceased. So it seems to me that today, Western Europe is the place where the famed American Dream is alive and (almost) well, where people best enjoy "certain inalienable Rights" along with "Life, Liberty, and the Pursuit of Happiness." Europeans have escaped the combination of morbid individualism, isolationism, anti-statism, frantic commercialism, philistinism, puritanism, intolerance, passion for quick fixes, violence, and the like that has generated what Henry Miller called the "air-conditioned nightmare." Europe could yet save its prodigal child, groping its way toward its elderly but wise and newly energetic parent.

In the twentieth century, much of the improvement on the eastern side of the North Atlantic was due to European borrowing from the American Dream and the American way of life. The time has now come for Americans to borrow from the European dream and the European way of life. Or else.

NOTES

1. *American Almanac: Statistical Abstract of the U.S. 1993–1994*, p. 18. Henceforth referred to as *AA*.

2. For more about U.S. cultural isolationism, cf. Bertrand and Bordat, 1994.

3. According to *AA*, an American is 70 times more likely to be shot dead than a Briton.

4. It should be remembered that Europe is the number one export market for the United States; 60 percent of the foreign profits made by U.S. films come from Europe.

5. As testified to by the films and documentaries about Europe shown during the war for propaganda purposes.

6. That is obvious from an alphabetical list of the names of European conductors who have prospered in the United States: Boulez, Giulini, Kousse Vitzky, Martinon, Monteux, Munch, Ormandy, Paray, Reiner, Solti, Szell, Stokowsky, and Toscanini.

7. In the early 1950s, the "consent decrees" separating the major studios from their chains of theaters led to a reduction in movie production, hence to an increase in European imports.

8. Their lateness in crossing the Atlantic reminds one of pop art, which, in the 1960s, reproduced the Dada innovations of the 1920s.

9. Like Julia Child's *The French Chef* on PBS from 1963 to 1973, which reappeared in 1978 as *Julia and Company*.

10. It was fascinating to read that U.S. consumption of red wine had gone up 30 percent after publication of a report on the low incidence of heart disease in southwest France.

11. Cf. my chapter on ideology in Kaspi et al., 1991.

12. Calvinist predestination was never popular in the United States.

13. A term not overladen with connotations, unlike "liberal," "left," or "socialist."

14. In popular culture, the shift was from self-reliant, efficient Mickey Mouse to bun-

gling, quick-tempered Donald Duck, who remains under the protection of his State-like billionaire uncle.

REFERENCES

American Almanac: Statistical Abstract of the U.S. 1993–1994, 113th edition, Reference Press Incorporated, edited by the U.S. Bureau of the Census Staff (Bowker, Ingram).

Bertrand, Claude-Jean (1987a). "American Cultural Imperialism—A Myth?" *American Studies International*, April: 46–60.

——— (1987b). *Les Médias aux Etats-Unis*, 3rd ed. Paris: Que sais-je?/PUF.

——— (1989). *Les Etats-Unis et leur télévision*. Paris: INA/Champ Vallon.

——— (1995). "Un Cas étrange d'insularité: les Etats-Unis." *L'Insularité*. St Denis: Presses de l'Université de la Réunion.

Bertrand, Claude-Jean, and Francis Bordat (eds.) (1994). *Les Médias français aux Etats-Unis*. Nancy: Presses Universitaires de Nancy.

Dennis, E. E. (1994). *Communiqué* (October). New York: Freedom Forum Media Studies Center.

Kaspi, André, C-J. Bertrand, and J. Heffer (1991). *La civilisation américaine*, 4th ed. Paris: PUF.

Part VI

Ethnic Cultures

16 "America" in Popular Irish Fiction and Drama: Elements of a Transcultural Discourse

Ciaràn Ross

"DOLLARS, BUCKS, AND NUGGETS": CULTURAL PREJUDICE AND RACIAL STEREOTYPES

American influence on Irish literature and drama goes back at least to the late nineteenth century. This can be seen in the way Irish political thinkers understood Ireland's most sacred concept, *republicanism*. As Fintan O'Toole points out, Irish nationalism adopted the vague and flexible American usage of the term rather than the radical and secular republicanism of France (O'Toole, 1985: 11–35). The model of the "Irish Ireland" nationalism of the early part of this century was a nostalgic utopia with its antibourgeois and antimodern bias tending toward a kind of Jeffersonian model. Both the United States and Ireland were founded on the belief that a paradise lost could be regained. However, for nationalist Catholic writers of the 1920s, it was America that proved to be a threat to such an Irish paradise, emigration being resented as an expulsion from an edenic state. Such a romantic conception of a pastoral Ireland dates at least as far back as the nineteenth-century intellectual Thomas Davis's view that the country was virtually the last bastion against "this thing, call it Yankeeism and Englishism, which measures prosperity by exchangeable value, measures duty by gain, and limits desire to clothes, food and respectability" (Brown, 1972: 78). By the turn of the century the rugged West of Ireland became a sanctuary for the romanticism of Yeats and Synge, because it was a reminder of what the world had elsewhere lost. To quote from Synge's preface to *The Playboy of the Western World*, Ireland (of the 1920s) still maintained qualities that had disappeared from a Europe where "the springtime of the local life had been forgotten, and the harvest is a memory only, and the straw has been turned into bricks."[1]

"America" as represented in the works of Séamus O'Grianna (*Caisleain Oir* [Castles of Gold], 1924), Peader O'Donnell (*Islanders*, 1928), Seumus O'Kelly and Daniel Corkery (*Munster Twilight*, 1917) was the perfect foil to set off romantic Irish virtues (Calahan, 1988: 184–185). In portraying America as anything but a romantic and exciting land where the experience of emigration turns out to be a spiritually debilitating one, the assumption was that Ireland was somehow different (Gonzalez, 1991: 33). The experience of emigration was nothing short of tragic for the hapless Irish emigrant. For example, in the story "Storm-Struck," Corkery's character, John Donovan—whose motivation for leaving Ireland is to earn money so that he can return and marry Kitty, his sweetheart—is blinded by an explosion in an American copper mine. Corkery's tone clearly places the blame on America. The new (American) Donovan pays the price for having emigrated, because on his return he discovers that his loved one no longer loves him and has already married; he is left alone to brood near some high cliffs, when a storm breaks out and he is saved by Kitty. The final blow comes when Kitty dies of exposure and Donovan is left with his guilt; exile to America comes across as the worst of all possible choices.

Such cultural prejudice must be seen against the romantic lure of life in a new and exciting land, the anti-exile posture being another specimen of the stifling cultural nationalism that marked the 1920s and not just a literary strategy on Corkery's part to counter such romantic idealizing. The cultural fantasy at play here is the undeveloped Irish West with an edenic existence doomed to extinction by the incursion of American materialism—unless Ireland can maintain its ideal. One is left wondering whether the debilitating aspects of the "land of the free" derided by Corkery are not rather an unconscious "dis-placement" of the ill-named Irish Free State, which following its inception rapidly degenerated into lethargy and disillusionment.

Similar cultural prejudices influenced attitudes toward theater. Although mass emigration was the central economic fact of Irish life from the nineteenth century onward, plays dealing with such a subject were disapproved of by Ireland's National Theater, the Abbey Theater. Indeed, the Abbey reflected the conservative nationalism of the dominant ideology, which was important to Irish self-understanding, that is, the need to produce realistic plays in English about ritual Irish and small-town life—what is cynically known as parish-pump theater. Such conservatism reflects the cultural isolation that prevailed, exemplified by the story often told about the Anglo-Irish Protestant writer, Lady Gregory, who wrote a play in the 1920s called *Fifty*, the title reputedly referring to the number of pounds with which the hero returns home after two years in America. However, the Abbey Theater objected that this might make America sound too attractive. Interestingly, it was the Catholic Church during the 1940s that encouraged the promotion of amateur dramatics within the local community as an alternative to the offerings of Hollywood (Brown, 1981: 178–179). Ironically, it was through local (amateur) drama, which greatly flourished in the 1960s, that the "emigration" plays of that same period—rejected by the Abbey—became familiar to many people: John B. Keane's *Many Young Men of Twenty* (1961), Tom Murphy's *A Crucial Week in the Life of a Grocer's Assistant* (1962), or Brian Friel's *Philadelphia Here I Come* (1964), to name but a few.

Returning to the 1920s, such disparaging sentiment and cultural ideology concerning America even found their way into Joyce's fiction, where, this time, it is the romantic lure of life in the new and exciting land of a child's imagination that is "repressed" by a Catholic priest figure. In Joyce's *Dubliners* story, "An Encounter," life has a way of imitating art. The child narrator has been introduced to the Wild West by his friend, Joe Dillon. They meet every evening after school and arrange Indian warfare, fighting pitched battles on the grass. But the narrator is also a *reader* of popular American literature, which is also part of the point Joyce is clearly making, namely, that it was not respectable for young Irish middle-class Catholic schoolboys to read popular American literature, such as detective stories or tales about the Wild West.

The young narrator's memory of the Wild West is a memory of books belonging to his friend, Joe Dillon:

He had a little library made up of old numbers of *The Union Jack, Pluck* and *The Halfpenny Marvel*. Every evening after school we met in his back garden and arranged Indian battles. . . .

The adventures related to the literature of the Wild West were remote from my nature but, at least, they opened doors of escape. I liked better some American detective stories which were traversed from time to time by unkempt fierce and beautiful girls. (Joyce, 1992: 11–12)

Having been caught by Father Butler reading "The Apache Chief" in class (the title of a story in *The Halfpenny Marvel* that presumably deals with the Amerindian wars), the child narrator is sternly admonished with: "What is this rubbish? he said. *The Apache Chief!* Is this what you read instead of studying your Roman History? . . . The man who wrote it, I suppose, was some wretched scribbler that writes those things for a drink" (12). Thus, a Catholic priest's deriding remarks about a popular American hack writer significantly offset the romantic appeal of the fictive America. This passage in Joyce's story is a powerful reminder of the realities, fears, and fantasies that marked the epoch. In reality, the notion of a pure peasantry had to be protected by the new Irish state (in 1922) from foreign influences, but in doing so the very basis of cultural independence was denied. The possibilities of a native literature were cut off by Catholic censorship; shelves emptied of banned Irish books were filled with American cowboy novels and their healthy, rural, asexual camaraderie.

So much for popular American literature and the dreams it may have represented for a mass Irish readership; but for social satirists such as Flann O'Brien (Myles Nag Copaleen) and Eimar O'Duffy, the American dream held few illusions.

They took pleasure in subverting the romantic stereotype of America as the land of the free and the home of the brave. In Flann O'Brien's *At-Swim-Two-Birds*, the "legitimate" inhabitants of the Irish cultural world in the years after independence (the 1930s) are Dublin cowboys, Slug and Shorty, who punch cattle along the Ringsend trail. O'Brien's parody of America as the land of the free is nothing more than a good Irish joke. This is seen in *The Third Policeman*, where the exchanges dealing with emigration to America speak for themselves. The narrator's ten brothers have all sadly emigrated to America. On hearing this, the police sergeant says:

That is a great conundrum of a country, a very wide territory, a place occupied by black men and strangers. I am told they are very fond of shooting-matches in that quarter. (O'Brien, 1988: 59)

The narrator replies: "It is a queer land." The narrator's "dadda" is in far "Amurikey" (60):

"Which of the two Amurikeys?" asked McCruiskeen.
    "The Unified Stations," said the sergeant.
    "Likely he is rich by now if he is in that quarter," said McCruiskeen, "because there's dollars there, dollars and bucks and nuggets in the ground and any amount of rackets and golf games and musical instruments. It is a free country too by all accounts."
    "Free for all," said the sergeant. (60)

Equally satirical is Eimar O'Duffy. In *Asses in Clover* (1933), he lets fly satirically at a variety of economic and religious issues in America; he vents his spleen over the American capitalist causes of the Great Depression. His fantasy figure, King Goshawk, sits in council in Manhattan, discussing the state of the economy in an American accent, pronouncing that "You can starve all of the people some of the time, and some of the people all of the time" (O'Duffy, 1933: 23).

"AMERICANIZED" IRELAND: EXPLODING THE AMERICAN DREAM

Popular Drama

From the 1960s onward, America ceased to be a mere source for fantasy or prejudice for Irish writers and their characters. America became gradually "integrated" into the Irish literary psyche to the extent that one finds "real-life" American characters inhabiting the fiction of John McGahern and Brian Moore. The obvious reason for this is that Irish society was being increasingly exposed to American culture not only through emigration but through the emergence of a substantial Irish middle class actively committed to consumerist values. Massive urbanization, the fading of nationalist ideals, and the decline of moral imperatives did the rest. Such changes were reflected not only by a general resurgence in drama and local drama in particular, but also by a profusion of new liberal and social themes in both drama and fiction: emigration, adultery, corruption, sex, middle-class consumerism, pornography. By the 1970s, it was generally recognized that American culture was having an open and *formal* influence on Irish writers, notably in Tom Murphy's use of the movie gangster genre in his play *The Blue Macushla*; Brian Friel's use of American idiom in his plays *The Loves of Cass Maguire* and *The Communication Cord*; and in Robert Patrick, Paul Durcan, James Simmon, and Roddy Doyle's respective uses of American musical rhythms and traditions. To this list I would add the influence of the Southern Gothic tradition on Ulster writers[2] and Samuel Beckett's use of Buster Keaton in *Film* (1963). I would equally suggest that such influences form a series that goes back a lot further than the 1960s. Here I am thinking of the Catholic novelist Liam O'Flaherty, who incorporated American idiom into literature with his celebrated novel *The Informer* (1925), by making a conscious use of the thriller genre that led to its subsequent immortalization by John Ford in the 1935 film.

What the drama of the 1960s and 1970s reveals is the fundamental disillusionment the American dream had come to mean for the Irish. The plays of the 1960s were all about separations, divisions, and the spiritual schizophrenia engendered by the pull between home and the small town versus dreams of big-city success (*Many Young Men of Twenty*, 1961; *A Crucial Week in the Life of a Grocer's Assistant*, 1962; *Philadelphia Here I Come*, 1964). Not surprisingly, the 1970s were marked by the fictions of homecomings, returns, disappointments, and irresolvable cultural clashes (*Bailegangaire*, 1978; *The Blue Macushla*, 1980; *Conversations on a Homecoming*, 1986—all three plays by Tom Murphy), or in the case of Robert Patrick, the death of the idealism of the Kennedy era as expressed in his play *Kennedy's Children* (1974), where the music of Don McLean plays a prominent part. However, what critics tend to forget is that there is nothing "new" about such material, given that as far back as the 1940s the theme of the "impossible return home" featured in Sean O'Faolain's final published novel, *Come Back to Erin* (1940). The hero, a disillusioned Republican, is taken outside the confines of a complacent petit-bourgeois Ireland to an emotional and intellectual awakening in America, which, when he returns to Ireland, can find no substantial expression within the social atmosphere of the country.

If the country in the 1960s fed itself on the American dream—with Ireland's real address being "Ronald Reagan Hill"[3]—such a "dream" turns out, however, to be effectively "written off" by Irish drama for present-day writers. In Murphy's plays, there is no return to some nostalgic whole or romantic transcendence. The American dream has exploded for both cultures, and Murphy is addressing America as much as Ireland when he constructs characters such as Liam in his play *Conversations on a Homecoming* (1986). As Shaun Richards points out (1990: 88), Tom Murphy's image of Americanized (postmodern) Ireland is economically dominated by a spurious, pseudo-American whose life-style is one of country-and-western music, cars without clutches, and, above all, the valuation of human relationships in terms of economic gain. Ireland is represented "as another commodity in the global market, for sale to any old bidder with a pound, a dollar, a mark or a yen" (68). The focus of the satire is Liam, described as "a farmer, an estate agent, a travel agent, he owns property . . . affects a slight American accent, a bit stupid and insensitive—seemingly the requisite to success" (10). The obvious parallel here is with Miller's *Death of a Salesman*: Murphy's character Michael Ridge has, like Willy Loman, also returned home in the expectation that its certitudes will provide solace for his personal insecurities and anxieties. The irony is that Michael is fleeing from an America that not only does not live up to the Kennedy-era idealism that first drew him there, but whose image is now projected onto an Ireland that is prepared to "follow to the death any old bollocks with borrowed image, any old JJ who has read a book on American politics or business methods" (50). What Michael has returned in search of is an idealism born of the Irish embrace of J. F. Kennedy's "New Frontier," but which has degenerated in both Ireland and the States into a vulgar materialism represented by Liam.

When social satire is aimed at an Irish bourgeoisie, it is shot through with the neurosis of the American middle-class type. In Hugh Leonard's historical farce, *The Patric Pearse Motel* (1971), Leonard exposes the vulgarity and idiocy of the nouveaux riches. The motel, where a sexual encounter is about to take place, has rooms named after the great Irish patriots (Pearse was a rebel executed after the 1916 Rising) and a restaurant hilariously called the Famine Room. Like their American counterparts, Leonard's nouveaux riches have no sense of history, as rapid social mobility ruptures their relationship with the past. Irony is driven home with the mythological names given to characters: Dermod, Grainne, Usheen, Fintan. Tradition is a joke, but materialist culture is even funnier. The American symbol of the motel offers the chance to stand outside of time within Ireland; yet the characters are terrified of materialism, of only being what they have, such as Grainne's dream of being identified merely with the material tokens of her wealth—her brooch and herring.

Popular Fiction

Moving from drama to fiction, the Irish find, through their American counterparts, idealized counterimages of themselves to represent sexual liberalism, corruption, materialism (as we have seen with Tom Murphy), ahistoricism, nostalgia, and ultimately schizophrenia.

For example, in Brian Moore's novels the characters increasingly look back nostalgically to the traditional values and sense of community left behind in Ireland. Moore's characters move between separation and nonseparation, or, to use a psychoanalytic concept, a "potential space" that is neither fully Irish nor American, but partly both.[4] Moore left Belfast for Canada in 1948, then moved to the United States in 1959, living in the East for some years before moving to California. The evolution of an Irish-American protagonist can be traced in the way he contends with the freedom offered by the New World (America) while remaining obsessed with memories of the Old World (Ireland). For example, *Cath-*

olics (1972), whose CBS television adaptation did much to increase Moore's reputation, is set on an island off County Kerry in the near future when the Latin mass and private confession are still practiced. Its abbot, Tomas O'Malley, is visited by an Irish-American priest, James Kinsella, a slick intellectual sent by Rome to bring reform to Muck Abbey. As indicated by James Calahan (1988: 270), *Catholics* is an allegory enabling Moore to look longingly to Ireland from America, like many an Irish American; and he makes the reader root for O'Malley, who finally discovers his own faith, rather than for the Americanized, secularized Kinsella. In *Fergus* (1978), Fergus Fadden, a serious novelist, hopes to strike gold as a Hollywood scriptwriter but is literally haunted in his California beach-house by ghosts from his Irish past. Moore's cultural dialectic is one between a futureless Ireland and a pastless America. The characters exist in the potential space of a "present" between Irish total recall and Californian amnesia.

But every dichotomy dichotomizes. The traditional contrast between the Americans as pastless and the Irish as obsessed with the past is exploded by John McGahern. In "Doorways" (1969), the narrator meets Kate O'Mara, a Catholic Irish-American journalist whose family "is rotten with nostalgia about Ireland."[5] Being sexually involved with someone who is fiercely anti-American—"he has this dream of an Irish Ireland, free of outside influences"—she is abused "all the time for being American" (McGahern, 1978: 73). Familiar and not so familiar dichotomies obtrude: Irish workmen are more servile than their American counterparts; the Irish lighthouse doesn't have a bell to warn ships, unlike those in America—"everybody comes to the beach and just sits around. In America they'd be doing handstands, playing volleyball, riding the surf" (McGahern, 1978: 86)— the suggestion is that if two different cultures cannot be bridged, neither can two different personalities. Equally, in the story "Bank Holiday," the myth of the non-intellectual American is exploded through the intellectual character of the American researcher, Mary Kelleher, who is from Mount Vernon, New York, and finishing her doctorate in Medieval Poetry at the University of Chicago.[6] Romantically, she wonders if there are poets still in Ireland, to which the male protagonist, Patrick McDonough, sarcastically replies: "They say the standing army of poets never falls below ten thousand in this unfortunate country" (McGahern, 1985: 146).

Fantasy is also to be found on the Irish side of the Irish-American divide. The image of the rich, liberal-minded, middle-class American lady with inevitably complex family problems and an experience of analysis is not just the product of American cinema, as Patrick, the Catholic schoolteacher of McGahern's novel, *The Leavetaking*, discovers to his surprise.[7] The novel tells of Patrick's disastrous return to Ireland after a year's sabbatical in London where he meets Isobel, a rich American divorcée, and marries her. Isobel's complex family history, as well as her expensive psychoanalysis and life-style, make Patrick realize that the world Isobel speaks about "was so outside [his] life, except in movies" (McGahern, 1974: 105). Yet there is nothing glittery about the story of Isobel's sexual turmoil as she tells it to Patrick and her expensive analysis paid for by her father, without which she claims she would never have worked past her sexual taboos. In exchange, Patrick's Catholic prejudice makes him jokingly remark that he would rather go to confession than face the expense and pain of analysis. On return to Ireland, the couple's landlady ribs Patrick ("O you blackguard") for having married an American rather than "one of our Irish girls" (McGahern, 1974: 149). The couple are ultimately thrown out of their lodgings and Patrick is fired from his job at the Catholic school, not only for having married an American divorcée in a registry office but also for not having married one of the "thousands of Irish Catholic girls crying out for a husband" (McGahern, 1974: 166).

CONCLUSION

Irish and American transcultural relations do not have to remain locked within inescapable dualities: the future (progress) *or* the past (regression), dream *or* reality, materialism *or* puritanism. Irish and American "opposites" turn out to be doubles; clichés employed by one side can be appropriated by the other. One side provides a space for the other to express its otherness. For me, the Irish do not simply adapt their own self-image to American models—inasmuch as such a self-image is inextricably linked to its model of "otherness."[8] In and through the space of American culture and idiom, the Irish find what I would call a cultural-social consciousness that attempts to transcend the previously perceived mutual exclusion between Irish and American identities. This is why the bankruptcy of the American dream (or is it the Irish dream?) as thematized in the drama of the 1960s and 1970s is doubly alienating. Not only is the future bankrupt, but so is the past. To borrow the old conceit, "You can't go home again"—especially when you were not really from there to begin with. In a way, disillusionment with America is disillusionment with the home one never had or the self one never was. Here we are back where we started with the nationalists in the 1920s[9] with the theme of exile, a theme hauntingly treated decades later in the poetry of the Northern Irish poet Louis MacNeice, one of whose characters says in the radio play *Columbus*:

"You know what it is to be homesick? Maybe you've been homesick for the home you never had."[10]

NOTES

1. J. M. Synge, *The Playboy of the Western World* (London: Methuen, 1991) 40.
2. In "Literature and Culture in the North of Ireland," Anthony Bradley shows how Ulster writers occupy an imaginative territory somewhere between Puritan New England and the Calvinist South. Similar to its American counterpart, the setting for Ulster Gothic is a brooding, rural landscape that emanates decay and corruption—the "good country people" are collectively involved in incestuous relationships, homosexuality, obsessive and compulsive behavior, violence, rape, and various forms of sadism and masochism: "The

area might be the rural Mississippi of American fiction rather than rural Ulster: it is a landscape of sleazy bars and dancehalls, failing stores" (Bradley, 1988: 51).

3. This term is used by the Irish poet Paul Durcan in his poem "The Haulier's Wife Meets Jesus on the Road to Moone" in *The Berlin Wall Café* (Belfast: Blackstaff Press, 1986) 4.

4. In *Playing and Reality* (London: Tavistock, 1971), Donald D. Winnicott describes an intermediate space for play between mother and baby that antedates any established reality-testing and is fundamentally illusory. Play then can be used to master the differences between the "mother-world" and the "non-mother-world." The play-space or transitional space that arises can be seen as both the child's separation and denial of this separation from the breast. The relevance of Winnicott's concept does not stop here. For Winnicott, the potential space does not—indeed, must not—disappear. It yields to cultural experience in general and to the art work in particular.

5. John McGahern, *Getting Through* (London: Faber, 1978) 72.

6. John McGahern, *High Ground* (London: Faber, 1985) 140–156.

7. John McGahern, *The Leavetaking* (London: Faber, 1974).

8. For example, the materialism of Tom Murphy's character, Liam, is not the expression of some self-image in which the American ideal counterpart plays a secondary part. *The image is the model* and vice versa. The fiction or rhetoric of Murphy's image reads as follows: the Irish, like their American counterparts, can also be materialist, stupid, and successful. With Brian Moore and Hugh Leonard, the Irish need to stand outside history and "forget" just as much as the Americans need to "remember" and have a sense of belonging. The Irish need to be "progressive" just as much as the Americans can be regressive and romantic. McGahern's Irish male protagonist is relatively free from family ties, whereas his American middle-class female counterpart is entangled in a family drama.

9. Interestingly, history seems to be repeating itself in contemporary Gaelic poetry where emigration to America is a major theme, as it was in the 1920s. Some of the "Imirce" poets and their poems (Imirce is the Gaelic for "emigration") include: Peadar Bairéad, "Trom Mo Chroí" [Heavy Is My Heart] (Dublin: Clo Ceilteach, 1990); M. B. (pseudonym), "Dom Dheirfiur in Amerioca" [My Brother in America] (Dublin: Clo Ceilteach, 1991).

10. Louis MacNeice, *Columbus* (London: Faber, 1944) 46.

REFERENCES

Barry, Frank (1987). "Between Tradition and Modernity: Cultural Values and the Problems of Irish Society." *Irish Review* 2.

Bradley, Anthony (1988). "Literature and Culture in the North of Ireland." *Cultural Contexts and Literary Idioms in Contemporary Irish Literature*, ed. Michael Kenneally. Gerrards Cross: Colin Smythe, 36–72.

Brown, Malcolm (1972). *The Politics of Irish Literature: From Davis to Yeats*. London: Allen & Unwin.

Brown, Terence (1981). *Ireland: A Social and Cultural History 1922–79*. Glasgow: Fontana.

Calahan, James M. (1988). *The Irish Novel: A Critical History*. Dublin: Gill & Macmillan.

Gonzalez, Alexander G. (1991). "A Context for Joyce: Seumas O'Kelly, Daniel Corkery, and the Nationalist View of the Irish Expatriate." *Etudes Irlandaises* 16.2 (December): 33–41.

Joyce, James (1992). *Dubliners*. Harmondsworth: Penguin.

John McGahern (1974). *The Leavetaking*. London: Faber.

———— (1978). *Getting Through*. London: Faber.

———— (1985). *High Ground*. London: Faber.

Murphy, Tom (1986). *Conversations on a Homecoming*. Dublin: Gallery Press.

O'Brien, Flann (1988). *The Third Policeman*. Glasgow: Paladin Books.

O'Duffy, Eimar (1933). *Asses in Clover*. London and New York: Putnam.

O'Toole, Fintan (1985). "Going West: The Country versus the City in Irish Writing." *Crane Bag* 9.2.

———— (1988). "Island of Saints and Silicon: Literature and Social Change in Contemporary Ireland." *Cultural Contexts and Literary Idioms in Contemporary Irish Literature*, ed. Michael Kenneally. Gerrards Cross: Colin Smythe, 11-35.

Pine, Richard (1983). "Cultural Democracy, Cultural Policy and Cultural Identity." *Crane Bag* 7.2.

Richards, Shaun (1990). " 'There's No Such Thing as the West Anymore': Tom Murphy and the Lost Ideal of the Land of the Free." *Etudes Irlandaises* 15 (December): 83–94.

17 Minorities in U.S. Films: The New Wave 1960s–1970s

Penny Starfield

Ethnicity and minority can be considered historically modern concepts. The word "ethnic," referring to a racial or national group, dates from the mid-nineteenth century; "minority," referring to a small group that differs from the dominant community through race, religion, language, and the like, from the early twentieth century. Apparently, just as the last nations were being formed in Europe, a need arose to define groups within the state or those that cut across boundaries, such as Polish minorities or Jews.

These concepts become important in postwar America with the rise of civil rights and the ensuing protest movements (students, youth, women, gays) of the late 1960s and early 1970s. This was also a pivotal period in terms of the representation of minority and ethnic characters in film.[1] Minority elements in American society appeared to be integrated, as it were, and shifts in character portrayal occurred on different levels. *Guess Who's Coming to Dinner* (S. Kramer, 1967) and *In the Heat of the Night* (N. Jewison, 1968) depicted blacks—both roles played by Sidney Poitier—in contemporary situations and as protagonists, not just secondary characters. Moreover, the subject matter was racism. Ethnic protagonists were often played by actors from the same group: Barbra Streisand in *Funny Girl* (W. Wyler, 1968) and *The Way We Were* (S. Pollack, 1973), Al Pacino and Robert DeNiro in *The Godfather* (F. Coppola, 1972), Dustin Hoffman in *All the President's Men* (A. Pakula, 1976). Ethnicity was the subject of *The Way We Were*, which shows conflict in a couple arising from social, economic, *and* ethnic difference. *The Godfather* in particular displays "the richness of the Italian-Catholic experience." (Erens, 1975).

Minority characters in American film can be divided into four categories: according to nationality (French people as seen by Americans); ethnicity (Jews, blacks, natives); gender (women); or social groups (homosexuals, disabled people). These characters can be considered minorities because they are seen in terms of the dominant culture that reflects white, male, Anglo-Saxon values. The idea of "minority" may vary in degree—from being on the fringe of society or a misfit, to an outsider[2] (one's own choice) or a pariah (excluded from society, e.g., prostitutes or homosexuals).

History and social structure have given rise to differences in European and American attitudes toward minorities. Americans tend to situate the discussion in terms of race, whereas, since World War II, the word "minority" has ceased to refer to any concrete concept for Europeans. Their minorities are composed of nationalist groups within the nations that make claims for autonomy (e.g., Bretons or Corsicans in France, or Scottish and Welsh people in Great Britain). Except for blacks and Native Americans, ethnic groups in the United States have been constituted through immigration, whereas ethnic groups in European states are usually nationals of former colonies or immigrant workers from Third World countries. Because of such differences, the particular expression minorities are given in American film often remains inexplicable for the European public. A European may be shocked at verbal practices of calling attention to ethnicity, often in a derogatory fashion, as in *Minnie and Moscowitz* (J. Cassavetes, 1971) or *Hustle* (R. Aldrich, 1975).[3] Instead of trying to soften racial issues, such invectives seem to increase tension. Generally, aspects of affirmative action escape Europeans, such as the quota system in job hiring that seems to insist on ethnicity. It could be argued that Europeans repress contentious issues. Religion has long sparked dissension and continues to do so in Northern Ireland. Bitter strife in Eastern Europe has recently proved the tenuousness of a non-ethnic supposition, and the term "ethnic" may no longer be acceptable since its association with the word "cleansing."

For the time being in Western countries, multiculturalism can be opposed to a nonracial society, flaunting ethnicity rather than repressing it—with the resulting consequences for both society as a whole and particular ethnic groups. The inception of the debate occurred when minority groups were coming to the fore and ethnic pride was establishing itself. I wish to examine the way in which minority and ethnic characters were depicted during this period (the 1960s–1970s) and to what extent these representations broke with former stereotypes. I will discuss some of the far-reaching effects of the changes and how minority representations have become a fixture in American film. I shall also point out what significance the emphasis on minority characteristics in film may have for Europeans.

Several American critics have expressed dissatisfaction regarding the extent of the changes in American film of the 1960s–1970s, noting a rather timid approach to ethnic and minority characters.[4] James Monaco argues that a lapse of roughly ten years was needed before the effects of, say, the civil rights or women's movements could be seen in film (Monaco, 1984: 56–57). This explanation seems unsatisfactory. Granted, film is a cumbersome medium and a delay may be necessary for contemporary events and trends to be expressed in it. Yet clothes and musical fashions enter film quickly, as do dramatic events (e.g., the Entebbe hijacking). In the 1960s–1970s, film depicted some of the more striking aspects of the social revolution of the late 1960s, such as drugs and youthful revolt.

Complex subjects such as minorities or the Vietnam War are more problematic. At the height of their presence in current events, they are conspicuous by their absence in film and are often addressed indirectly. Vietnam was, as Monaco says, "almost totally ignored by the film industry during its interminable duration." One is struck by the lack of Oriental-type characters in general during this period and, when they do appear, the treatment they receive. It seems that not only are ethnic and minority characters linked to social changes, but their film representation calls into question their previous images and stereotyped conceptions regarding them.

Bringing his European point of view to bear in his discussion of national character types in American film of the 1930s and 1940s, Siegfried Kracauer indicated how American culture fixes and appropriates representations:

The American screen image of the English is more or less standardized. True as this image is to reality, as a stereotype it has also a life of its own, a life independent of that reality. The English snob, as he appears in Hollywood films, is a figure which has in some degree drifted away from its original to join those mythological figures that people the world of American imagination. Whether angry at him or fond of him, Americans consider this kind of Briton one of theirs. He "belongs"; like Huckleberry Finn or Mickey Mouse, he is part of their universe. (Kracauer, 1949 as reprinted in Rosenberg and White, 1957: 267)

I would say, "True as this image *may be* to reality," because I do not believe that a stereotype is the exact replica of reality. The autonomous nature of these stereotyped representations in relation to the original models is to be noted, as well as the idea that American culture absorbs foreign or marginal elements, making them "one of us," as Tod Browning expressed it in *Freaks* (1932).

Film seems to require something more solid (and to obtain it, may indeed need more time than other media and artistic forms). It demands a transitional space before ethnic and minority characters can be integrated. A useful concept for describing this intermediary stage between reality and representation could be Michael Riffaterre's "sociolect," which he defines as:

language both as grammar and repository of the myths, traditions, ideological and esthetic stereotypes, commonplaces, and themes harbored by a society, a class, or a social group. . . . Aside from syntactic structures, the sociolect contains ready-made narrative and descriptive models that reflect a group's idea of or consensus about reality. (Riffaterre, 1990: 129)

The sociolect is the area in which ethnic groups become fixed, if not stereotyped, and in which they acquire acceptability. This is exemplified by the young

Jewish women played by Barbra Streisand. Fanny Brice in *Funny Girl* and Katie Morosky in *The Way We Were* have traits that denote the "Jewish woman" (Katie's obsession with food) or Jews in general (Fanny and Katie's humor, Katie's intelligence); neither character, nor the actress who portrays them, complies with the canons of beauty, but they compensate with their strong personalities (they are full of energy and talk a lot). These characteristics are also found in popular reading of the time (e.g., Dan Greenberg's 1964 bestseller *How to Be a Jewish Mother*, and Philip Roth's novels) as well as Woody Allen's films (Dundes, 1985). Stereotyped notions about Jewishness were already present in the sociolect and were relayed to the films, where they became a stereotyped aspect of the characters in question (only in relation to the sociolect, of course). In terms of American film, young Jewish women as central characters break with previous stereotypes. The novelty of the characters in the films decreases their stereotyped aspects. At the same time, the presence of these ethnic aspects in the sociolect facilitates the passage of this type of character to film.

Freaks is in fact all about otherness. It contrasts society's physical outcasts with "normal" people. Otherness is to be found in the oppositions inherent to American film in general. At a given moment, it has a given expression and certain groups are chosen to represent it. Previously, the tendency was to express otherness indirectly. Erens observes that former films often minimized the ethnicity of characters; she compares the gangsters of films in the 1930s to those of *The Godfather*.[5] Similarly, Jewish characters in a variety of films did not display any distinctive features that singled them out as belonging to a particular ethnic group. In my opinion, this neutrality of ethnic characteristics was to a large extent superficial. The "Italianness" of the early film gangsters can be seen in their relationships with their mothers and sisters. Many negative signs set them apart as "non-American": their brutish way of talking and gesticulating, their garish nouveau riche dress.[6] I feel that these film gangsters and their violent actions were possible *because* they were enacted by an ethnic group, a foreign element within American society, and were subsequently denounced and punished by American justice.

Otherness enables an American to assume traits that might pose a difficulty, as Julia Lesage indicates in her study of *Broken Blossoms*, a film directed by D. W. Griffith in 1919. Through the character of a Chinese man the romantic hero, a cultivated and sensitive man with an artistic temperament, could be presented (Lesage, 1985: 248). Roles that may be taboo for American characters still tend to devolve onto foreigners. Despite the "permissiveness" of the mid-1970s, the director Robert Aldrich believed the American public would reject a love story between an American policeman (Burt Reynolds) and a prostitute in *Hustle*. To make it credible, Aldrich had a foreign actress, Catherine Deneuve, play the role, thus complying with the traditional image of the French prostitute.[7] The choice of an actress with a glamorous image does soften up the character; but considering the film as whole, one wonders about the necessity of doing so. The supporting characters are full of explosive violence: Reynolds feels crushed by the "system"— to which much of the wrongs of the period were attributed—and his black partner bears a grudge against whites. Nevertheless, the narrative of "American policeman in love with prostitute" makes their love impossible, and Reynolds dies in the end.[8]

François Géré demonstrates how American film integrates the positive-negative opposition of otherness into the narrative with, on the one hand, "humanness" represented by whites, and on the other, "non-humanness" represented by Indians or Orientals, for example. Whites are fleshed-out characters, particularized by their differences and their oppositions, as in the beginning of *The Deer Hunter* (M. Cimino, 1978). They are individuals with whom we can identify. The "other," however, remains indivisible, without individuating facets (e.g., South and North Vietnamese combine in a single image of the cruel Oriental). This opposition functions through an excess on one side and simplification and uniformity on the other.

Attempts were made in the 1960s–1970s to do away with polarizations of this type. In *Too Late the Hero* (R. Aldrich, 1970), humanness is restored to Oriental characters by having the Japanese soldiers speak in conversational tones instead of the usual guttural utterances accorded to them in war movies. However, in *There was a Crooked Man* (J. Mankiewicz, 1970), the mark of the "other" falls on the Oriental character, who, in his refusal to speak and the need for his thoughts and feelings to be interpreted by another character, becomes very much the "illiterate savage cum faithful dog," a role that usually devolved onto black characters. The same film went to great lengths to break with traditional stereotypes regarding black people. Using a method typical of the times, the opening sequences deconstruct the traditional filmic southern Mammy and Griffith's "Old Faithfuls," giving a more "realistic" portrait of these characters. Later, another black character, the madam of a whites-only brothel, illustrates a second way of rethinking existing film stereotypes: a character that had previously been presented negatively is given a positive charge. She complies with what Edward Mapp terms the "Hot Mamma," a positive female version of Laurence D. Reddick's "sexual superman"; and she is not subservient: she gives orders to the white men.[9] The film also shows latent and overt homosexuality as well as a "twist . . . to the good-guy-versus-bad-guy mythology of the traditional Hollywood Western" (Geist, 1978: 371–372). Thus, although some stereotypes were revised during this period, otherness remained and its characteristics were shifted from one group to another. Stereotypes are thus transferred (e.g., cruelty taking on the form of Nazis, or Japanese or Russian spies), depending on the times.

The originality of the otherness expressed in the 1960s–1970s was an attempt to come to terms with the "other" within American society: *Easy Rider* (D. Hopper, 1969) and *Five Easy Pieces* or *Duel* (S. Spielberg, 1971) show protagonists in search of the "other America." *Hustle* and *The Deer Hunter* indicate how this period was drawing to a close and how, in many respects, American film was picking up the old strands of Hollywood tradition. The former illustrates that amid a selection of paradigmatic possibilities regarding minorities, film was emphasizing national belonging instead of choosing from a social minority (e.g., a prostitute).

The characters in *Easy Rider* or *Midnight Cowboy* (J. Schlesinger, 1969) seek a mythical escape within the United States (Florida). Through its French female character, *Hustle* is forced to construct an imaginary world in Europe—needless to say, based on American stereotypes. In *The Deer Hunter*, the shifting of otherness onto characters outside the United States serves to assert the Americanness of the characters within, who are themselves descendants of Russian immigrants. That the "other" was increasingly found outside American society had been shown in benign fashion in the previous year with *E.T.* (S. Spielberg, 1983) and would recur more menacingly in science fiction films of the decade to come—such as *Alien* (R. Scott, 1979). The "other" was thus taking on more imaginary representations.

Previously, a particular actor had tended to play a certain type of character: Kirk Douglas, a sensitive intellectual; Gregory Peck, a man of integrity; John Wayne, a moral cowboy. Now, characters as well as the actors that animate them tend to represent the group to which they belong. Even Robert Redford appears as a WASP, the role he plays in *The Way We Were* and in *All the President's Men*.

Some critics have noted a shift in the way characters are depicted in film during the period under consideration. According to Leo Braudy (1976), characters in films of the 1930s–1940s were subordinate to the plot; but starting in the 1960s, the tendency began to be reversed.[10] In this light, we can see the new emphasis on characteristic traits of ethnicity as dependent on the desire for fully rounded characters. Patricia Erens (1975) notes that one of the aims of the focus on ethnicity is to depict the diversity of the United States. Moreover, belonging to a minority or ethnic group has become an important element of a character's identity. This ethnicity presents itself through physical appearance (bumpy nose and kinky hair) as well as cultural traits thought to be specific to a particular group (language, food). The "ethnic experience" is part of a character's "whole personality," what makes him/her exist as a person, with good and bad sides, and not as a flat type.

It seems to me that two innovations took place regarding central characters in films of the 1960s–1970s. One was a desire to deepen them, and the other to diversify them. Regarding the first, efforts were made to give greater psychological veracity to characters and to describe their development. This can be seen in the use of psychological explanations for characters such as the male prostitute in *Midnight Cowboy* and/or the depressive model in *Puzzle of a Downfall Child* (J. Schatzberg, 1970). Just as "psychology" may flesh out a character, so does the integration of an ethnic background give it substance. In both cases, American film of the 1960s–1970s tried consciously to attack the problem of film stereotypes and to provide a wider range of characters. It sought to present those who were excluded from previous films (i.e., the "other"), offering portraits of more sensitive men and the evocation of different milieux with drug takers and prostitutes. Jane Fonda's tough Bree Daniels in *Klute* (A. Pakula, 1971) contrasts with Shirley MacLaine's idealized prostitute-with-a-heart-of-gold. The character of Daniels also presents a reversal to a 1950s film such as *River of No Return* (O.

Preminger, 1954). In *Klute*, the "loose" woman is not morally condemned by the man and does not have to prove herself to him in order to win his respect.

Films of the 1960s–1970s emphasized the need to replace previously negative images with more positive ones. In *Stars*, Dyer (1986) situates the debate on positive rethinking of film stereotypes within the context of criteria of verisimilitude and the fully rounded character. In another study about the representation of homosexuals in dominant cinema, Dyer favors a positive image whereby homosexuality would not be considered deviant from a heterosexual norm.[11] In contrast, the American Diane Waldman questions the criteria that determine a positive image and the very notion of positive image (Waldman, 1978). She points out that what is favored as a positive image is often based on an ideal conception of reality and not on reality itself; that people do not always take into consideration the possible diversity of positive images according to one's socioeconomic group and the commercial structures within which these images function; and finally, that the notion of positive image assumes that the spectator will identify with the character but does not take into account the mechanism of identification, especially within the codes of realism. To date, the debate over positive-negative image remains unresolved. As Waldman indicates, positive images frequently end up conforming to new, updated stereotypes.

What interests me is how "positive" images were expressed during the 1960s–1970s and whether they met expectations or instead side-stepped issues. Generally, there seems to be a difficulty in representing ethnic and minority groups as self-sufficient in film. The black protagonist of *In the Heat of the Night* requires a white fellow traveler; the minority characteristic of male sensitivity portrayed by Jack Lemmon in *The Odd Couple* (G. Saks, 1968) must be matched to Walter Matthau's gruff he-manness. The dual male protagonist configuration, which I call the "odd couple," replaces the former solitary hero and reflects the period's outward tendency of encompassing the "other." It provides an outlet for ethnic and minority characteristics, but it tends to deny them autonomy. Its main function is to reconcile fringe characters with the mainstream.[12]

Frequently, the transformation of stereotypes presents a revised image within existing narratives, as was seen with the Mammy in *There Was a Crooked Man*. The image of the Native American is mainly revised within the western. Few contemporary American Indians are to be found. A noticeable exception is *One Flew Over the Cuckoo's Nest* (1975) by the Czechoslovakian director Milos Forman.

Another means of portraying minority characters is to situate them in the past. This is often the case where women are concerned—for example, the strong Jewish women played by Streisand or the women portrayed in *Julia* (F. Zinneman, 1977). As *Julia* shows, the past also allows more acceptable and traditional film images to be continued—the 1940s provides a more glamorous image of women than the more contemporary period of, for example, *Alice Doesn't Live Here Anymore* (M. Scorsese, 1974). A more attractive image of women can also be projected through present-day glamorous personae, such as the model in *Puzzle of a Downfall Child*. Female protagonists were generally scarce during the 1960s–

1970s, as were feminist issues. Women were often excluded in favor of the odd-couple configuration; and despite sexual liberation in society, films of this period tend to condemn women who seek to reverse traditional roles (*The Graduate*; *Puzzle of a Downfall Child*; *Looking for Mr. Goodbar*—R. Brooks, 1977). The paucity of women directors throughout American film and in the world at large is a known fact, although some change has occurred in the United States over the last ten years. During the 1960s–1970s, women directors were generally independents (e.g., Joan Micklen Silver, whose 1974 film *Hester Street* centers on a Jewish woman in the immigrant community of New York at the beginning of the century). Women tended to make documentaries, often concerned with women's issues (Monaco, 1984: 260). A similar situation existed in Europe: in France, for example, women directors such as Agnes Varda or Marguerite Duras could find a place within the avant-garde but not elsewhere.[13] If women actresses have lost their previous goddess-like status in American film, they remain the mouthpieces of male directors, through whom they generally express themselves—as, for example, Jane Fonda (Dyer, 1986: 73–98; Gledhill, 1991: 237–250) or, more recently, Susan Sarandon in *Thelma and Louise* (R. Scott, 1991).

Paradoxically, the attempt to do away with stereotypes through a greater representation of minorities has brought out other types. In his discussion of Orrin Klapp's methodology, the British critic Richard Dyer points out that Klapp's social types include few minority members (women, homosexuals, workers, ethnic minorities) and that his point of view is that of the dominant ideology (Dyer, 1986: 54; cf. Klapp, 1962). Klapp's types are indeed no longer in tune with the anti-hero of the 1960s–1970s or the perspective this period gives to American film in general. Donald Bogle, for instance, has defined five broad categories for black characters: the good *Tom*; the funny *Coon*; the tragic *Mulatto*; the asexual *Mammy*; and the supersexual *Buck* (or *Black Beauty* for women characters). For Bogle, the stoicism of the Sydney Poitier characters of the late 1960s, even if they are central, define them as *Toms*.

Ethnic and minority representation can be seen in terms of film as upward and downward mobility. If in fact many minority members were at the time aspiring to rise in social spheres or simply to attain equality, many members of the white middle class were dropping out of society, refusing to assume the role they had been socialized to play. This meant that in film, their former unquestioned position in dominant roles was not being revised. Conversely, black characters were acceding to roles previously reserved for whites, such as the detective or the gangster of *In the Heat of the Night* or *Shaft* (G. Parks, 1971).

The foregrounding of ethnicity of character, which had previously been a secondary characteristic, is particularly noticeable in films that portray a group of people from different backgrounds—such as *The Poseidon Adventure* (R. Neame, 1972), in which Shelley Winters plays a Jewish mother. Formerly, in films presenting several characters, personality differences were the main distinguishing feature—as in *The Magnificent Seven* (J. Sturges, 1960). *Twelve Angry Men* (S. Lumet, 1957) provided its characters with a socioeconomic context in which each character's profession was defined. Physical characteristics also situated a character. The baldness of Telly Savalas in *The Dirty Dozen* (R. Aldrich, 1967) and Ed Begley in *Twelve Angry Men* denoted, respectively, perversion and racism (Cieutat, 1988: 207–208). Such characteristics became accessories in forming a character's identity. Now ethnicity is at the center and determines the physical *and* personality characteristics of the character (e.g., Shelley Winter's Jewish mother). Thus, in later films presenting an assortment of characters, ethnicity is the character's primary trait and other characteristics (e.g., profession, milieu, physique) are secondary. In this configuration of the "mixed bag," which presents an array of characters from varying ethnic backgrounds, depth is eliminated as ethnicity becomes an automatic character trait. Ethnic representations tend to become superficial and display a pretense at diversity. Once ethnicity becomes an established fact in American film—from the late 1970s onward—the previously mentioned diversity and dimension of character fall away. Gradually, films with multiple characters see a single hero, usually male and white, coming to the fore again, and the other characters—each with an ethnic identity—provide a frame or background for this central character.[14]

Another later development concerns ethnicity as "plot." In films with ethnic questions as subject matter, the suspense was organized around the exposition of ethnicity. Toward the end of the 1980s, suspense begins to be organized around the treatment of racial issues. This phenomenon can be seen in *Bonfire of the Vanities* (B. De Palma, 1990), *Do the Right Thing* (S. Lee, 1989), and *Homicide* (D. Mamet, 1991). In these works the different ethnic groups are pitted against each other and the theme of racism becomes part of the diegesis. Recent changes have also been found within the odd-couple structure, with both members of the couple belonging to different minorities. In *Carlito's Way* (B. De Palma, 1993), one group dominates the other. In *Philadelphia* (J. Demme, 1993), two kinds of discrimination are paralleled: against a man with AIDS and against a black man. The irony is that the latter character represents the majority point of view.

Why do ethnic and minority types continue to exist over and above the sociopolitical needs defined by affirmative action? In the early 1950s, Marshall McLuhan attacked the loss of individuality as represented by America's "homogenized Dagwoods." Now it seems that the distinctive features of entire cultures have disappeared and that cultural homogenization is the result of the 1980s and 1990s. This leveling process has made it necessary to stress differences and define sociocultural or ethnic groups according to the most plain and simple stereotypes. Despite the desire to transform former stereotypes in film, the 1960s–1970s only provided a partial solution to the problem. Other questions were in fact revealed, linked to the way in which characters themselves are represented. Replacing a negative image by a positive one does not necessarily avoid stereotyping. The promise of diversity that brought minorities out of obscurity led to characters being given a fixed identity according to their ethnic group.

This poses a basic problem for stereotypes in the cinema. In the 1960s–1970s, it was a liberating process to present characters of an ethnic type, a sign of optimism that minorities could exist in their own right as main characters. But this presentation was essentially visual and was mainly based on physical recognition. With ethnicity as identity, there has been a return to the use of basic character types whereby characters—their identities and personalities—are recognizable through physical appearance. The identity of American cinema has now come to include ethnic or minority characteristics as the defining element of character and has become for Europeans one of the bases of what they see as the "American film."

NOTES

1. The change in the representation of ethnic and minority characters in American film from 1967 was part of a general reaction to the former Hollywood system. The revival, which continued for almost a decade, was characterized by a younger generation of directors with a more personal viewpoint, different types of actors, new roles and stories, and cinematic innovations. It has been called the American New Wave (under the French influence), new Hollywood, or Hollywood Renaissance. For convenience, I shall refer to this period as the 1960s–1970s.

2. To this must be added the existential connotations, important during the 1960s–1970s, suggested by one of the translations of the title of Albert Camus's *L'Etranger*.

3. This practice intensified in film and novels of the 1980s. See, for example, *Bonfire of the Vanities* (T. Wolfe, 1987), *Do the Right Thing* (S. Lee, 1989), and *Homicide* (D. Mamet, 1991).

4. See Mapp, 1972, and Bogle, 1973, on black characters; or Haskell, 1973, concerning women. The new directors depict people dropping out (*The Graduate*, M. Nichols, 1967) or on the fringe of society (*Five Easy Pieces*, B. Rafelson, 1970) but center on the emotional fluctuations of the young white male heroes.

5. A French version of this film, *Le grand pardon* (*The Day of Atonement*, Alexandre Arcady, 1981), was set among the Sephardic Jewish gangsters of Paris, complete with patriarchal figure and gang warfare between Jewish and Arab communities.

6. Similar characteristics are found for the protagonists of early 1930s gangster films: Catholics and immigrants; "expansive, vulgar and garrulous" and "abnormal" sexual relationships. Cf. McArthur, 1972: 35.

7. See J. O. Thompson, "Screen Acting and the Commutation Test," in Gledhill, 1991: 192. Difficult themes often gain acceptability in a foreign film, which could account for the considerable American success of *Les Valseuses* (B. Blier, France, 1974). To the American viewer, this film may be bordering on the pornographic.

8. For how the story is contained in the narrative, cf. Riffaterre, 1990: 131–132.

9. Mapp uses Reddick's classification of 19 black stereotypes to indicate the changes of black characters in the 1960s–1970s. See L. D. Reddick, "Educational Programs for the Improvement of Race Relations: Motion Pictures, Radio, the Press and Libraries," *Journal of Negro Education* 13 (Summer 1944).

10. Cf. Braudy, 1976. However, Kracauer already described characters in terms of psychological consistency in 1949.

11. Dyer, 1978: 16. First published in *Gay Left* 2 as "Rejecting Straight Ideals." Dyer analyzes *Sunday Bloody Sunday* (Schlesinger, Great Britain, 1971).

12. In contrast, the German director Rainer Fassbinder not only depicts characters on

the fringe but seeks to bring out the "fringe" elements in society's seemingly established members. His characters' exhibitionism aligns him more with Andy Warhol. Wim Wenders's films are closer to mainstream films of the period, although his heroes express an angst that is not entirely resolved.

13. Independent directors have a more prominent position in France, and over the last decade a number of women directors have appeared.

14. For example, *The Warriors* (W. Hill, 1979), the *Alien* series (female protagonist), *The Champions* (S. Herek, 1992).

REFERENCES

Bogle, Donald (1973). *Toms, Coons, Mulattoes, Mammies, and Bucks: An Interpretive History of Blacks in American Films*. New York: Viking Press.

Braudy, L. (1976). *The World in a Frame*. Garden City, NY: Anchor Press/Doubleday.

Cieutat, Michel (1988). *Les grands thèmes du cinéma américain. Tome I: Le rêve et le cauchemar*. Paris: Septième Art/Editions du Cerf.

"Cinéma américain: aux marches du paradis" (1993). *Revue Française d'Etudes Américaines* 57 (July). Nancy: Presses Universitaires de Nancy.

"Cinéma et judéité" (1986). *CinémAction* (February). Paris: Cerf.

Dundes, Alan (1985). "The Jewish American Princess and the Jewish American Mother in American Jokelore." *Journal of American Folklore* 98: 465–475.

Dyer, Richard (1978). "Gays in Film." *Jump Cut* 18.

———— (1986). *Stars* [1979]. London: British Film Institute.

Erens, Patricia (1975). "Gangsters, Vampires, and J.A.P.s: The Jew Surfaces in American Movies." *Journal of Popular Film* 4: 208–222.

———— (ed.) (1990). *Issues in Feminist Film Criticism*. Bloomington: Indiana University Press.

Geist, K. L. (1978). *Pictures Will Talk: The Life and Times of Joseph L. Mankiewicz*. New York: Scribner.

Géré, François (1980). "L'imaginaire raciste: la mesure de l'homme." *Cahiers du Cinéma* 315 (September): 37–42.

Gledhill, Christine (ed.) (1991). *Stardom, Industry of Desire*. London: Routledge.

Haskell, Molly (1973). *From Rape to Reverence*. New York: Holt, Rinehart, & Winston.

Klapp, O. E. (1962). *Heroes, Villains and Fools*. Englewood Cliffs, NJ: Prentice-Hall.

Kracauer, Siegfried (1949). "National Types as Hollywood Presents Them." *Public Opinion Quarterly* 13: 53–72. Reprinted in *Mass Culture: The Popular Arts in America*, eds. Bernard Rosenberg and David M. White (New York: Free Press, 1957), 257–277.

Lesage, J. (1985). "Artful Racism, Artful Rape: Griffith's *Broken Blossoms*." *Jump Cut: Hollywood, Politics and Counter-Cinema*, ed. P. Steven. Toronto: Between the Lines.

Mapp, Edward (1972). *Blacks in American Films: Today and Yesterday*. Metuchen, NJ: Scarecrow Press.

McArthur, Colin (1972). *Underworld USA*. British Film Institute, coll. "The Cinema One." London: Secker & Warburg.

McLuhan, Marshall (1951). *The Mechanical Bride: Folklore of Industrial Man*. Boston: Beacon Press.

Monaco, James (1984). *American Film Now: The People, the Power, the Money, the Movies* [1979]. New York: New American Library.

Riffaterre, Michael (1990). *Fictional Truth*. London: Johns Hopkins University Press.

Starfield, Penny (1993). "Le stéréotype au cinéma: le cinéma américain de 1967 à 1977."
      Ph.D. thesis. Paris: Université Paris VII.

Waldman, D. (1978). "There's More to a Positive Image Than Meets the Eye." *Jump Cut*
      18.

18 America on My Mind

Lazare Bitoun

It all began the day I saw Burt Lancaster grin his wide, white, toothy smile and quote his friend Ace Hannah, who always had an appropriate saying for whatever was happening. It was at the Rialto, the theater where they showed American movies in Casablanca—the town, not the film. I was ten years old and the movie was *Vera Cruz*. All of a sudden, the stories my father had been telling about the war began to make sense: Gary Cooper and Burt Lancaster had saved the Mexicans from the rule of Maximilian, their French emperor; in turn, the GIs had saved the Jews from Pétain and the Franco-Germans. We were the Mexicans, for three years my family had lived in fear and had lain low, then the Americans had come to save us. They feared nothing; they had arrived with their cigarettes, their chewing gum, and their Coca-Cola; and while they were at it, they had also brought their Winchesters and killed the dragons. They were our freedom and our future, just like in the movie.

With *The Man without a Star, The Big Sky, Red River*, and *Shane*, I became at the same time a cowboy, a sheriff, a trapper, and an outlaw. On our farm in the drylands of Morocco, the cows grew long horns, the sheep became buffaloes, and the donkey that I rode everyday, without bridle or saddle, to school and back, changed into a wild mustang. After this, of course, I never went anywhere without sticking my gun into my belt, a crooked piece of dead wood I had found at the foot of an olive tree. My cousin Jojo and I set traps for wild animals (hens and rabbits), ambushed our enemies (sisters and cousins), and once, we even captured two calves that had strayed onto our property. To this day I can remember the angle of my father's thick eyebrows and the stinging of his belt, when the neighbor, an old schoolmate of his, came to get his cattle back. I only read western comics (in French)—Kit Carson, Buffalo Bill, Red Ryder, and Buck John (he was the Sheriff of Alkali City). I cut off the sleeves of an old jacket to make it into a vest, and I was able to wear my father's hat after wrapping a scarf three times around my head to bring it up to size.

I had gone overboard; I was hooked on America.

Meanwhile, back at the Rialto, they were now showing Dean Martin and Jerry Lewis movies. Forget the song and dance, or the humor, or the crooner and dimwit act: we liked these movies because the two actors were Jewish. Yes, of course Dean Martin was Jewish. He was teamed up with a Jew, and in those postwar days you had to be a Jew to work with one. That Jews could be in a movie was to our parents a miracle beyond comprehension, and sending the children to watch "their" movies filled them with pride and was considered a mitzvah. So every Saturday afternoon, along with the money for the tickets (and through this, somehow, for the children of Israel), they gave us their blessing as we shot off to the Rialto. For two hours we would be transported into a fantasy world where our two Jewish heroes avenged us for all the vexations we had endured and sometimes still endured in the schoolyard. Dean Martin and Jerry Lewis turned the world on its head and ridiculed everything, from the U.S. Navy to boarding schools and the Wild West when they took Irma there. They were kings of the screen, the world belonged to them, they were what we longed to be, and they called God by his first name. "Only in America," our parents would say—that place was the new Eden to which the Messiah had come.

Then I met the McGintys.

They came from Wisconsin, he had opened a toy store in downtown Casablanca, she worked at the American cultural center, and they loved the idea of living on what they called "a farm" and in what we called "a country house." They were gods fallen from the sky. They had two huge American cars (a Buick sedan and a Nash Ambassador coupé) plus an orchard, a lawn, a swimming pool, a real bathroom with a bathtub and a shower, a generator for electricity, and a refrigerator. They also had a pedigreed dog, Mitzy; a son my age, George; and a daughter, Vicky, the first love of my adolescent life. With George I discovered baseball, model airplanes, blue jeans, Arrow Egyptian cotton shirts, Superman, and the inside of a golf ball. With Vicky it was another story; she was 12 and I was 13 and we were going to be married when we grew up. For the time being, since we were so young, we only did as if, which meant we kissed a lot (French kisses, of course) and played often at my finger on your bellybutton. With both of them, besides friendship and the first tinglings of libido, I discovered James Dean, Elvis Presley, "Passion Flower," "Day-O," and Paul Anka, Kellogg's corn flakes, Bazooka bubble-gum, hamburgers, and portable radios. The first time our two families went to the beach together, I think I was never more ashamed in my life: us on one side with a kerosene stove and a huge pot for the *tajine*, because, as my father would say, going to the beach didn't mean you had to starve; then on the other, each with two square sandwiches cut into perfect triangles, neatly wrapped in wax paper. Our only common ground was a case of Coca-Cola.

I didn't marry Vicky. Instead I moved to France.

The King of Morocco had come back; we had to pack our bags and go. If the family had left only a farm, I had left a ranch on the Rio Grande of my childhood. Now we lived in two tiny rooms above the café into which my father invested everything he had—and didn't have. I missed the space; I missed the light in the air, the whitewashed houses, the scarce vegetation, and the dry beauty of the landscape. Here everything was either disgustingly grey (grim houses and cloudy skies) or disgustingly green (the dark shutters and whatever grew in the ground). There was nothing in that village, and you had to travel 20 miles to the nearest town if you wanted to buy a record, see a movie, or watch people in the street. When we did go those 20 miles—by train, for we no longer had a car—all you could buy in the stores was Edith Piaf records and all you could see were stupid Saturday night French family comedies. There were no McGintys, either. I was miserable, I hated France, I hated the French, and all I wanted was to go back where I came from.

Until I discovered the American airbase 10 miles away.

Airmen and NCOs came to the café. I served them beer and red wine, and we talked. I had been learning English at school for four or five years, but over the next four years it was GIs who taught me the language and most of what I now know about America and the Americans. Like me, my new friends were far from home; somehow, we had something in common—a lost paradise of some sort or another, I suppose. With them I discovered a microcosmic America; it was made of the commissary from which they brought me corn flakes, pancake mix, corn chips, and peanut butter, and of the PX that provided the rest: bluejeans, T shirts, portable radios, and pretty soon cigarettes. To the same airbase I owe my acquaintance with bowling alleys, cafeterias, clubs, slot machines, Harley Davidson motorcycles, fried onion rings, *Playboy* magazine, the L. L. Bean catalogue, Charlie Parker, Count Basie, Ray Charles, Frank Sinatra, and the novels of Mickey Spillane, Ross McDonald, and Carter Brown. I remember the cover of *Walk Softly Witch*; it showed a pair of long, shapely, nylon-sheathed legs at the end of which feet sunk deeply into a 3-inch-thick carpet.

The PX also made my first two years at the Sorbonne possible; it allowed me to pay my way through school. My friends bought the goods, I sold them, then we would split the profits: cigarettes and whiskey for my teachers; American shirts, Levi's jeans, fatigue pants, watches, radios, and records for my classmates.

I went on reading *Playboy* for quite some time—for the interviews and the short stories, of course—and I quickly graduated to Hemingway and Steinbeck. Then somebody gave me *Dangling Man* and *The Tenants of Moonbloom*. Somebody else gave me *The Naked and the Dead* and *Goodbye, Columbus*. I discovered that there were Jews in America who were Jewish the way I felt Jewish, without the superstitions, without the narrow-mindedness, outside of the synagogue and the repetitious chant of the prayers. It opened a whole new world to me. I discovered unknown writers and encountered my first reformed Jews as well as strange words such as "lox," "gefilte fish," "gewalt," and "mishpuchah."

Soon after, I went to New York. It was 1964. It blew my mind.

By the time I came back, de Gaulle was closing down all the U.S. Air Force bases and Army posts in France. After all, it wasn't such a bad thing for me. I might otherwise have ended up in jail: the penalty for contraband was pretty stiff.

On the return flight I had met Jimmy. He was from Boston and he was coming to study in France for a year—he has remained here to this day. Together we listened to the records of Leadbelly and Woody Guthrie and went to hear Joan Baez and Pete Seeger when they came to Paris. We were sure we would overcome. For the time being, we linked arms, asked LBJ how many kids he had killed that day, and hopped along the streets of Paris to the sound and ideology of "Ho, Ho, Ho Chi Minh!" As the years went by, we marched against the Vietnam War, for women's rights, for abortion, against racism, and for or against at least 250 other more or less lost causes. We loved Stewball who was a good horse, we said farewell to Angelina and laughed with Tom Lehrer and Lenny Bruce. We went to rallies for the Chicago Seven, the California grape pickers, the Black Panthers, the Chicanos, and the Indians; we recited the music of The Last Poets; went to Marx Brothers, Mae West, and W. C. Fields movies; and religiously attended the performances of the Living Theater and the Bread and Puppet people. In due time we grew beards and long hair, got more or less married, finished our doctorates, and began to work.

Today, America is in France and France is in America: both countries have lost their exotic charm.

My friends now teach at Queens, at City, at New Paltz, or at Berkeley. I am now at a large university in the Paris suburbs, where I teach American literature. We have, over the years, exchanged jobs, apartments, and cars, and we are now even beginning to exchange our children. We see each other here or there; we gather around food and talk endlessly about our work, politics, our computers, and ourselves; and we complain about taxes, cholesterol, and students. Here or there is the same world now; you can eat croissants and buy French designer clothes in New York; fast-food joints, Levi's jeans, and baseball caps have invaded the streets of Paris.

I do not watch westerns any longer, ideologies have gone out of business, Joan Baez has cut her long hair, and Bob Dylan has lost his voice; I now love Mozart, good wine, and *gratin dauphinois*. But two things still give me a kick: the view of the Statue of Liberty as the boat sails in from Staten Island, and the taste of a New York bagel.

Part VII

Americanization

19 A Taste of Honey: Adorno's Reading of American Mass Culture

Kaspar Maase

During the 1950s, Max Horkheimer and Theodor Adorno, together with other European emigrants to the United States such as Hannah Arendt, Günter Anders, and Leo Löwenthal, became protagonists of the theoretical critique of contemporary mass culture.[1] Their philosophical study on the "Dialectic of Enlightenment" was first published in German in the United States in a mimeographed version in 1944; slightly revised, it came out as a book in Amsterdam in 1947. Without a doubt, this essay has proved to be one of the most influential intellectual works in the second half of our century. The broad reception, however, inevitably implied that much of the complexity of thought was lost in favor of stereotyped judgments.

The book's chapter on the culture industry has shared the fate of being misread quite often. The authors, so it was perceived, absolutely condemned all manifestations of mass culture by applying the standards of autonomous art and of the good life in the decidedly moral sense of the term. "There can be no good life in the wrong"—Adorno's aphormism of 1944[2] was cited frequently; it served to foster a fairly shallow reading of a highly dialectical critique. In the end, the anti-fascists' essay on the aporias of progress and enlightenment was adapted to the mainstream of predominantly conservative theories of mass society.[3]

In this discussion I want to recall that Horkheimer and Adorno had a much more differentiated understanding of mass culture, especially of its material and sensuous satisfactions. In a hitherto unpublished lecture, Adorno sketched what he regarded as positive aspects of American culture; his argument culminated in the thesis that the affluence on which mass consumption is based contained an element of realized utopia. The importance of this idea for the necessary reshaping of our way of life will be the topic of a short final consideration.

THE RIGHT TO HAPPINESS AND THE MISREADINGS OF CRITICAL THEORY

Dialectic of Enlightenment is a very complex text, and it is hard work to reconstruct its intellectual architecture. The book's effect is not in the least due to a pervasive rhetoric leaving the underlying argument in some ambiguity and hermetic darkness. Much could be said about the authors' motives for this style of presenting their critique of the spiritual foundations of modern society,[4] but this discussion is not the place to do so. It is beyond doubt, however, that Horkheimer and Adorno's work in itself contained some starting points for the conservative reading that dominated its reception in the 1950s and 1960s, and that in some regard is still influential today.[5]

Above all, two lines of historical experience can be traced in the *Dialectic of Enlightenment*. First, Horkheimer and Adorno tried to understand how the rise to power and the barbaric crimes of fascism had been possible. Second, their fate as Jewish expatriates made them highly sensitive to any sign of marginalization of autonomous thinking and autonomous individuality—and they perceived an alarmingly high number of such signs in contemporary American society. This was why they took up de Tocqueville's argument that democracy (in America) would facilitate a new kind of dictatorship by means of a most powerful social pressure toward conformism. Their essay pointed out two concrete historical preconditions for such a development. One was a monopolized culture industry subjugating intellectual and artistic production to the laws of making profit, of mass markets and of mass consumption. The other prerequisite was a relatively high standard of living that had made traditional conceptions of impoverishment and class struggle baseless.

The core argument of *Dialectic of Enlightenment* is political and humanist, not cultural. "What matters is not culture as a value . . . a critical self-reflection of enlightenment is necessary, rather, if man shall not be betrayed altogether."[6] Horkheimer and Adorno never intended to denounce the betterment of living conditions of the working class as generating a threat to culture. They violently attacked the total transformation of intellectual creativity into a branch of industry catering to the most comfortable consumption of cultural commodities. They deeply despised the mainstream of slick entertainment, and they joined the critics judging that popular music, pulp literature, and Hollywood movies only served to make people forget about their social situation and to make light of human suffering by the stereotyped way of showing it.[7] But the dark side of mass culture became a cause for being alarmed only within the social and political trend to barbarization. The problem was an absurd state of conditions "turning even the good things in life into elements of disaster" (Horkheimer and Adorno, 1971: 4f). It is only within this very distinct context that we find critical commentary on mass consumption, for instance, the remark that "the powerlessness and tracta-bility of the masses are increasing with the amount of goods apportioned" (4).

Reading a text means adapting it by framing it with the reader's view of life. The intellectual elites on both sides of the Atlantic were no exception to the rule. They perceived the dialectical critique of the Frankfurt School as a well-formulated variation on the traditional theme of "the uneducated masses wasting their time and money on the vulgar satisfactions of the body instead of lifting themselves up to enjoy the longlasting pleasures of the spirit." Pointed catchwords such as that of "the people's wicked love for what is done for them" (Horkheimer and Adorno, 1971: 120) were grist on the mills of those who cynically defended their cultural privilege. By isolating such remarks, Horkheimer and Adorno's cri-tique was watered down and misinterpreted along the lines of the "bread and circuses" stereotype of mass culture and mass society (Brantlinger, 1983).

In their preface to the *Dialectic of Enlightenment*, Horkheimer and Adorno dis-sociated themselves unmistakeably from the contemporary criticism of culture (*Kulturkritik*). Authors such as Huxley, Ortega y Gasset, Jaspers, and others wor-ried that culture as a value in itself was being threatened. Horkheimer and Adorno, however, started from the conviction that it was humankind that had to be safe-guarded and that to this end it was not the past that had to be conserved but the hopes of the past that had to be redeemed. In their view, outstanding among these hopes was the idea of a state of fulfilled human existence integrating all sensuous joy.[8]

Martin Jay has pointed out that "the claim to happiness has always been a relevant and basic element of Critical Theory" (Jay, 1981: 217; Wiggershaus, 1986: 205–208). Horkheimer's outstanding essay entitled "Egoism and Emanci-pation Movement" pleaded emphatically for "unrationalized free pleasure aspired without any justifications" and for the legitimacy of an "absolute desire for hap-piness" (Horkheimer, 1936: 170, 171). According to the author, modern bour-geois thinking, religious or not, was grounded on an ascetic anthropology and had effectively informed people's attitudes with the "disapproval of 'vulgar' lust" (Horkheimer, 1936: 172). The denouncement of natural drives and basic human desires conflicted most sharply with the materialistic and hedonistic traditions to which Horkheimer and Adorno referred.

From this point of view, an incessant dialectic pervaded all forms of individual consumption. Criticizing Veblen's concept of conspicuous consumption as one-dimensional, Adorno stated that there was a presentiment of real happiness even in such a highly alienated activity. Adorno spoke of the "dialectic of luxury"; it meant that the satisfaction drawn from the idea of gaining status was spoiled through and through by barbaric social relations, but even this experience of joy inevitably transcended the status quo by the promise of some other, different happiness (Adorno, 1977: 86f).

Public as well as academic reception tends to underestimate or even ignore the fundamental role of the idea of uncurtailed happiness in Critical Theory. This fact is partly due to the specific method of argumentation preferred by the authors.

Especially in the *Dialectic of Enlightenment*, Horkheimer and Adorno strictly refrained from positively developing their concept of a free and humane society. They attempted to apply the method of "particular negation" (*bestimmte Negation*) to analyze the mechanisms responsible for the self-destructive and barbaric dynamics of bourgeois society up to the point where a possibility of sudden change (*Umschlag*) appeared.

"MORE ICE CREAM, LESS FEAR"

I must admit that for quite some time I had adhered to the opinion that with respect to mass culture, Horkheimer and Adorno shared many judgments put forward by conservative cultural criticism—and in my view this meant no recommendation. So I was most surprised when I came across a newspaper report of a lecture held by Adorno in 1957; the journalist summarized Adorno's assessment of American culture with the headline: "More ice cream, less fear."[9] What made me extremely curious to know more about this lecture were the reported views on the utopian dimension of American mass culture. My own studies on the image of America among the German working class had led to the assumption that the popular perception of the American way of life bore distinct connotations of the land where milk and honey flow[10]—and here it seemed as if Adorno could be a most unexpected representative of such a view.

Adorno held his lecture on German and American culture at least 13 times between 1956 and 1966. The only printed version is from a tape recording slightly revised by the author (Adorno, 1959);[11] the text has not been included in his *Collected Works* (*Gesammelte Schriften*). Adorno's foreword stresses that the small brochure was just meant to support his listeners' memory and that he was not taking any responsibility for the text. Nevertheless, the lecture contains a unique sketch of what might have been the content of an essay on the "positive aspects of mass culture," which Horkheimer and Adorno had announced in their preface to the 1944 version of *Dialectic of Enlightenment* (Wiggershaus, 1986: 360). Thus, reconstructing Adorno's argument does not mean paying tribute to an academic cult of personality. Treating mass consumption as a materialization (although deeply perverted) of the pursuit of happiness means intervening into a highly topical contemporary debate.

Adorno's starting point was the decisive difference between the European and the American notions of culture. On the Old Continent, and most prominently in Germany, "culture" fixed on a canon of excellent intellectual works and implied an ideal of spiritual self-development. In America, the idea of culture was related to the practice of shaping reality: forming social relations as well as taming nature and mastering natural resources by means of technology. Both of these dimensions were rooted in the meaning that the notion of culture gained in early modern Europe. "Culture" derives from the Latin verb "colere," which means to cultivate, to care for something. One interpretation of this basic meaning was man taking control over nature in the sense of governing the resisting forces of nature outside as well as controlling the natural urges within himself—the human drives and the unconscious. But cultivation is not tantamount to ruling. Cultivation of nature also included maintaining the essence of all that is appropriated and molded for human use. This kind of relationship with nature demanded contemplation and self-reflection of human praxis; it demanded a kind of spiritualization in order to civilize the power exercized on external and internal nature.

According to Adorno, the different accentuation of culture in America and Germany was due to the different historical experience of the middle classes in the two countries. American society was based on a purely bourgeois foundation, and here the principles of middle-class culture were realized in the most conse-quent way. Germany, in contrast, had never experienced a successful bourgeois revolution, and in 1918 the foundation of a democratic civil society was distorted by the paramount middle-class fear of socialism. Under these circumstances, cul-ture assumed a highly spiritualized character, thus compensating for the lack of opportunities to shape German society according to middle-class ideals. This con-centration on intellectual and spiritual refinement facilitated the achievements of German music and philosophy; but the price for setting free the absolute powers of the human mind was a significant deficit of contact with reality.

As a result, most German intellectuals have tended to denounce the alleged rule of "materialism" in the United States. Adorno confronted them with his di-alectical view of mass production and mass consumption:

Probably one of the most intense experiences for a person coming to America is the over-whelming wealth of goods presented there. Sometimes I feel suspicion against the idea that a world capable of producing so many goods should be solely materialist. I hear the well-known overtones of the grapes hanging too high. For this reason we should judge extremely cautiously and delicately. This amount of goods has got a certain feeling to it . . . which you can hardly explain to anyone who has not himself had the experience; but we should not deny this impression, and, above all, we should not value it too lowly. There is a touch of the land of Cockaigne in it. Just pass through one of the so-called American supermarkets only once, and somehow you will feel—however deceitful and superficial this feeling may be—: there is no more deprivation, it is fulfilment, boundless and perfect fulfilment of all material needs. (Adorno, 1959: 7)

Of course, Adorno added, nothing was free in monopoly capitalism. In America, as in any other country, the aim of the most rationalized and reckless methods of production was profit, not human well-being. But then we find a statement that may sound very simple and commonsensical from a liberal point of view; but—as far as I can see—it is unique in the context of Critical Theory and it means a kind of break with the principles of the postwar Frankfurt School. Adorno noted that the production system in the United States was so enormously effective that despite the profit orientation, each single person got an overwhelming amount of consumer goods. By taking the perspective of the common people's individual experience, Adorno not only contradicted traditional Marxism but opposed the entire discourse of conservative cultural criticism that dominated in West Germany until the mid-1960s. He connected individual material well-being with the fact that in America the principle of bourgeois culture—which he saw as closely interwoven with the principle of humanity—not only had been radically thought but had been realized with final consequence.

Adorno gave an example. In America, the mass media successfully popularized some ideas of modern psychology and so-called progressive education. Not all results were pleasant:

But the fact that each American child may actually eat a so-called ice-cone incessantly . . . thus finding a kind of fulfilment of children's happiness at any moment, that happiness for which our children once craned their necks in vain—this is really a part of utopia come true.

It has got something of that peacefulness, that absence of fear and threat which we would imagine to prevail in a chiliastic kingdom. The abundance of goods, the fact that deprivation diminishes . . . —this brings into everyday experience a trait of that peacefulness and unaggressive behaviour which we have lost nearly totally in Europe. It is a kind of friendliness that you may observe especially with so-called common people . . . , pervading the whole society with humanity in behavior itself. This makes up very well for the fact that the people in question may perhaps not pronounce the names of Bach and Beethoven in the correct fashion which we believe to be indispensable for real refinement. (Adorno, 1959: 7f)

Today, the image of American society is generally associated with the omnipresence of violence in the media as well as in the streets. Against this background, it is most enticing to brush aside Adorno's observations: a German philosopher, incurably romantic, confusing a Norman Rockwell painting with reality. But, strange as it may seem to an American public, you will find similar impressions in the reports of Germans who have traveled through the small towns of present-day urban America. In fact, the frightening increase of aggression and violence in everyday life is much more apt to corroborate Adorno's notions on the correlation between the satisfaction of material needs and a peaceful social climate than to refute it. And, apart from this empirical problem, the point of Adorno's theoretical argument is as keen today as it was in the 1950s: humanity in behavior is a social value ranking high above the knowledge of even the greatest works of art; and peacefulness is not tied to the European concept of cultural refinement.

In exploring the utopian potential of mass culture, Adorno had not deserted his critical point of view. In the United States, so he told his audience, the bourgeois principle of a society solely based on market exchange had been realized with utmost consistency. This resulted in cutting off all institutions that might reach beyond the exchange principle and beyond the closed circle of pragmatic activity. Thus nowhere in society could a critical spirit be rooted, and the expanding apparatuses of mass production, mass consumption, and mass communication exercized a most effectful pressure toward intellectual conformity.

But as a dialectical thinker Adorno insisted on his thesis that the American way of life had to be understood as a "universal victory of enlightenment in the sense of the all-European process of enlightenment" (Adorno, 1959: 10). American preoccupation with the practical dimensions and consequences of intellectual work and philosophical ideas made it possible to transfer the demands of "culture" from the spiritual realm to the outside world.

Adorno sharply distinguished between two dimensions of mass culture, which the common discourse on the topic united indiscriminately. The sphere of material reproduction of human beings and the patterns of everyday behavior connected therewith were following a logic quite different from that inherent in mass communication and mass entertainment. The argument is in some way related to the Marxist view of material basis and ideological superstructures. Mass consumption—by fulfilling the needs of human beings as natural, sensuous beings—was always related to the basic dimensions of human happiness. This truth could by no means excuse or even justify a type of rationalized, monopolized production subduing its objects as well as its agents to a logic of domination. Defending the human right to freedom of material privation could never legitimize destroying external nature, human nature, and the large majority of people outside the highly industrialized countries. On the other hand, Critical Theory had to delimit its radical negation of capitalist economy from the religious struggle against earthly satisfaction and sensual joy and from the conservatives' contempt for the striving of the masses for a life of modest abundance. For Adorno, returning to a standard of living typical of the early twentieth century was out of the question. The barbarism inherent in the spiral of mass production, the shaping of needs, and mass consumption was obvious. But the philosophical bias for dealing with these flagrant contradictions from a progressive point of view was to stick to the material, sensuous foundations of any ideal of human happiness.

According to Adorno, the same way of looking at things was to be applied to the cultural relevance of another founding element of American culture. The exchange principle had penetrated the farthest corner of American society informing even the most sublime interpersonal relations. The entire range of intellectual production was evaluated by its capacity for bringing profit or becoming a success on the market. This is why autonomous philosophy and arts in the European sense of culture remained marginalized in the United States, surviving only in the niches of nonconformism. Children were socialized toward an ego-ideal of success, thus preparing them to accept the pressures of social adjustment and conformism. But for Adorno there was yet another side to the domination of the exchange principle: it supported the social rooting of democracy and a certain openness in social behavior: "The omnipresence of exchange activity means at the same time that all people are there for all other people. No one will harden himself in the limitations of his individual interest in the way you find in . . . Europe" (Adorno, 1959: 8). In Germany, the ideal of self-identity often produced a type of character with a grim, chilly appearance, indicating to all other people from the start that they actually did not matter for him and that they should not interfere with his precious and precarious inwardness (Innerlichkeit). This attitude was responsible for an internal distance from democracy, especially among the intellectuals. However, the American accent on adjusting to a social standard of "being there for other people" generated a further positive trait in American culture if compared to German *Kultur*. Adorno supposed "that a person educated with some social pressure to behave in a friendly fashion is yet more likely to practice a certain humanity in his relations with other people" (Adorno, 1959: 10).

A SLAP IN THE FACE OF CULTURAL ANTI-AMERICANISM— OR MORE?

Here, Adorno probably by far overshot the mark. If things only were so easy! Nevertheless, we have to ask why the critical philosopher got carried away enough to praise American mass culture in such a manner. There are two answers, one more global and one concretely historical. From about the middle of the 1950s, tendencies of pragmatism grew in Adorno's attitude. During those years he prepared his most radical book, *Negative Dialectic*, in which he worked out that the only authentic way of referring to society was to negate it. As a social science professor, however, he became involved in discussions about practical measures of cultural betterment, for instance, media pedagogics (Kausch, 1988: 197–214).

However, the decisive motive for touring the country with such a provocative lecture was Adorno's conviction that "the global historical trend will boil down to an Americanization of Europe" (Adorno, 1959: 14). He did not hide his criticism of this development; but he was above all worried that in response, the strong attitude of cultural anti-Americanism among German intellectuals would be radicalized.[12] This, he was afraid, could only strengthen the disastrous antidemocratic undercurrent of German thinking that had always expressed its hostility to Modernity by hateful attacks on Western civilization (Adorno, 1971: 137). In order to shatter his listeners' stereotyped convictions that *Kultur* was so much superior to American culture, Adorno answered rudeness with rudeness. He presented American supermarkets and ice cream for children as the realization of the innermost motives of spiritual creation. "Does not any culture in our European sense of spiritual culture contain something like a reference to this utopia of fulfilment?" he asked. Taking *Romeo and Juliet* as an example, Adorno insisted that all great works of art drew their power from the dream that "there shall be happiness, people shall give themselves to each other, there shall be fulfilment, not prohibition" (Adorno, 1959: 7).[13]

By praising the utopian elements in American mass culture, Adorno tried to shake the self-righteousness of his German contemporaries. I think it is to this historical and presumably also emotional confrontation that we owe the disclosure of some motives that Adorno used to cut down nearly to invisibility in his writings.

CONCLUSION

With the omnipresence of the culture industry and with the spreading of prosperity in West Germany, anti-sensual, ascetical critique of mass culture lost ground. But since the late 1970s, the tradition of German cultural criticism has made an impressive comeback. Today, cultural and pedagogical elites draw on irrefutable ecological arguments to prove that the standards of material convenience and the alleged hedonistic way of living of the "masses" in the highly industrialized countries are immoral and self-destructive. Undoubtedly the habits of private everyday life in the so-called affluent societies do waste limited resources, pollute the environment, and deepen the gap between the inhabitants of the "First World" and the expanding dominions of misery and starvation on earth. But among those who are calling for a radically new design of our way of life, I hear a lot of voices asking directly or indirectly: "Haven't we always told you that unlimited mass consumption and the hedonistic chasing after ever new thrills are the cause of evil, that you should turn to the immaterial riches of life?"

Actually, those voices are sounding much more often and much louder in Europe than in America—as they have always done throughout the nineteenth and twentieth centuries. But the general question remains: Where do intellectuals and scholars rank the material conveniences and sensual satisfactions of mass culture when debating the necessity to reshape our way of life? Do the pleasures of the body and of the senses just make up the lowland of contemporary culture, prominent only because of the dubious influence of uneducated masses and without any substantial value? Or should we stick to the hedonistic tradition that goes back to ancient philosophers such as Aristippus and Epicurus? Critical Theory insisted that any disrespect for the natural needs in man would inevitably damage human culture as a whole and could only result in a deformation of our spiritual heritage. In my view, this remains a very serious contribution to the debate on the future of mass culture.

NOTES

1. Since the late 1930s, the attitude among radical American intellectuals toward modern mass media and its aesthetics had turned from hope to fear. The convergence of this criticism with the theoretical framework of the European scholars becomes evident in the classical readers: Rosenberg and White, 1957; Jacobs, 1961; another example is Dwight MacDonald's 1960 text "Masscult and Midcult" reprinted in MacDonald, 1982: 3–75. For an outline of the intellectual development, cf. Richard Pells, "Die Moderne und die Massen. Die Reaktion amerikanischer Intellektueller auf die populäre Kultur in den dreißiger Jahren und in der Nachkriegszeit," in Krenzlin, 1992: 102–117.

2. "Es gibt kein richtiges Leben im falschen." *Minima Moralia. Reflexionen aus dem beschädigten Leben* (Frankfurt: Suhrkamp, 1987) 42.

3. Cf. Giner, 1976: 166–182.

4. Cf. Wiggershaus, 1986: 338–390; Jay, 1981: 253–259, 297–326.

5. Cf. Kausch, 1988; Kellner, 1982: 508–515.

6. Horkheimer and Adorno, 1971: 4 (preface).

7. Cf. the chapter "Culture Industry: Enlightenment as Mass Deception" in Horkheimer and Adorno, 1971.

8. Translating German philosophers into English is itself quite presumptuous, and with the writings of Horkheimer and Adorno one feels doomed to failure. A central notion for this discussion is that of *Glück*, generally translated here as "happiness." In the discourse of the Frankfurt School, *Glück* is a concept of highest philosophical dignity; it is a kind of short formula for the quality of existence in a free and humane society. *Glück* includes the sensations of the body from sexual lust to the pleasures of eating and drinking, the satisfactions derived from any intense activity, as well as the spiritual joy of art and thinking. Depending on the context I am using terms such as "joy," "pleasure," or "fulfilment," but I ask the reader to be aware of the overtone of *Glück*, of happiness in the full philosophical sense.

9. "Mehr Eiscreme, weniger Angst. Professor Adorno zur deutschen und amerikanischen Kultur," *Frankfurter Rundschau*, 16 May 1957.

10. Cf. Maase, 1992: 42–46, 186–190.

11. Newspaper reports on 12 additional public lectures are collected at the Theodor W. Adorno Archives, Frankfurt; I am very grateful especially to Henri Lonitz for supplying these materials.

12. For European anti-Americanism, see Henningsen, 1974; Kroes and van Rossem, 1986. For Germany, see Fraenkel, 1959; Berg, 1963; Schwabe, 1976; Maase, 1992.

13. This corresponds surprisingly to the tenor of Jean Baudrillard's account of his travels through the United States in *America*. In his view, American culture is the carefree materialization of ideals that had been articulated in Europe; on the Old Continent, in contrast, justice, affluence, equality, and freedom were regarded as final goals of history, and the realization of this utopia was postponed to a distant future.

REFERENCES

Adorno, Theodor W. (1959). "Kultur und Culture." Vortrag, gehalten am 9. Juli 1958 bei den Hochschulwochen für staatswissenschaftliche Fortbildung in Bad Wildungen, Sonderdruck, Bad Homburg u. a.: Gehlen, no date.

———— (1971). "Was bedeutet: Aufarbeitung der Vergangenheit." *Eingriffe: Neun kritische Modelle*, 7th ed. Frankfurt: Suhrkamp.

———— (1977). "Veblens Angriff auf die Kultur." *Gesammelte Schriften*, vol. 10.1. Frankfurt: Suhrkamp.

Berg, Peter (1963). *Deutschland und Amerika 1918–1929. Über das deutsche Amerikabild der zwanziger Jahre*. Lübeck: Matthiesen.

Brantlinger, Patrick (1983). *Bread and Circuses: Theories of Mass Culture as Social Decay*. Ithaca: Cornell University Press.

Diner, Dan (1993). *Verkehrte Welten. Antiamerikanismus in Deutschland*. Frankfurt: Eichborn.

Fraenkel, Ernst (1959). *Amerika im Spiegel des deutschen politischen Denkens*. Köln: Westdeutscher Verlag.

Giner, Salvador (1976). *Mass Society*. London: Robertson.

Henningsen, Manfred (1974). *Der Fall Amerika. Zur Sozial- und Bewußtseingeschichte einer Verdrängung*. München: List.

Horkheimer, Max, and Theodor W. Adorno (1971). *Dialektik der Aufklärung: Philosophische Fragmente.* Frankfurt: Fischer. Translated as *Dialectic of Enlightenment* (New York: Herder & Herder, 1972).

Horkheimer, Max (1936). "Egoismus und Freiheitsbewegung. Zur Anthropologie des bürgerlichen Zeitalters." *Zeitschrift für Sozialforschung* 5.2.

Jacobs, Norman (ed.) (1961). *Culture for the Millions?* Princeton: Van Nostrand.

Jay, Martin (1981). *Dialektische Phantasie: Die Geschichte der Frankfurter Schule und des Instituts für Sozialforschung 1923–1950.* Frankfurt: Fischer. First published as *The Dialectical Imagination: A History of the Frankfurt School and the Institute of Social Research, 1923–1950* (Boston: Little, Brown, 1973).

Kausch, Michael (1988). *Kulturindustrie und Populärkultur. Kritische Theorie der Massenmedien.* Frankfurt: Fischer.

Kellner, Douglas (1982). "Kulturindustrie und Massenkommunikation. Die Kritische Theorie und ihre Folgen." *Sozialforschung als Kritik. Zum sozialwissenschaftlischen Potential der Kritischen Theorie,* eds. Wolfgang Bonß and Axel Honneth. Frankfurt: Suhrkamp, 482–515.

Krenzlin, Norbert (ed.) (1992). *Zwischen Angstmetaphor und Terminus: Theorien der Massenkultur seit Nietzsche.* Berlin: Akademie-Verlag.

Kroes, Rob, and M. van Rossem (eds.) (1986). *Anti-Americanism in Europe.* Amsterdam: Free University Press.

Maase, Kaspar (1992). *BRAVO Amerika. Erkundungen zur Jugendkultur der Bundesrepublik in den fünfziger Jahren.* Hamburg: Junius.

MacDonald, Dwight (1982). *Against the American Grain.* New York: Da Capo Press.

Rosenberg, Bernard, and David M. White (eds.) (1957). *Mass Culture.* Glencoe, IL: Free Press.

Schwabe, Klaus (1976). "Anti-Americanism within the German Right 1917–1933." *Amerikastudien* 21.2: 89–107.

Wiggershaus, Rolf (1986). *Die Frankfurter Schule: Geschichte—Theoretische Entwicklung—Politische Bedeutung.* München/Wien: Hanser.

20 The Experience of Freedom and Vacuum: An Anthropologist at Euro Disney

Marc Augé

When Catherine de Clippel (a filmmaker and photographer) offered to follow me to Euro Disney,[1] I was pleased for two reasons. I was wondering whether I had made a good decision when agreeing, in a euphoric moment, to go into that odd place to act as an anthropologist of Modernity. For a few days, I had been telling myself it was a deceptively good idea: Euro Disney is nothing more than the *Foire du Trône*[2] out in the countryside. Besides, on Wednesday—I had been able to take only Wednesday off—I was doomed to bump into all the country's school-children. The mere thought of their ceaseless chatter around me gave me the shivers. It was too late to back out. I could already glumly picture myself standing by myself in the crowd for hours on end, scared by the prospect of the Ferris wheel, or scratching Mickey Mouse between the ears. Catherine's company and support would definitely be an asset. Moreover, she offered to take photographs and film my rambling, just in case. The prospect of being Disneyland's Monsieur Hulot (à la Jacques Tati's 1958 comic film *My Uncle*) was about to change the day of ordeal into one of fun. Still, I was worried; stage fright is known to plague great actors—besides, Catherine and I were wondering if we could walk into Disneyland with our equipment without making the local authorities suspicious. They were aware of the kind of scorn that French intellectuals commonly lavish on entertainment imported from America. Were they not going to oppose the presence around their premises of Catherine's sophisticated and subversive camera?

When you drive to Euro Disney (a friend had agreed to give us a lift and pick us up in the evening), your first impressions stem from the landscape. Suddenly, in the distance, looming on the horizon yet already close (it is reminiscent of the visual sensation experienced elsewhere, as in the instant one catches the first glimpse of Mount Saint-Michel or the Chartres cathedral), Sleeping Beauty's castle stands against the sky with its towers and domes, so much like the pictures published in the press and shown on television.

That was probably Euro Disney's first pleasure; we were being offered a sight perfectly identical to the one advertised. No surprise here, as at New York's Museum of Modern Art, where one cannot get over how much original works look like their copies. As I thought afterwards, that was undoubtedly the key to a mystery that struck me at once—why were there so many American families visiting the park, whereas they had of course already visited its U.S. counterparts? Well, they were enjoying what they already knew, savoring the pleasure of cross-checking, the joy of recognition, a bit like the foolhardy tourists who quickly become bored with the local color of the exotic world in which they are stranded until they find their way around it among the anonymous crowd of a glittering superstore: from one supermarket to another.

Besides the subtle pleasure we experienced because the place met our expectations so perfectly well, we were very soon overcome by a feeling of relief. First of all, our photographic equipment went unnoticed. We quickly realized that its absence would have been more conspicuous. You don't visit Disneyland without at least one camera; all children above age 6 have their own. Better cameras are generally owned by fathers, who share their interest between intimate moments (Snow White's kiss to the little one) and more ambitious camera work (traveling on the great parade, or the landing of the paddle-wheel *Mark Twain* at Frontier Land).

I gather Catherine got a bit upset because her equipment aroused no curiosity whatsoever. To prove to herself that she was not simply shooting everything, like everybody else, she proceeded (as a true professional) to film the people filming. I moved closer to them to make it easier for her and remind her I was the film hero. But this attempt failed to set her off a great deal from the others. The population density of cameras was so high that it was rather difficult to keep them out of the picture. For a while, I looked down on this sight from the top of the Swiss Family Robinson tree (reminiscent of a four-room apartment with mezzanines). Unquestionably, every one of those who were filming or photographing was being filmed filming, filmed photographing, photographed filming, or photographed photographing. You go to Disneyland to be able to say you have been there and produce relevant evidence. It is a visit in the future perfect; it becomes meaningful later, when relatives and friends are shown (with comments) the little one's pictures of Dad filming the little one, then Dad's film as crosscheck.

Another reason for relief was that children were not as numerous as I had feared initially. Obviously, there would always be a few kids to ask Mickey or Minnie for autographs on Main Street. But all in all, there were many more grown-ups than children. You were sometimes under the impression that whole families had gotten together to accompany the kid. It was not so much the king-child as the pretext-child. Indeed, the pretext was optional to a majority of visitors who

You don't visit Disneyland without at least one camera . . .

indienne
en SARi

060792

p 39

Indian woman in a sari

only found serious, tense faces to shoot. But let's not be mistaken: it is their fun they took so seriously.

I had time to imagine the exciting comparative anthropology studies that could be conducted in such a cohabitation space. For a while, I gazed at a party of young Arab women wearing scarfs and long dresses, who hurried from one attraction to another with charming enthusiasm, and Japanese businessmen in three-piece suits (the only persons *not* dressed up as Americans), who did not hurry because they were too busy filming and photographing everything, as if they were indulging in industrial espionage. I lingered in front of a group of African dancers and musicians (somewhere around Adventure Land, between the oriental bazaar and the pirates' den). Without overdoing it, their leader, a tall and burly man, would invite some women from the audience—English, Italian, Spanish—to dance with him; then their husbands or boyfriends would film them snuggling up in his arms and shrieking in fear or pleasure. French-type machismo at its best.

Suddenly, I seemed to understand what it was all about, what made this whole show so attractive—the secret of the allure it created in those who let themselves be overcome by it is the reality effect, the surreality effect produced by this place of all tales. We are living in an epoch in which history is staged, turned into a show, and in this way de-realizes reality, whether it be the Gulf War, the Loire castles, or the Niagara Falls. This distancing, this entertainment-ing, is never so perceptible as in travel commercials that advertise "tours" and sequences of "snapshots"—which will never be more actual than when we see them "again" during the slide shows (with comments) that we will impose on a resigned circle of nearest and dearest.

At Disneyland the show itself is turned into a show. The scenery reproduces what was only scenery and fiction in the first place: Pinocchio's house or the *Star Wars* spaceship. Not only do we cross into the screen, backward from Woody Allen's *Purple Rose of Cairo*, but we find another screen beyond the screen. A trip to Disneyland is arch-tourism, quintessential tourism. What we have come to visit does not exist; we only meet with the memory of our dreams. What we experience there is pure freedom, without object, reason, or stake. We find neither America nor our childhoods there, but an absolutely unwarranted set of images into which all people around us (although we will never see these people again) can posit whatever they like. Disneyland is today's world, its worst and its best: the experience of freedom and vacuum.

Final counterpoint. On our way out, we stopped at the Newport Hotel, which tried very hard to look like an actual hotel. But we won't get fooled again; even though the waitress kept us waiting half an hour for a beer, as if to get us back to earth, and made us feel that we had left the fictitious world where doormen, sheriffs, and hostesses never stop wishing you a good day, we did not buy into it. Actually, nobody was to be seen in the hotel. Outside, fake sailing ships pretended to sail on a fake ornamental lake. We drank our beer—real beer, I must

Minnie and the cripple

say. Inside there were only fake ones, alcohol-free. We stuck out our tongues at
the waitress, who pretended to look offended. She could have been real.

Translated by Jean-Paul Gabilliet

NOTES

"L'expérience du vide et de la liberté. Un ethnologue à Euro Disneyland" was published
in the August 1992 issue of *Le Monde diplomatique*. We wish to thank Marc Augé and
Ignacio Ramonet, editor of *Le Monde diplomatique*, for authorizing us to publish an English
translation.

Artwork © Jean-Pierre Cagnat.

1. Since the Fall of 1994, the park's name has become Disneyland Paris. [Editors' note]
2. A famous Parisian amusement park. [Editors' note]

21 Popular Culture and Mass Culture: A Franco-European Dilemma

Jean-Marie Domenach

Words stand in mutual opposition in the first place. "People" is a term that, in the modern epoch, has become loaded with emotion. It used to name a community of inhabitants; in revolutionary language, it went on to designate the mythical subject pertaining to the nation's soul. Conversely, "mass," which in Latin refers to "paste," "dough," "magma," is a flat, often scornful word in contrast to such a glorious term as "people." A similar ambiguity is found in "culture": in the French usage, it is closer to *culte* (worship) than to agriculture; it evokes a corpus, a hierarchical *body* of works, whereas in English it designates all the types of behavior of a human community. The phrase "popular culture" typifies a built-in challenge, that of the people invited to appropriate something hitherto owned by the bourgeoisie. Popular culture relates to a universe still "casted," to the ideological reflection of a class society that has almost vanished. "Mass culture," on the contrary, is a contemporary phrase, democratic on two accounts: through the popularization of culture, and the transition from people to mass.

How could "culture," the offshoot of time-honored tradition and continuous labor,[1] end up appended to "mass," which signifies *indistinction*? This contradiction sticks in the French people's unconscious, if not their consciousness. Paradoxically, our most radical intellectuals are steeped in this contradiction as well. How could I have not been myself, at least partially? Any reflection on culture should take into account the "hermeneutic circle"—only through one's own culture does one perceive the differences that set one apart from other cultures.

It should be noted that the constitution of the people's culture as weapon of democracy dates back to a very distant past. A genuine popular culture used to exist in France from the twelfth through the sixteenth centuries; cathedrals, fabliaux, and mystery plays attest to its vigor. But that culture was oral, iconic, and did not necessitate the command of reading. Grounded in Christian mythology, it was shared by all. The rupture occurred with Modernity, when the State came into being, towns increased in size, and religion started losing influence.[2] A "cultivated culture" drawing on classical sources took shape in collèges, universities, courts, and salons—one could not claim to be "cultivated" without a smattering of Greek and Latin.[3] Clerics were gradually replaced by humanist scholars; the latter originated a clerisy who were eventually called intellectuals in the late nineteenth century. Priests, aristocrats (then bourgeois), academics—this triangle contains culture. The people have been excluded from it and their culture folklorized. Only a handful of authors—Molière, Charles Perrault, Jean de la Fontaine—could be called "popular" legitimately. This rift is in keeping with the one separating Paris from the province. France was made up of heterogeneous communities; its unification relied on the imposition of a national language that pushed back all dialects.

The controversies addressing the cultural role played by the French state fail to take into account that historical necessity; those fragments of people, dispossessed of their original culture (often of their own volition), were able to coalesce into a nation only under the aegis of and aided—sometimes constrained—by a centralizing state (Fumaroli, 1991). This is the root of what was called the "French exception" during the December 1993 GATT negotiations. The country's linguistic unification, however necessary, resulted in nefarious consequences; it aggravated the folklorization of regional cultures, hence the break between high and low cultures. It was the ruthless doing of compulsory, state-supervised school attendance. Around the turn of the century, when close to half of all French people could not yet speak French, education inspectors realized that French was much better written in areas where local dialects still prevailed. It was learned as a "distinguished" language, untainted by usage. Nonetheless, the upshot was that the rural population that moved to the outskirts and suburbs of cities brought along dated folklores and expressed themselves in a cultural language that was anything but their own. The awareness of this sort of alienation originated the culture populaire movement: animated by socialist and Christian activists, it endeavored to give underprivileged classes access to the vaults of Culture.

I took part in it. At age 17 I studied under Jean Guéhenno,[4] the high master of culture populaire. The son of a craftsman, he attended the Ecole Normale Supérieure, an examplar of socially promoted boursiers de la République[5] who meant to introduce the people to liberal arts. In 1941 and 1942, I would go to plants to educate apprentices. But my most rewarding experience in this domain was my participation in the Uriage[6] équipes volantes (mobile teams), which, in 1943, would go to the Alps Maquis camps to educate young men condemned to idleness by their insufficient number of available weapons. Between sessions of military training, I would animate periods of poetry and singing. There I became aware of the gap between my liberal arts culture and their culture, which was limited to some popular tunes. Poetry was all but inaccessible to most of those young men; I had to fall back on Louis Aragon's texts and some of Paul Eluard's, two communist poets.

Therefore, one understands why *culture populaire* movements and subsequently André Malraux, who became the Minister of Culture after Charles de Gaulle's accession to power in 1958, endeavored to introduce "the people" to French high culture. Nowadays, it has become fashionable to slander this enterprise despite its original greatness and efficacy of sorts. But it did come too late. The people did not really crave what we wished to give them—the two cultures were too far apart by then.

The painful paradox of that time was that "the mass" started re-emerging out of the rubble of old social classes. When living conditions started becoming more unified along the social spectrum, when television sets entered households, French culture became more learned, more esoteric—in a word, more elitist than ever before. That was the time when fiction experienced incipient exhaustion, when the novel's language took refuge in preciosity. This happened around the 1960s.

During the same period, mass culture, invented and packaged in the United States, swept across Europe. We were not prepared; our minds were on the Algerian war and we believed that intellectuals were still arbiters of culture. Left- and right-wing intellectuals were caught napping amid a democratization of culture that they had never entertained, and they responded by denouncing "Americanization." Hostility to overpowering technology had been strongly voiced in the second quarter of the century by French writers (ranging from George Duhamel to George Bernanos); it was now aggravated by Heideggerianism gone fashionable. Our culture was withdrawing into itself, vilifying humanism and its universal claims (although the latter had propagated French culture beyond the country's borders), incapable of winning over a new audience—that selfsame mass of individuals who were force-fed U.S. products by television. Yet back in the 1930s and into the 1950s, great novelists and great filmmakers produced works that met the expectations of a mixed public. But *nouveau roman* and *déconstruction* theories inhibited creation while cinema was withdrawing in on intimism and folklore. This is why, despite the French exception's recent, hard-won victory, the crisis of creation has left bloodless a culture that has caused its own paralysis.

The detractors of a culture attached to traditionalism, impervious to technology and innovation, esoteric and aristocratic, fail to take into account a history that does not compare with that of the United States. France sustained technological progress as a trauma, because its culture's links to peasants and landscapes were exceptionally strong. From Pierre de Ronsard to Jean Giraudoux, how many writers would not have existed without this particular trait, the French countryside, an earth that everywhere carries the imprint of Man? But between 1960 and 1990, France went through a genuine upheaval: consumer society, urbanization, rural exodus, mechanization of agriculture. A bulldozer fits into the U.S. landscape; it seems monstrous and out of place in Touraine. Hence the sensation that each technological breakthrough entails aesthetic deterioration and, more seriously, mauls our collective imagination. The obsession with decadence, the foreboding of impending doom, shroud this inconsistent civilization in a lugubrious atmosphere.

Theories proliferate about a living-dead artform, the French novel. They prevent us from perceiving the truth that Van Gogh expressed about painting: "Let's hurry—things themselves are about to disappear." In dark periods, the French used to hang onto what the historian Pierre Nora has called "the national novel," their nation's legendary history. Through this imaginative space, elite and popular cultures met several times. But the 1940 defeat cast a mourning veil on this glory. France's culture did suffer from the wane of her power. Whereas the strength to convince and assimilate others has declined, a clear political purpose is still to emerge from the newly created European Community.

This outline points out why the French, unlike the Americans, have been incapable of meeting the challenge of a mass culture consistent with structural and behavioral mutations and instrumental in fitting cultural commodities into the cycle of mass production-consumption. Whatever we interpreted as loss and mutilation was congruent with a belief that did not experience the burden of history in North America. As Fernand Braudel put it: "Louis XIV's France was already an elderly person." The American nation was born a century later, at the same time as industrialization and urbanization. What France's "culture vultures" experienced as an aggression, America experienced as symbiosis.

Nevertheless, social conflicts were fierce over there, and great works have testified to the nostalgia of aristocratic culture in the South. The myth of the land survived for a long time. But expansive space has always enabled conflicts to evolve. Space fosters motion; novelty arises constantly, only to wear off and make room for new trends. Technologies' adequacy to space and human multitude allowed U.S. culture to follow the development of the nation's power and embark on a tremendous growth of cultural means and equipment, ranging from audiovisual technology to libraries and museums. Culture has remained consistent with the nation. The American collective imagination did not go through such ruptures as the technological and historical shocks inflicted on Europe. Although the United States eventually ran out of fresh space, although the western movie faded as a genre, other resources were brought to bear; and, despite deconstruction theories' one-time paralyzing effect on the U.S. novel, it has reconquered its fertility, its playful and sometimes comical creativity (Chénetier, 1989). Such vitality contrasts with the exhaustion of French fiction. The test seems conclusive, if one agrees that the novel is *the* democratic genre.

Above all else, the American imagination has been capable of holding on to what the Europeans have lost in the horror of wars and dictatorships: a belief, which the French regard as naive, in the certainty of good's triumph over evil. Conversely, Europe has remained dominated by the sense of tragedy. But the sense of tragedy is no sentiment for the people. And nihilism, which recurrently plagues European cultures, seems exotic to the Americans. The people have remained lyrical; they relish grandiloquence in any form and want a clear-cut distinction between heroes and villains—incidentally, this is why Victor Hugo is probably our last great popular writer. Hence the relief the French public experiences when they are given simple feelings and moving stories, even in mediocre American movies. However, the contemporary vogue of violence may herald the return of a coarse and vulgar form of the tragic sense to the United States. Could there possibly be such people as natural-born killers? I sometimes wonder whether Louis Hartz was not right to contend that the United States has remained in the European eighteenth century (Hartz, 1964). If it is true, violence may eventually counteract the vital optimism that has enabled American culture to permeate a population that came from Europe in search of utopia. Religion played a major part in this integration; the Bible has remained much more present in the United States than in France and, as Walter Benjamin said, the Bible is the book to which all Westerners refer. There is a marked contrast between Europe's all-out secularization and the pervasive religious sentiment that is the common beacon of U.S. politics and culture.

The explosion of mass culture has renewed hostility to "American imperialism" in France—the famous stage director Ariane Mnouchkine has called Euro Disney a "cultural Chernobyl." Such responses are over-simplistic. U.S. products make up the largest segment of mass culture in France for three reasons: the superior financial and technological means of which the Americans can take advantage; the generally high quality of some of this output; and finally, the failure of France and other Western European countries to develop a culture in step with our time.

By way of closing remarks, I offer a few questions:

- Can this superiority last? American production has drawn considerably on European material. Won't this supply run dry one day?

- Will American mass culture continue to integrate the several million migrants who have entered the United States in the last few years? Aren't "people's cultures" impervious to integration looming in the future?

- Isn't the popularity of reality shows and live TV (of the CNN ilk) conducive to the confusion of reality with fiction, thereby depriving the latter of its creative potential?

- Does mass culture contain elements necessary to the individual's cultural promotion? If the marginalization of writing continues, won't culture risk toppling into indistinction? Who will maintain hierarchies and orient choices, if education fails to do it?[7]

- Whereas nobody questions the quality of the foremost U.S. universities, the average educational level of American students is declining. France's culture and that of most of Western Europe hold up because of the quality of its secondary education. If this segment of the curriculum is collapsing in the United States, what will be the fate of culture as a whole?

Only the future has answers.[8]

Translated by Jean-Paul Gabilliet

NOTES

1. The Latin verb *colere* referred to religious worship; later, to the peasant's labor.

2. That regional culture survived in the most remote areas until the late nineteenth century. Calvaries were built in Brittany until the 1880s, when the first consumer goods shipped from the capital (*articles de Paris*) reached the region thanks to railway transportation.

3. In France, Latin remained a social hurdle into the early twentieth century. It was crossed of the subject list of the Ecole Polytechnique entrance examination only in 1910. In his biography—Roselyne Chenu, *Paul Delouvrier, ou la passion d'agir* (Paris: Seuil, 1994)—P. Delouvrier, a French high-level civil servant, recalls being told by a Christian unionist: "We don't belong to the same race; *you* studied Latin."

4. This French essayist (1890–1978) was among the foremost Catholic intellectuals in pre- and post–World War II France. The son of a shoemaker and a seamstress, he entered the French Academy in 1962. [Editors' note]

5. The phrase means "government scholarship holders," but it conveys much stronger connotations in French. It traditionally refers to children from the urban or rural underclass whose entire schooling—from kindergarten to higher education institutions—is funded by the French government on the basis of academic achievement. [Editors' note]

6. The École des Cadres of Uriage was founded in 1940 after the defeat to train *animateurs* (social workers trained for cultural activities). After the school defected to the Résistance in December 1942, its research department organized *équipes volantes* to educate underground fighters hiding in the Maquis.

7. I laid the foundations of a popular culture for the future in a 1991 report to the French Ministère de la Jeunesse et des Sports (Ministry of Youth and Sports). Cf. "La culture, patrimoine et développement" in *Pour un Renouveau de la culture populaire*, ed. Jean-Marie Domenach (Paris: INSEP/Ministère de la Jeunesse et des Sports, 1991).

8. Many of the points addressed in this text are examined in a more thorough manner in my book *Le Crépuscule de la culture française?* [*The Twilight of French Culture?*] (Paris: Plon, 1995).

REFERENCES

Chénetier, Marc (1989). *Au-delà du soupçon. La nouvelle fiction américaine de 1960 à nos jours*. Paris: Seuil.

Domenach, Jean-Marie (1995). *Le Crépuscule de la culture française?* Paris: Plon.

Fumaroli, Marc (1991). *L'Etat culturel*. Paris: de Fallois.

Hartz, Louis (1964). *The Founding of New Societies*. New York: Harcourt.

Index

academic traditions, xix

Adorno, Theodor W., 69, 201–211. *See also* Frankfurt School; Horkheimer, Max; *Kultur*

advertising: American food in, 121; for the Barbie doll, 141, 144; P. T. Barnum as inventor of, 8; for Coca-Cola, 129, 132; of Harlequin books, 92, 95; ideology and esthetics of, 14; as market principle for rock music, 69; pressure of advertisers, 103; as a sign of cultural erosion, xxxvi, xlii; travel commercials, 218; in *USA Today*, 165

Alien, 13, 14, 188

Allen, Woody, 186, 218

Americanism, xxxv–xxxvii, 132. *See also* anti-Americanism

Americanization, xix, xxi, 30, 56, 58, 127, 159, 208, 223

Americanness, 128, 132, 188

American Psycho, 150, 152. *See also* serial killing

anti-Americanism, xxvi, xxx, xxxvi, xl, xlvi, 128, 208. *See also* Americanism

aristocracy, xxx, xxxiv, 5, 6, 163, 222, 223, 224. *See also* elite

audience reception, xvi, xviii

Austria, xxii, 131, 153

auteur, 14, 20

Babette's Feast, 124

baby boom, 58, 71, 140

Barbie doll, 139–145

Barnum, P. T., 8

Barthes, Roland, 128, 164; on food, 131–132, 134 n.1, 135 n.9, 10, 19

Basic Instinct, 16

Baudrillard, Jean, xl, xliii, xlvii, xlix, 19, 151, 164

Beatles, 72, 80, 163

Belgium, xviii, xxxiv, 6, 24–32, 38, 40

Berkeley, Georges, xxix–xxx

blacks, 63, 82, 113, 162, 176; black Barbies, 141, 142; blackface minstrels, 3–11; black rock 'n' roll, 61; fears of African, xxviii; in movies, 183–191; Netherlands, 64; on television, 17, 163; traditional music of, 73

B-movie, xxvi, xlvii, 112

Bourdieu, Pierre, vii, xx

Britain, xix, xxix; American crime fiction in, 109–113; British pop music in the

States, 161, 163, 165, 166. *See also* pornography
Shakespeare, William, xxviii–xxxi
The Silence of the Lambs, 16, 152, 155. *See also* serial killing
Simon, Paul, 72, 80, 83, 86
Spain, 24, 128
Spengler, Oswald, xxxiv, xxxvii, xliii
Spielberg, Steven, 13, 14, 20, 187, 188. *See also* E.T.; *Jurassic Park*
Spirou (comic strip magazine), 24, 27, 28, 40, 42
sports, 20, 72, 128, 161, 165, 166
Springsteen, Bruce, 57, 59, 82
stereotype: according to Adorno, 202, 203; in cinematic depiction of minorities, 183–192; cultural stereotypes in minstrel acts, 4; differences between Europe and America, xlix–l; French opinion of American food, 119–120; Irish stereotypes on America, 173–180; in 1970s television, 14; shallowness of Americans, xxxii; social rituals, 124
Switzerland, 40

taste: in American food, 160; bad taste of American customs, xvii; in cuisine, 119–125; cultural, xxxiv, 69, 166; dictates of good, xxxviii–xl; national, 132; people with, 104; popular, 81; smallest common denominator, 15; threat to foreign, xxvi
technology, 3, 153, 159, 204; dehumanizing, xxvii; hostility to, 223; in nineteenth-century entertainment, 9–10
television, xlii, 55, 58, 156, 214; American TV as a threat to national media systems, xvi, xxvi; audience, xli; Barbie ad on, 141; and cinema in the United States, 13–20; and neutralization of susceptibility to violence, 152–154; penetration in France, 223; as propagator of Dutch rock music, 60; reality shows, 18–19, 225; serial mentality, 150; series, 30, 121, 163; soap operas, 93; TV culture as mainstream culture in the

West, 57; in the United States, 162–166. *See also* video
Ter Braak, Menno, xxxv–xxxvii, lii
terroir, 123, 132
Thompson, Jim, 109, 155
Tintin (comic strip character and eponymous magazine), 24, 25, 27, 28, 30, 41. *See also* Hergé
Tocqueville, Alexis de, xxxiii–xxxiv, xxxvii, xxxviii–xli, 202
translation, 91–98

Valérian (comic strip character), 32–35. *See also* Mézières, Jean-Claude
Veblen, Thorstein, xxxviii, 69, 203
video, 82, 142, 149; clip syndrome, 15; as a new media, 16, 20; pornography, 166; rock-related sales, 71; as tool of virtualization, 153. *See also* cinema; movie industry; movies; television
Vietnam, xviii, 15, 162, 185, 187
violence: contemporary vogue of, 225; denial of, 105; in the media, 206; in *Miami Vice*, 17; of movies and rap, xvi; in serial killing and roman noir, 148–156; as a surrogate for sex in the U.S. media, 161
vulgar, xlviii, xlix, 7, 10, 20, 97, 178, 203

Warhol, Andy, 120, 149
Wells, Herbert George, xxx, xlv
western, 195, 198; comics, 25, 27, 28, 196; decline of genre, 224; decline of TV series, 165; *Gunsmoke*, 14; influence in *Star Wars*, 13; material initially published by Harlequin, 92; music, 216; as originated by a concern for reality, 19; revised stereotype of Native Americans, 189; spaghetti, 56; twist to traditional,187
women: in films, 183, 184, 189–190; Harlequin readership by, 91, 93; as a minority, 1, 198; work, 122
Woodruff, Robert, 129–130. *See also* Coca-Cola

youth culture, 65, 70, 74, 81

About the Editors and Contributors

KARL ADAMS is a graduate of the University of Utrecht, the Netherlands. In 1993 he completed a doctoral dissertation in American Studies entitled "Alienation and the Lyrics of Paul Simon." He has been an active singer/songwriter since 1988.

MARC AUGE is President of Ecole des Hautes Etudes en Sciences Sociales in Paris. For a decade, this anthropologist has devoted himself to developing a new theory of Modernity based on the "anthropology of everyday life." His latest publication is *Pour une anthropologie des mondes contemporains* (1994).

DANIEL BAYLON is Professor of American Literature and Civilization at the University of Nantes, France. His main field of research is the American media, particularly magazines. He is currently studying the status of elderly people in America through such magazines as *Modern Maturity*.

CLAUDE-JEAN BERTRAND is quondam Professor of Media Studies at Université Paris II and a leading figure in American Studies in France. He has written and edited numerous books on European, American, and global mass communications, most recently *Les Médias français aux Etats-Unis* (1994, with F. Bordat), *La Civilisation Américaine* (4th ed. 1991, with A. Kaspi and J. Heffer), and *Les Médias Américains en France* (1989, with F. Bordat).

LAZARE BITOUN is a professor of American Literature at Université Paris VIII–Saint Denis. An author, editor, and radio commentator, this specialist of the American novel produced in 1995 the highly regarded French translation of Philip Roth's *Operation Shylock*.

JOHN G. BLAIR has been Professor of American Literature and Civilization at the University of Geneva, Switzerland, since 1970. He has published books on W. H. Auden's poetry; confidence men in modern fiction; and *Modular America: Crosscultural Perspectives on the Emergence of an American Way* (Greenwood, 1988), a crosscultural analysis of organizational modes. His next major project addresses the cultural work of nineteenth-century American drama.

FRANCIS BORDAT is Professor of American Civilization and Film Studies at Université Parix X–Nanterre. He is the author of numerous articles and books on U.S. cinema, most recently *Cent ans d'aller au cinéma: l'exploitation cinématographique aux Etats-Unis 1898–1995* (1995).

JEAN-PIERRE CAGNAT regularly contributes cartoons to the French daily *Le Monde* and its international issues–related spinoff, the monthly magazine *Le Monde diplomatique*.

ANNICK CAPELLE is a linguist and specialist of Western European popular fiction at the Facultés Universitaires Notre-Dame-de-la-Paix in Namur, Belgium.

CLAUDE CHASTAGNER is professor of American Studies at Université Paul Valéry in Montpellier, France. He specializes in Anglo-American popular music. He has co-authored *The American Dream: American Popular Music* (1995, with Margaret M. Mayer). His forthcoming study, *Rituel Rock*, will be published in 1996.

ROBERT CONRATH is a Franco-Canadian-American citizen. He is professor of American Studies at Université Paris VII and the Paris Institute of Political Studies. He specializes in the sociology of literature and anthropology of cultural production.

JOHN DEAN is a professor of American civilization and mass media studies at Université Strasbourg II. The author of *American Popular Culture* (1992) and *Education in the United States* (1990), he is currently at work on *The Diffusion of American Popular Culture in Western Europe since World War II*.

MARIANNE DEBOUZY is Professor of American Studies at Université Paris VIII–Saint Denis. She has written extensively on U.S. labor history and working-class culture, most recently in *Le Capitalisme sauvage aux Etats-Unis (1860–1900)* (1991).

LAURENT DITMANN attended Université Paris X–Nanterre, the Saint-Cloud Ecole Normale Supérieure, and Brown University. He is currently professor of French Literature and Civilization at Spelman College in Atlanta, Georgia. A researcher in comparative cultural studies, he is working on a biography of French-born Civil War generals.

JEAN-MARIE DOMENACH is Honorary Professor of Sociology at the Ecole Polytechnique in Paris. A prominent figure of the post–World War II French intellectual scene, he was the editor of the Catholic review *Esprit* for two decades and has written several books about the impact of Modernity on contemporary society.

His latest major work is the controversial essay *Le Crépuscule de la culture française?* (1995).

HENRI DROST is a graduate in both Communication Studies and American Studies of the University of Utrecht, the Netherlands. His main focuses of interest are American popular music and mythical America.

MIREILLE FAVIER works in the English Division of the Duperré School of Applied Arts in Paris. She recently contributed to the Louvre catalog for the 1993 Veronese exhibition. Her forthcoming study on food representations in still-life painting, *L'Oeil gourmand*, will be published in 1996.

JEAN-PAUL GABILLIET is professor of English and North American Studies at the Strasbourg Institute of Political Studies. He is the author of an unpublished doctoral thesis about anthropological aspects of comic books and comic-book reading in North America, as well as of numerous articles on North American popular culture and United States–Canada relations.

ROB KROES is Head of the University of Amsterdam's Amerika-Instituut and current President of the European Association for American Studies. He has written and edited numerous prestigious studies about the United States, most recently *Cultural Transmissions and Receptions: American Mass Culture in Europe* (1993, with R. Rydell and D. Bosscher).

KASPAR MAASE is a sociologist and full-time researcher at the Institute for Social Research in Hamburg, Germany. In 1992 he published *BRAVO Amerika*, a well-received study of youth culture in modern West Germany.

JEAN-CLAUDE MEZIERES is the co-creator of the best-selling French comic album series "Valérian." A key figure of the French comic strip scene since the late 1960s, he has recently published a new artwork collection entitled *Les Extras de Mézières* (1995).

ANDREW PEPPER is a Ph.D. student working in the field of contemporary American crime fiction, race, and the city at the University of Sussex.

CIARÀN ROSS is a graduate of Dublin's Trinity College. Currently a professor of British and Irish Studies at Université Strasbourg II, he is working on a book entitled *Samuel Beckett and Psychoanalysis: Playing and Thinking*.

PENNY STARFIELD was born in South Africa and has lived in France since 1978. An American cinema specialist at Université Paris VII, she has written numerous articles on the topic and is the author of an unpublished doctoral thesis about minority representations in American films.

MEL van ELTEREN is Associate Professor of Sociology of Culture at the University of Tilburg, the Netherlands. He has taught and written widely on theories and histories of the human sciences, social history, and American popular culture. His most recent book is *Imagining America: Dutch Youth and Its Sense of Place* (1994).

EUGENE VAN ERVEN holds a Ph.D. from Vanderbilt University. He teaches American Studies and Drama at the University of Utrecht, the Netherlands. He has published several articles and books on theater and has been involved in various musical, theatrical, and cinematographic productions.

ISBN 0-313-29429-1

9 780313 294297

HARDCOVER BAR CODE